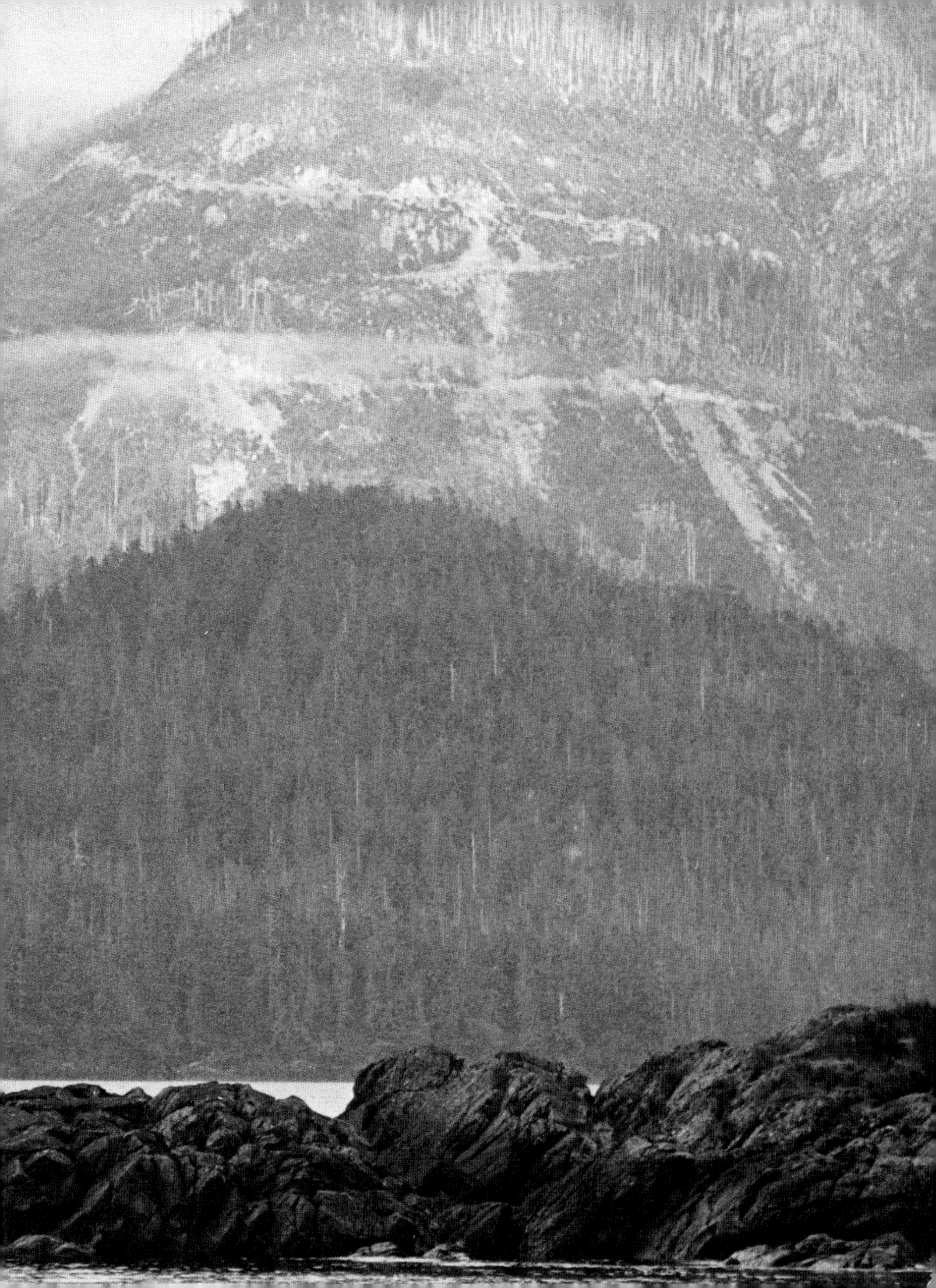

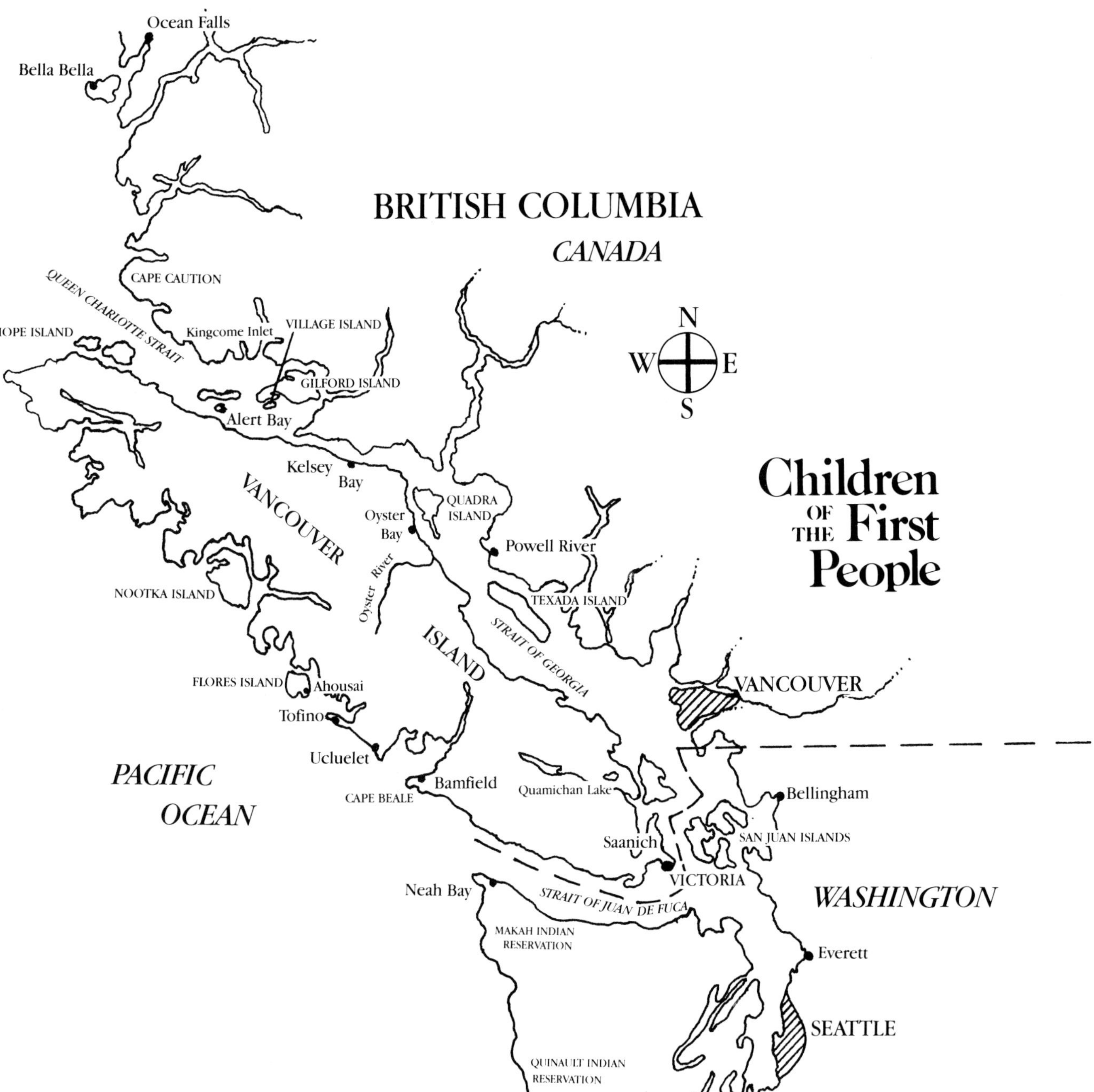
Children of the First People
BRITISH COLUMBIA
CANADA
N
W
E
S
Ocean Falls
Bella Bella
CAPE CAUTION
QUEEN CHARLOTTE STRAIT
HOPE ISLAND
Kingcome Inlet
VILLAGE ISLAND
GILFORD ISLAND
Alert Bay
Kelsey Bay
VANCOUVER ISLAND
QUADRA ISLAND
Oyster Bay
Oyster River
Powell River
TEXADA ISLAND
NOOTKA ISLAND
STRAIT OF GEORGIA
FLORES ISLAND
Ahousai
Tofino
Ucluelet
VANCOUVER
PACIFIC OCEAN
Bamfield
CAPE BEALE
Quamichan Lake
Bellingham
Saanich
SAN JUAN ISLANDS
VICTORIA
Neah Bay
STRAIT OF JUAN DE FUCA
WASHINGTON
MAKAH INDIAN RESERVATION
Everett
SEATTLE
QUINAULT INDIAN RESERVATION

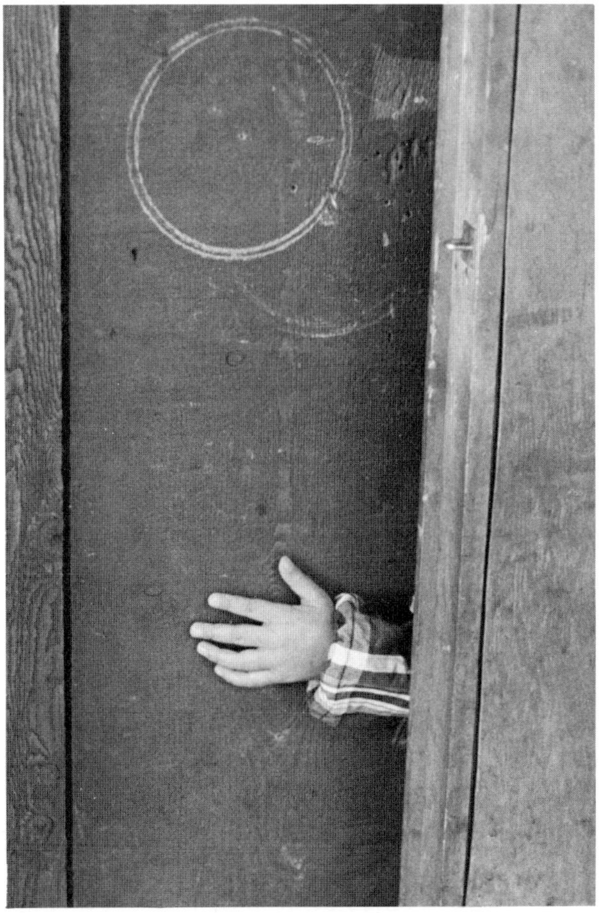

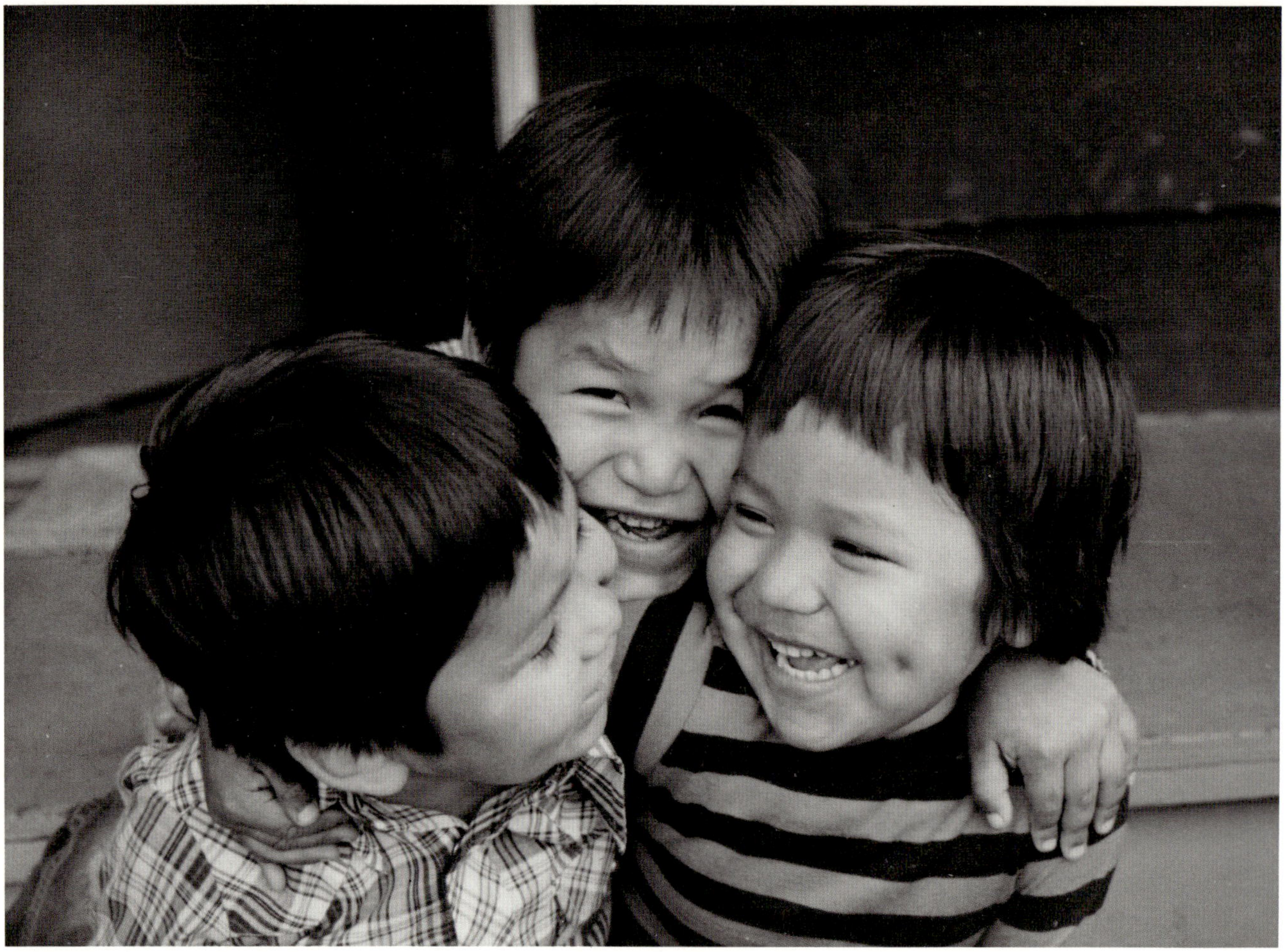

Children

Dorothy Haegert

Tillacum Library

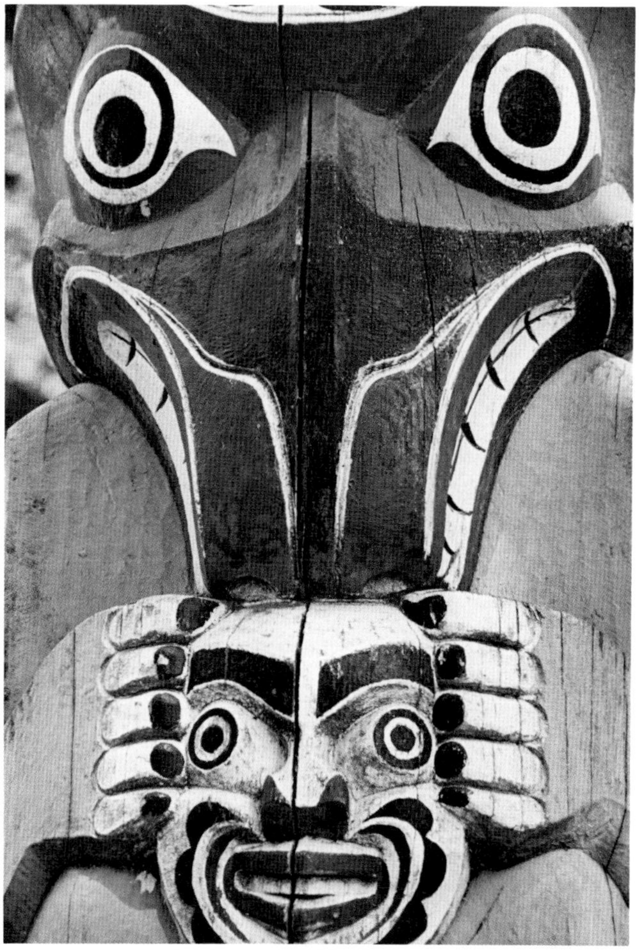

OF THE First People

CHILDREN OF THE FIRST PEOPLE

Second Edition Published 1989

TILLACUM LIBRARY
100-1062 Homer Street
Vancouver, B.C. Canada V6B 2W9
A Division of Arsenal Pulp Press Book Publishers Ltd.

The publisher gratefully acknowledges the financial assistance of The Canada Council.

COVER DESIGN: David Lester
TYPESETTING: Baseline and Vancouver Desktop Publishing Centre
PRINTING: Hignell Printing
PRINTED AND BOUND IN CANADA

CANADIAN CATALOGUING IN PUBLICATION DATA:
Haegert, Dorothy, 1938-

ISBN 0-88978-217-2

1. Indians of North America - British Columbia - Vancouver Island - Children - Portraits. 2. Indians of North America - British Columbia - Vancouver Island - Biography. I. Title.
E78.B9H33 1989 971.1'3400497 C89-091559-8

CONTENTS

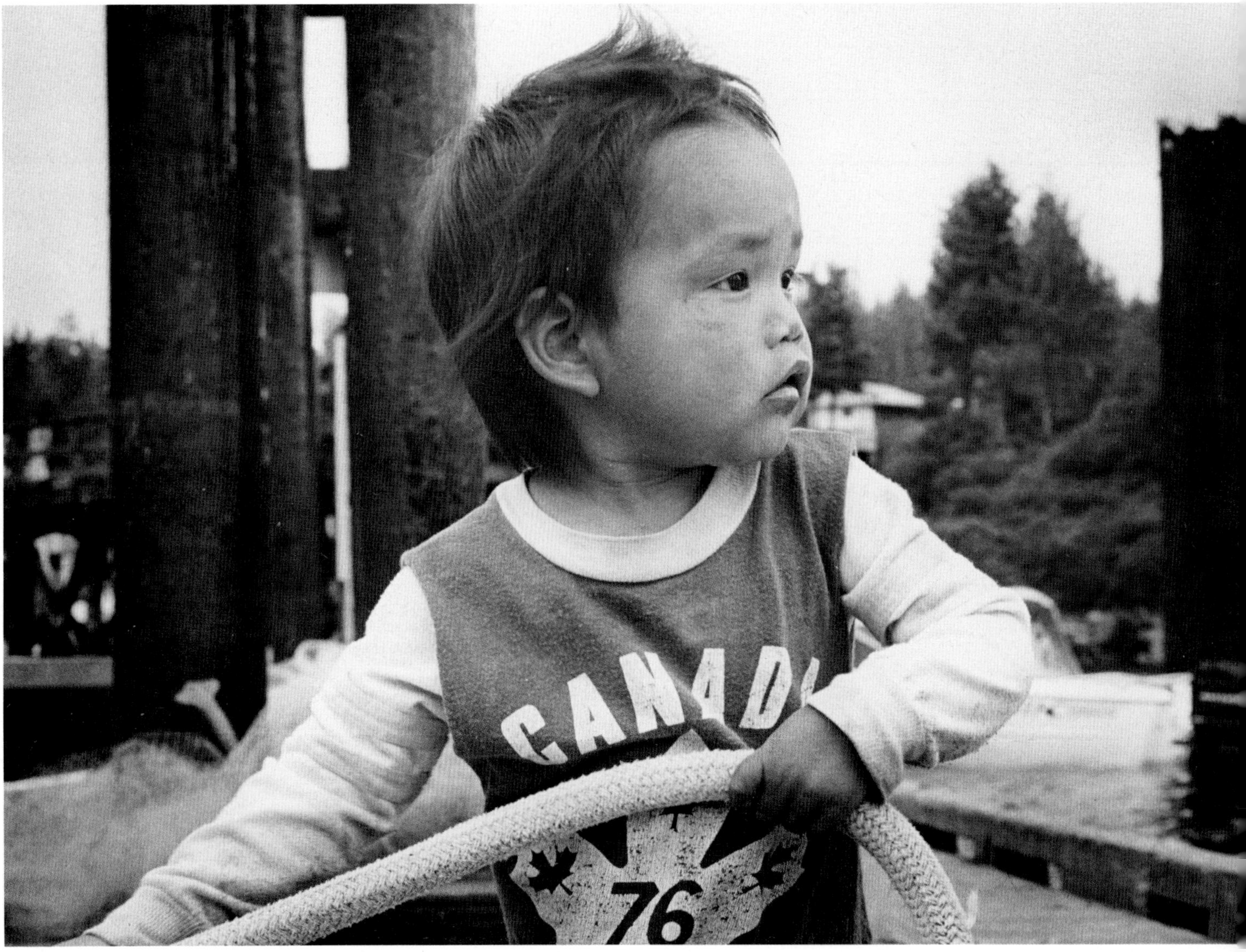
CANADA
76

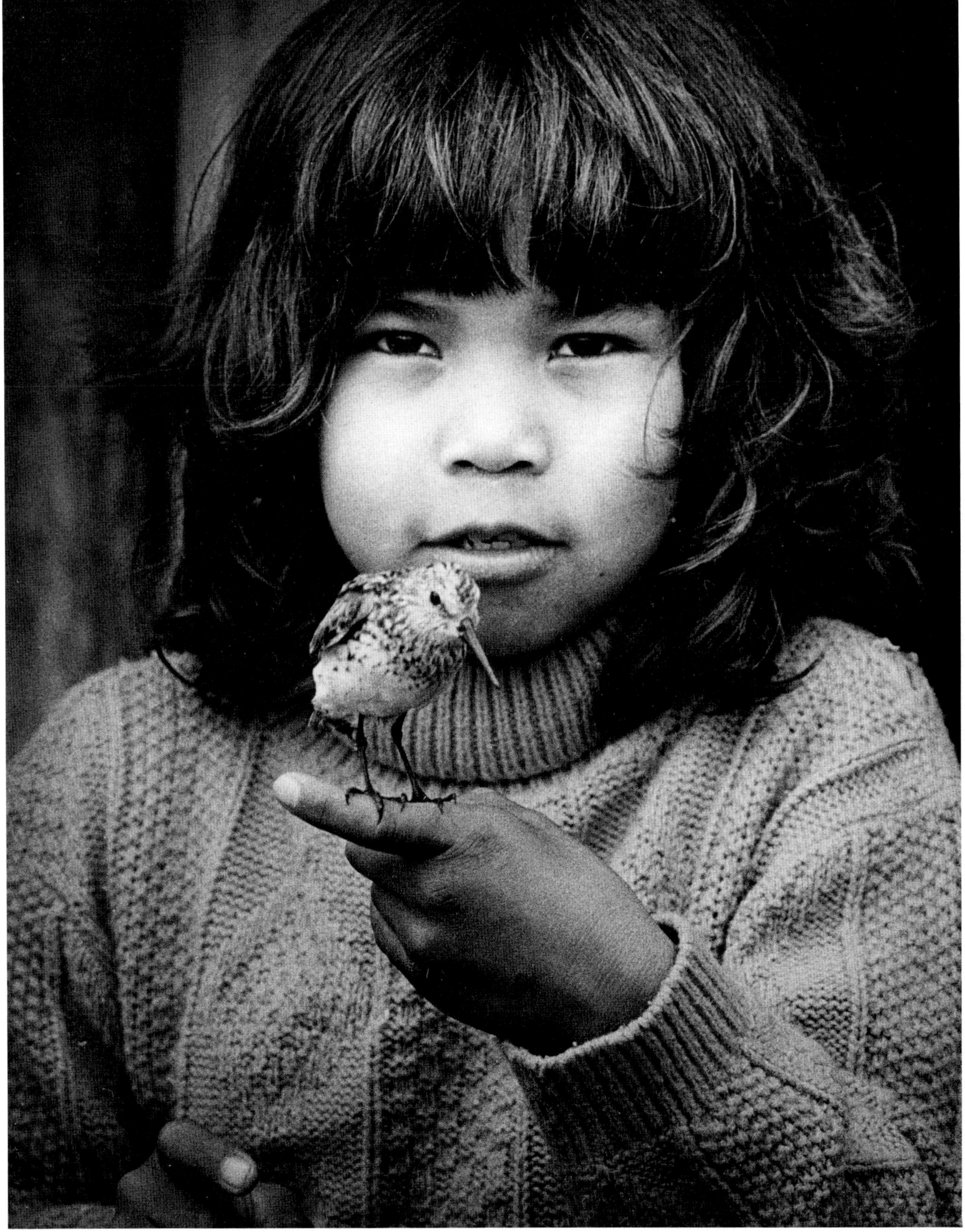

Introduction *by Dorothy Haegert*

THIS BOOK IS THE CULMINATION OF FOUR SUMMERS SPENT TRAVELLING UP and down the British Columbia coast, visiting and photographing Native Indian children in their villages. I met and befriended many people on these journeys, allowing me a rare glimpse into their unique and largely unspoiled way of life. Their reverence for tradition and a culture steeped in history is reflected in the upbringing of the children, who are instilled with the same values and beliefs as their forefathers, and in the love and respect shown for the elders, who have much to offer.

After my portfolio was largely complete, I enlisted the support of those elders, who shared their own stories of the Native way of life as it was during their own childhoods. We should not forget that, less than one hundred years ago, their indigenous world was still intact and vital, not as yet greatly affected by white society. The personal recollections gathered here are a testament to remind us of what these people, and all of us, are in danger of losing, as the beautiful children may give us hope for what endures and what is to come.

Sadly, since this book's first publication, three of the contributing elders have passed away: Dorothy Sanvidge in 1983, Dave Elliott in 1985, and Alex Amos in 1987. Their deaths are a great loss, as there are so few people left who remember "how it was." Luckily, some Natives are striving to keep their languages and traditions alive—people like John Thomas of the Makah Language Program in Neah Bay, Washington, and Dr. George Louis of the Ethnology Department at the Royal British Columbia Museum. George Louis received an honourary law degree from the University of Victoria in 1987. Ruth Cook is working in the Greater Victoria school system as a member of the Native Indian Education Division; Helen Alphonse continues to knit her beautiful Cowichan sweaters; and Stan James continues to carve. Both Francis Charlie and Peter Webster have retired.

I wish to thank the ten contributing elders who were willing to share their fascinating stories. And, of course, I am deeply grateful to the children whose images are recorded here, and to their families for allowing me to photograph them. Of the many people who gave me help and support throughout this project, the following deserve special mention and thanks: Sue Vollert (Carmichael), who accompanied me on several journeys; Bill Conconi, whose sailboat took us, on more than one occasion, to Alert Bay, Gilford Island, Village Island, Kingcome Inlet, Hopetown, and Friendly Cove; Dave and Flora Dawson for their hospitality in Kingcome Inlet; Sharon Paul; Ray and Teri Williams of Friendly Cove; Elsie Williams of Hopetown; George and Doris Smith of Gilford Village; Dorothy Sanvidge of Oyster River; the Johnson family of Bamfield; Sophie Shaw of Bamfield; Flora Tom of Saanich; Florence Charlie; Julie Alphonse of Quamichan; Ronny and Nancy Alphonse of Komiachan; Lucy Alphonse; Harvey and Frieda Alphonse; Violet Alphonse; Bob and Muriel Titian. I must also thank Marie Cooper for her support and for the opportunity to photograph students of the Native Indian program in Victoria and Tsartlip Elementary School in West Saanich.

There are many others. But above all, finally, it is the faces and voices of the First People which enabled this document to come into being.

—Victoria, B.C.
Summer 1989

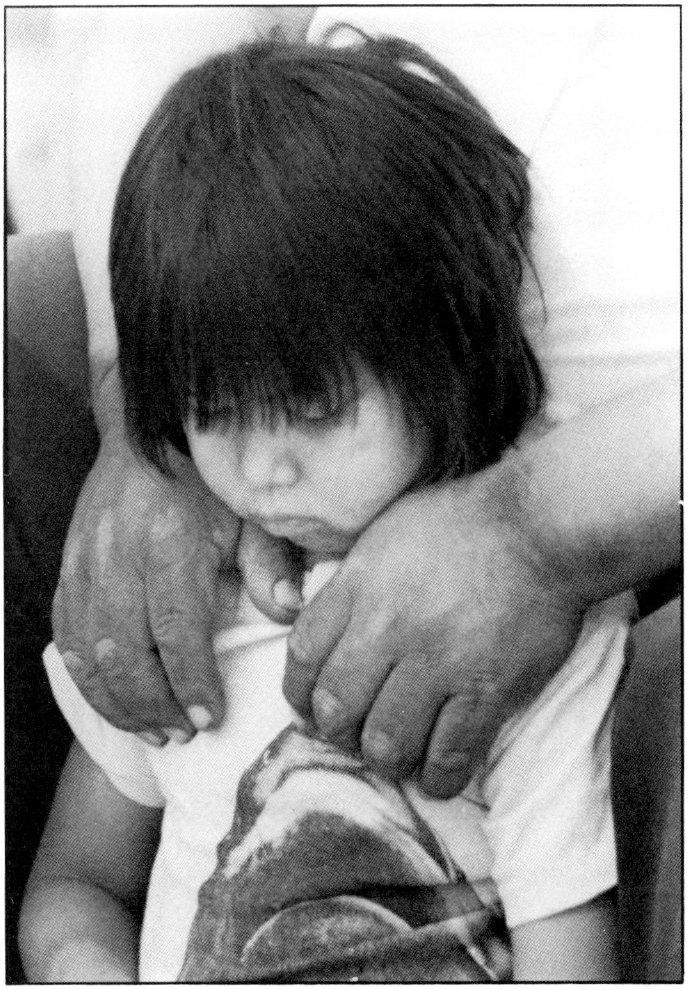

For Joey, John & Anne
& the Children of the First People

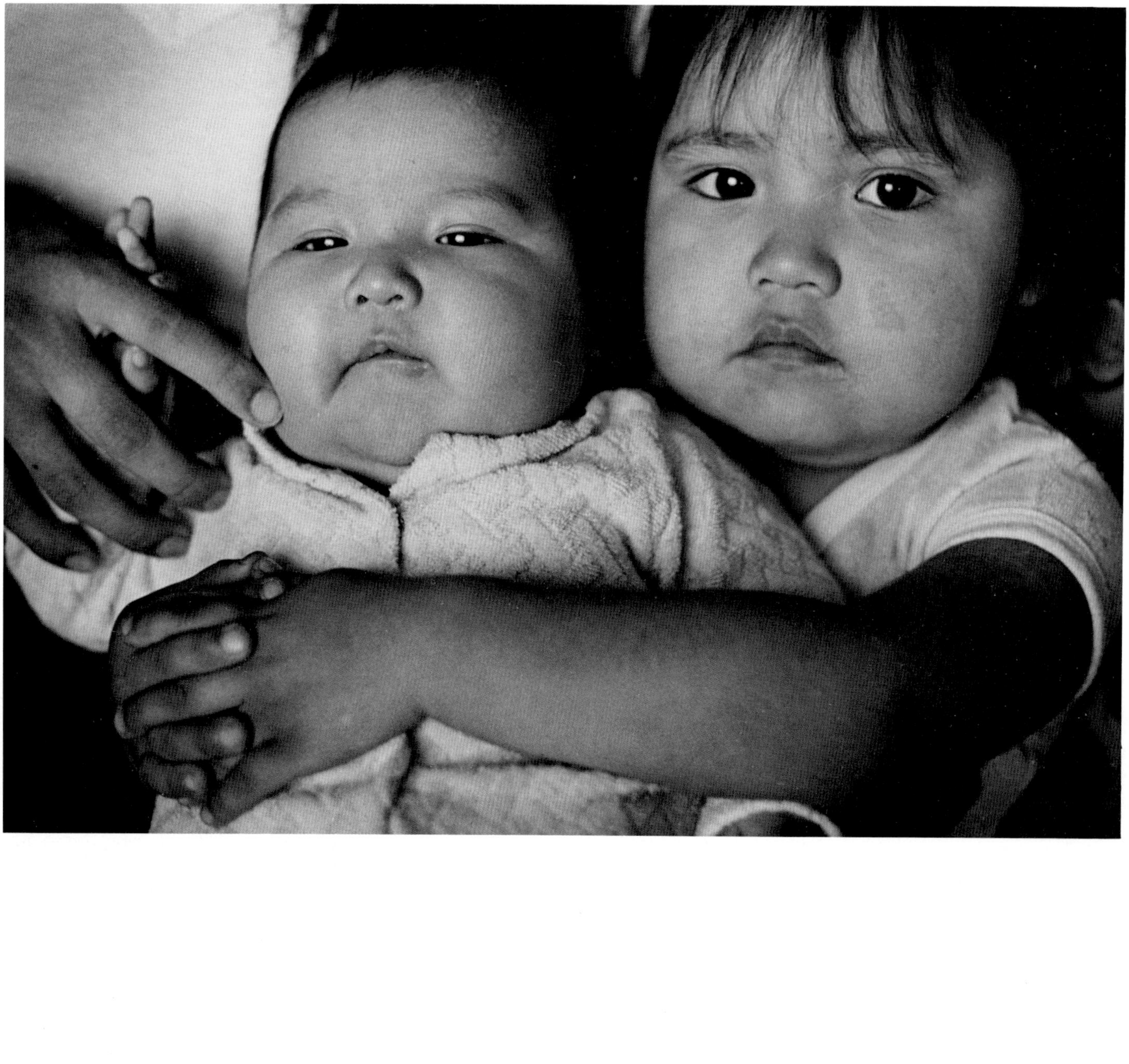

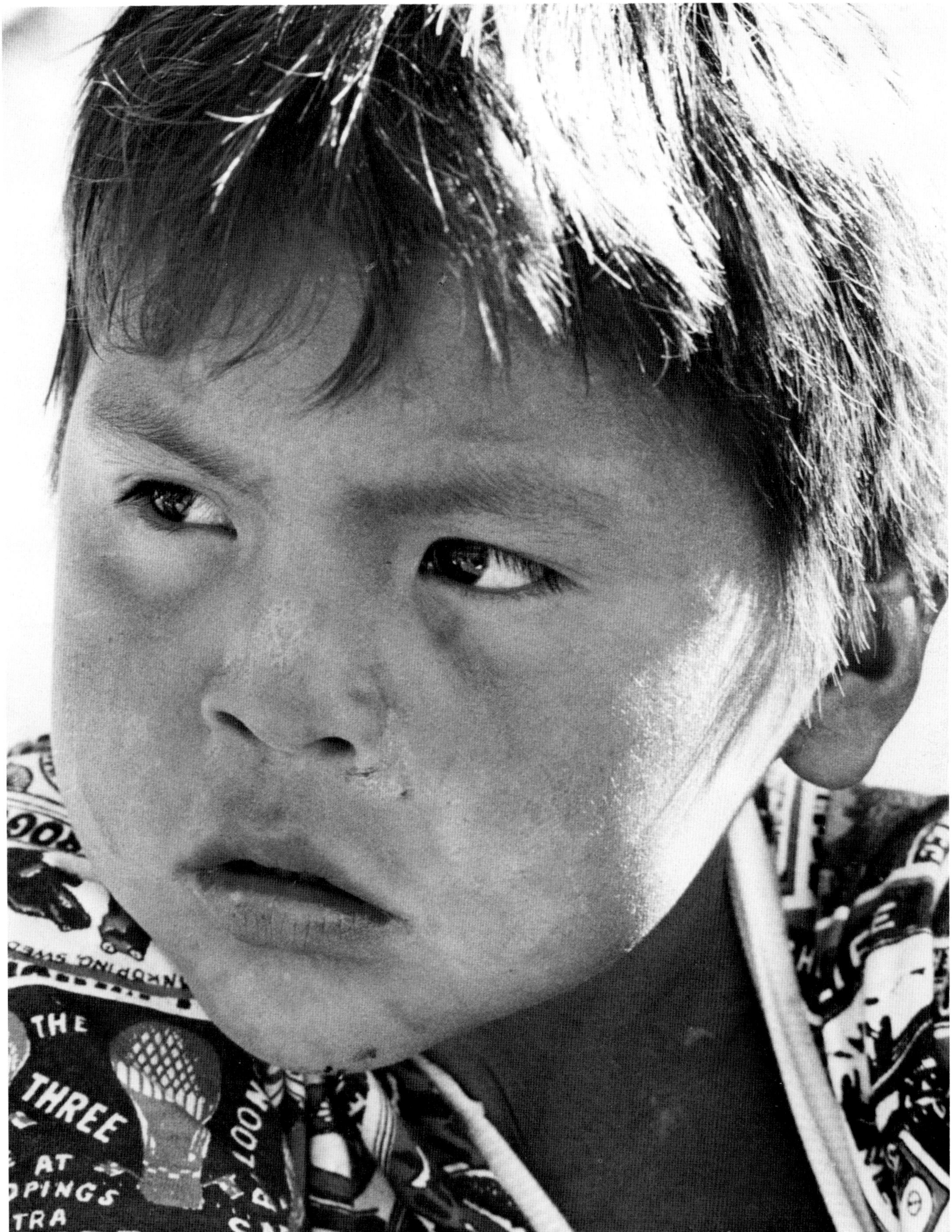
THE
THREE
AT
LOON

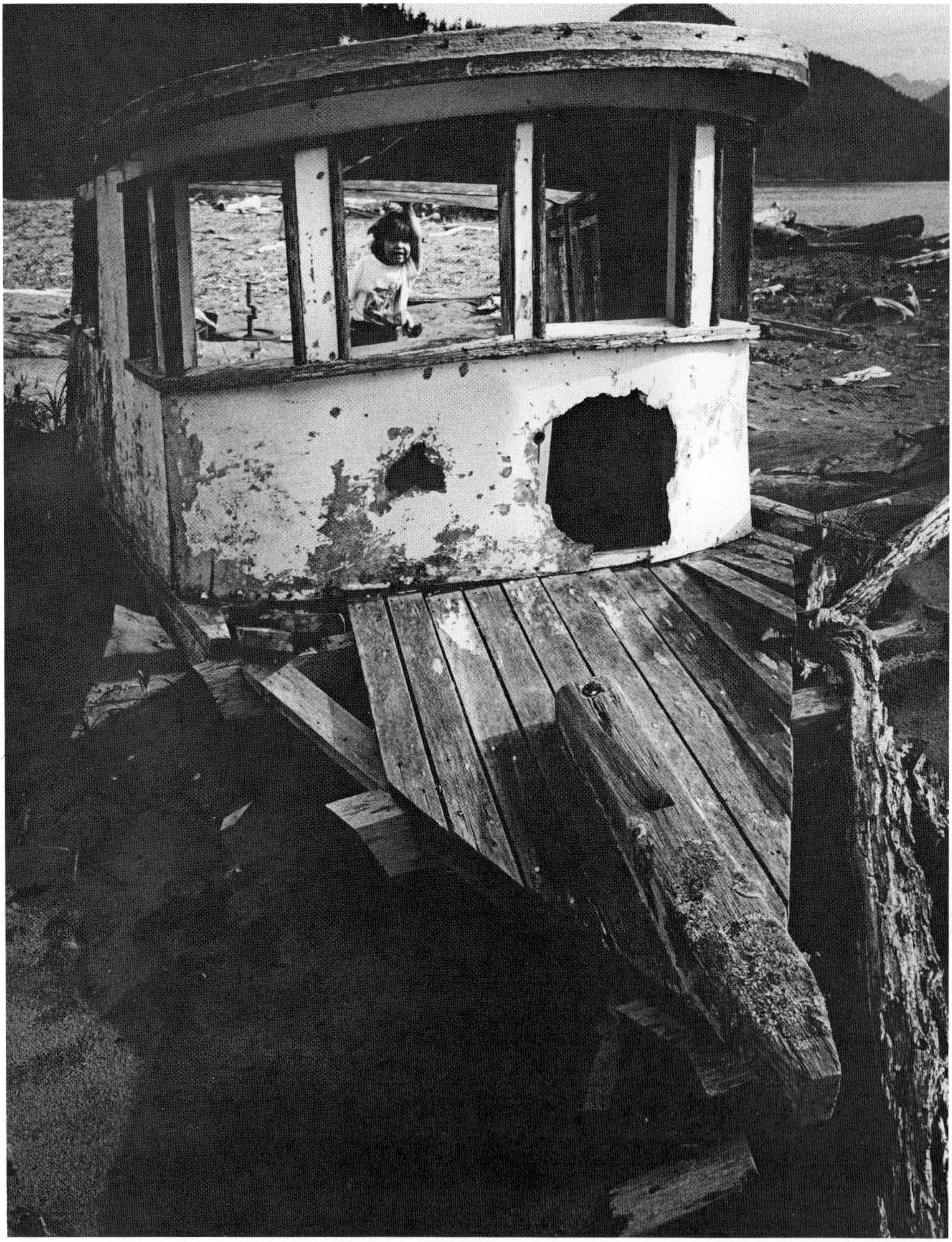

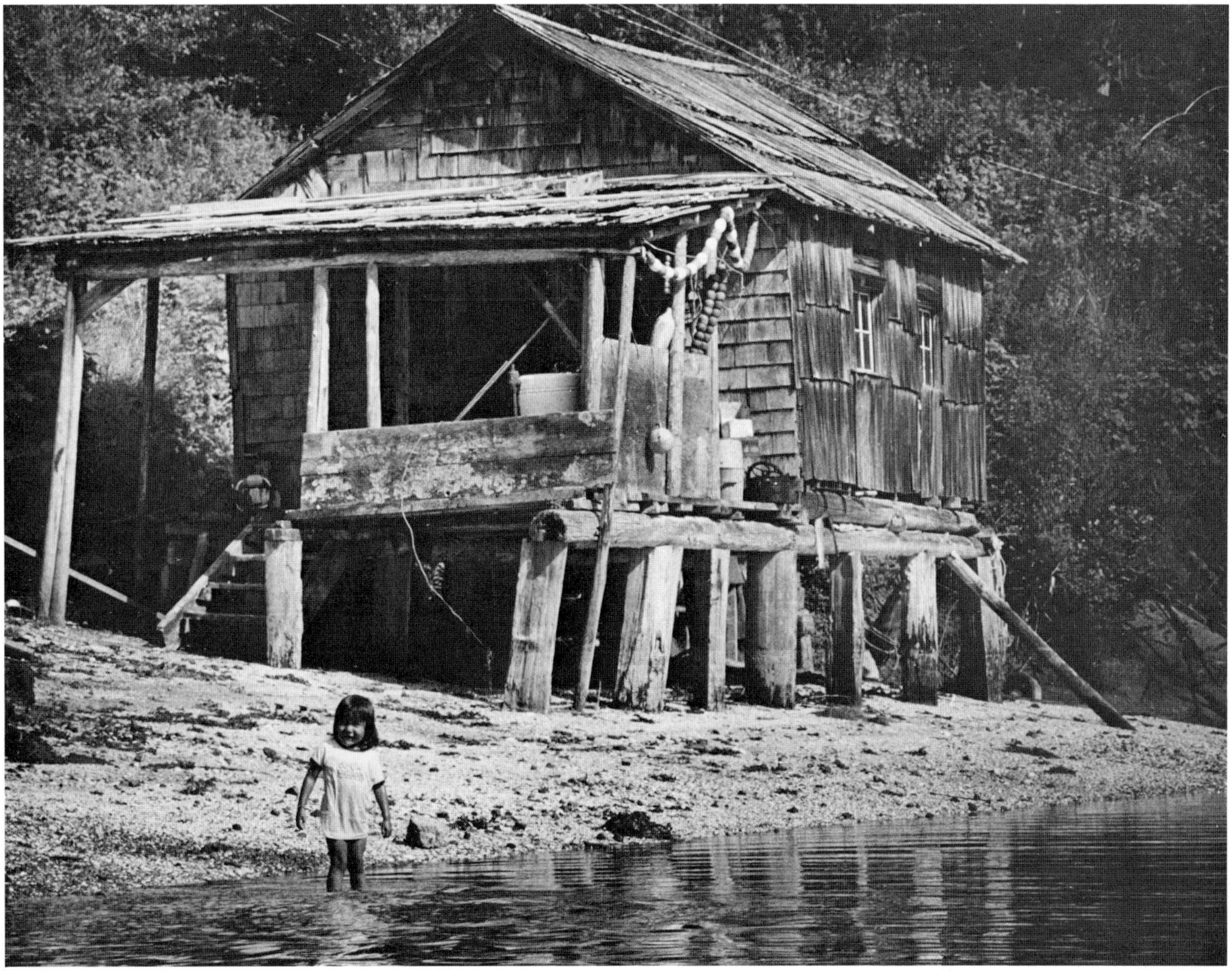

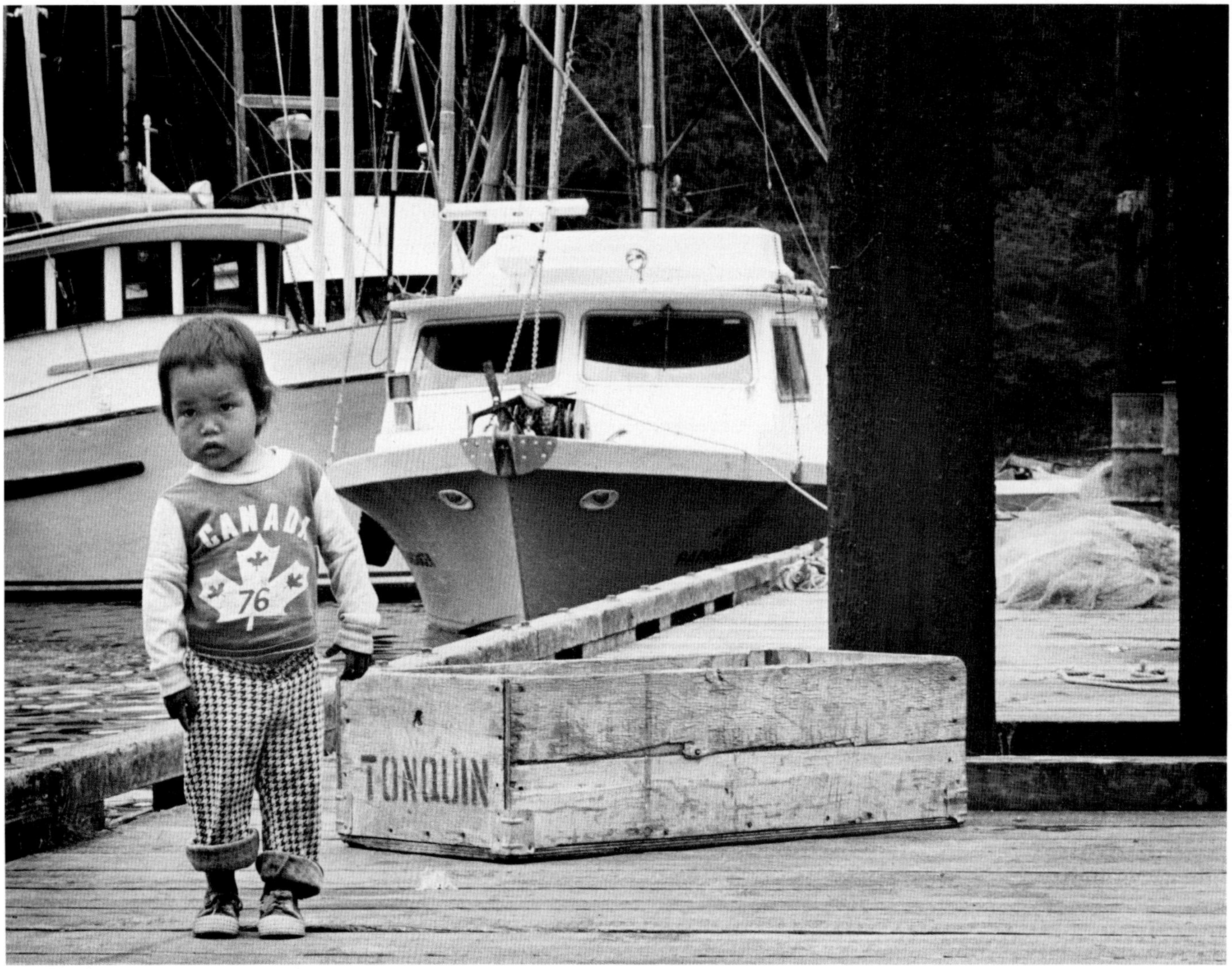
CANADA
76
TONQUIN

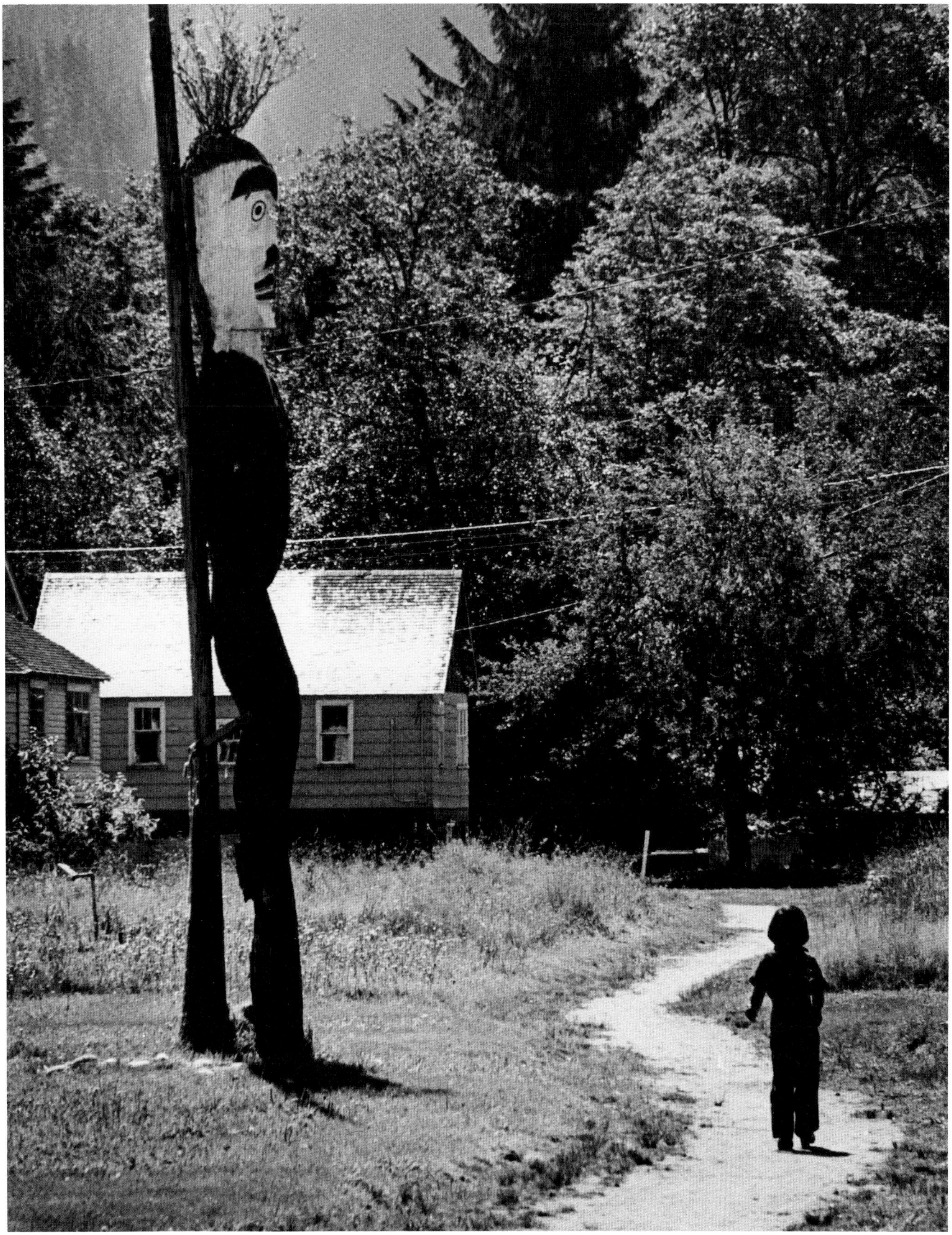

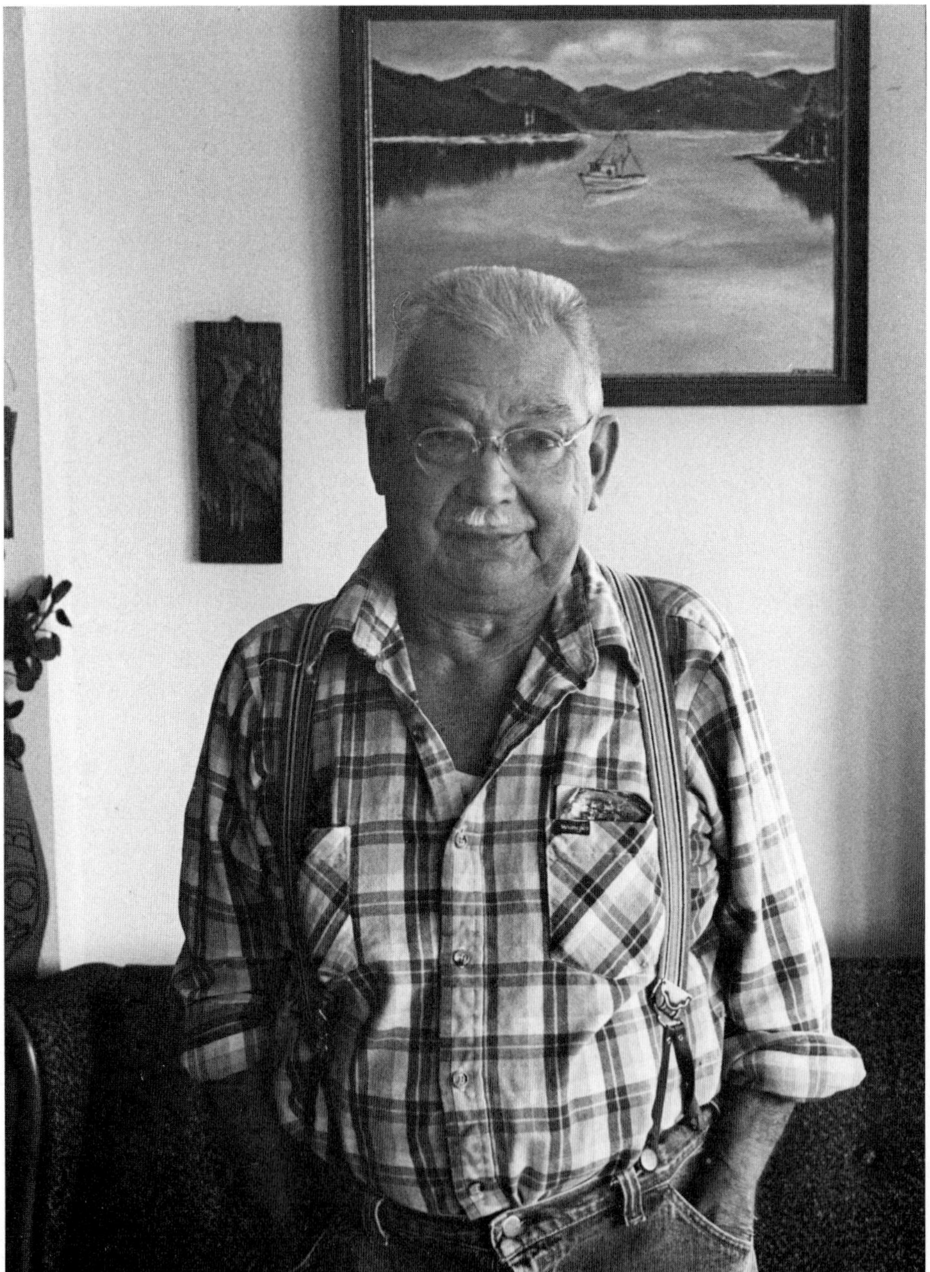

DAVE ELLIOTT

Saanich

When the Europeans first came, our people were here, well established, living good, sensible lives, living in a beautiful way. I'll say in a way that has never been equalled, never touched before. We believed that we came from a higher order of intelligence. We realized that what was here was put here for a purpose. That's why the people respected all life—the birds, the fish, the trees, even to the streams and lakes. They believed everything had a right to live just the same as we did. We used, respected, took only what we needed. We made full use of everything in the materials.

Sometimes when I think of my people, I realize how good they were, how honest, how kind, how just they were. I have to think that. They must have walked hand in hand with the creator.

Living the way we did, close to nature, we belonged to the land and the land belonged to us. Land wasn't something to be exploited, bought and sold for profit or gain. Everybody had a right to it whether it was a man or a woman, a bird, an Indian or a white man. The land was here first and it wasn't just for the powerful, corrupt, greedy, dishonest people. Those are the people that now own the land—while some people don't even have a home to go to. They'll never have a home as long as they live. Why? How come? So when I think of our people, who realized all this—there had to be an order far beyond us. Anyone with half a brain would have to believe that. We weren't savages running through the bushes. We couldn't say we completely understood it. But we knew there had to be a strength, an intelligence, a power, way beyond ourselves.

My people never killed a tree unnecessarily. Once in a while the need was so great they would cut a tree. When this had to happen they would speak to the tree. It had a sacred name. Every living thing had a sacred name—streams, lakes, trees, flowers, birds, everything. When your need was great you had no choice. You would stand before the tree and talk to it and tell the tree how sorry you were to take its life. When we took the life of a tree, we used every scrap, every shred right down to the last bit. We used it all. It was wrong to waste something that had been provided for us by this intelligence we didn't quite understand. This is why our people didn't just kill. Sure, they killed ducks, they killed deer, they killed fish and other animals, for eating, for food and other necessities. When they ate the fish they ate the whole thing—the head, tail, skin, many parts of the innards—liver, milt, roe. The head was lovely eating, wonderful taste, very nourishing. When we killed a deer, we ate every bit of it that was edible. When there was nothing left but the bare head, we would burn it so it would not be carried around by dogs or lie there in disrespect.

We lived in big houses, huge houses, some of them a hundred feet long and forty feet wide. Huge. It was just like bringing the environment inside in the winter time. It was airy and pleasant and just lovely to live in with lots of freedom to move about, many people to move about. Sometimes in this big house there would be three or four fires. We had a special word for when your fire went out and you had to go to your grandfather's fire or maybe your uncle's fire and get some coals. You would go with a couple of sticks and get coals from the other fire because in those days there were no matches to start a fire. Often they would send a little boy to get the coals.

This is where the way of life began, in the big houses. They went right around the bay, around the harbour, along the shore. Our villages were in beautiful places because we had the first choice. Lovely beaches, good shelter, plenty of sunshine in the winter. Inside there could be three, four, five families all living together. Mother, father, sons, daughters, aunts, uncles, grandparents, great-grandparents. I lived with my great-grandfather and saw how he lived.

As children we learned from the very beginning, by teaching and discipline, and later on through lecturing—and also by example. You saw how your elders lived, how respectful they were of one another, and how they loved one another. I used to see the old people when they would meet after not seeing each other for a long time. They would hug and embrace each other and the tears would roll down their cheeks. It was one of the finest qualities of life. Leaving, parting, was just the same. It was a sad time, a sad parting. Maybe they were going off to another place, far away, and they would hug each other again.

The training went on as a child grew older, became more severe, harder, tougher. Girls were taught to keep busy all the time, even while sitting their hands had to be going. It became a habit to live in a sane, sensible way, an intelligent way. Discipline took a step up when a girl was turning into a woman and the same with a young man. And on up through marriage. In the old days not only your own elders would discipline you, but also an outsider would come in and lecture the young. This could happen anytime, just happen naturally.

I remember when I was a grown man, out of the blue my mother says, 'Sit on the chair!' and she ripped me up and down. And when she was through talking, she said, 'I'm not mad at you, I like you. I love you—that's why I want you to grow up to be a good person. What will it be to me—I won't even be here. I want you to be a highly honoured, respected person.'

Our people were salt water people, salt water fishermen, boat builders, travellers of the sea, hunters of the sea. Our people hunted seals, porpoises, sea lions, whales and all the fish in the water. They excelled in fishing. Their halibut hook has never been equalled in intelligent structure. They were completely made for halibut—didn't even look like a regular hook. You had to find a log completely rotted away till there was nothing left, and then look for the root. It was hard as steel—that's what you made the hook from. Of course there were all kinds of other ways of catching fish. I used to be taken fishing as a kid. I can remember sitting in the stern with the fish flapping over my face. My mother was good at fishing.

Materials for tools didn't come from a store. You had to go and find the materials. So a child early in life would learn by going along, being with their parents or their elders, gather roots or bark or different things. Early in life a child would learn where to go, what to get, what quality to get, how much. Lots of stuff had to be seasoned. Stored, dried out and so on. Gathering usually took place in the spring. It was a busy time when the sun began to shine and spring got underway.

We're going through bad times now, really bad times. Our people are caught between two ways of life. The old way is gone and we haven't gotten into the new way. We still don't understand. Many of us still don't want it, but what do you do when you're forced into it? You have to. Everything is gone from the past. The hunting's gone, the fishing's gone, the land is gone, the timber, the streams are spoiled, the lakes are spoiled. Forbidden, outlawed, legislated away, harrassed away. My people are caught right in the middle, between two great walls, big bare walls. Not even the past, nothing you can lean back on, no place to go. My people today know too much poverty, chaos, destruction. We are living in the shadow of rubble, the destruction of the beautiful land.

All the tests we've been through. It's a long story.

Some of our young people rebel against education. They don't want it. It's something they have no feeling for. But we're so lacking in education that we can't see what's wrong and how to cope with it. If we had education we could cope. We have to cope with this society. We have to conform to it, adapt, in our own way. Otherwise, we won't survive.

I'm a kind of a throwback to the old ways. I realize I'm a different kind of person because of the time I was born, where I was born, what I was born into. I often think of myself as having one foot in the last century and one in this one. I can cope with the white society. Not all my people can. I know where I come from and where I'm going – not like these people caught between two blank walls. Too often I see my people standing there, caught.

If I told you what they've been through, you'd understand.

RUTH COOK

Village Island

I used to feel so lucky, growing up where my parents came from – this neat village where I grew up with my mother, and my father's country where we went up and made the oolichan oil. I was living in Village Island with my mother and when she got sick for a couple of years with T.B., my English godmothers took us in and looked after us. They really lived their faith – Anglican missionaries who came out and went to live right in the village among us. I was with them for a couple of years. Then I went home back to my mother for two or three years. They took me back again when I was six and kept me till I was going to school that following summer, at residential school in Alert Bay.

They prepared me months ahead for it, but I was still excited. At the same time I was scared of a big school. I didn't want to leave my village. What for? I'm happy here. Why do I have to go? My mother could see that the changes were coming and we were going to have to have some education. And she explained, 'I can see the days are changing. I'm not going to bother teaching you any of our old Indian ways.' She meant the Potlatch ways, because she could see that would be phased out too. It wouldn't be that important for us, anyway. Maybe to other people, but not to us. That was my mother's personal view. She said, 'You're going to have to learn to read and write because when you grow up you're going to have to get a job. It's time.' So she was open enough to see that we were going to be living in different days.

I can remember when I was about eleven during the summer holidays when we were home for the summer. The other kids would be playing outside after lunch and my mother would sit us down and say, 'Now you're going to learn to knit.' And we had to sit and learn to knit and embroider, and bake. 'What good are you going to be if you don't learn these things now? Because when you grow up and have a family you're going to know nothing, so it's my duty to teach you.' She was a great woman and she was consistent when she made rules. I was a stubborn child. We'd go home in the summer and I still had to go to bed at seven-thirty when the other children were still out playing. I never gave up trying. 'Mom, please just once can I stay up till eight o'clock?' 'No, you're going to bed at seven-thirty.' And she never gave in to me and I never stopped trying. So that helped her in her discipline of us.

The pace of living wasn't like it is today. Our village life was placid. There was such a serenity there because it wasn't rush, rush, rush. You just got up in the morning, lit your fires, got your breakfast, did your washing, and then whatever

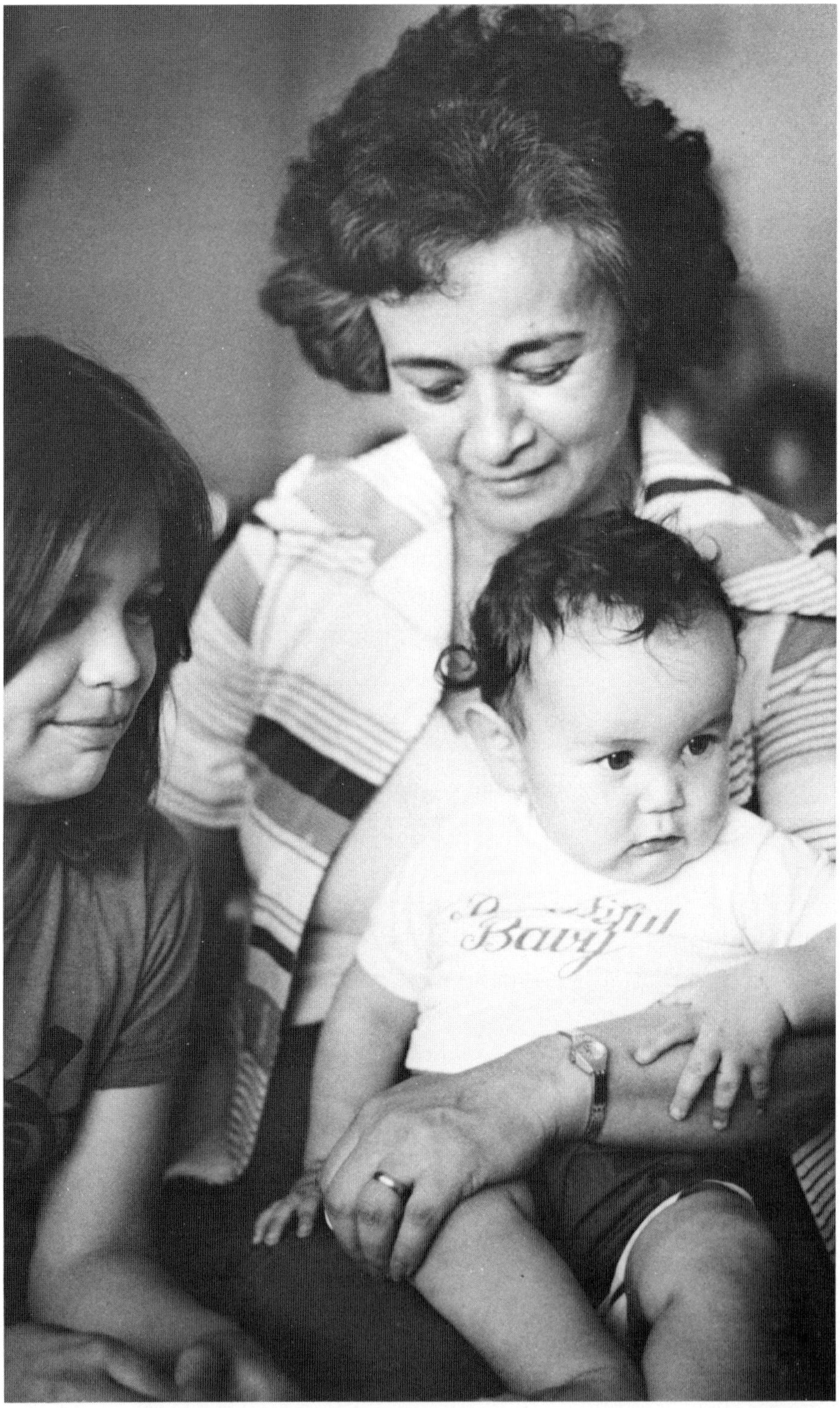

needed to be done—which was mostly picking berries. You packed your lunch and away you went for the whole day—came back with your berries, cleaned it, prepared it, jarred it, whatever you had to do with it. And this would go on till the weekend when the men would bring the fish home. While they're out fishing, you're home picking berries. And then when the fish came you barbequed it and you canned it, and you smoked it. So that you were having a holiday as well as preparing your food for the winter. In winter, about November, the fall fish would come. You'd wait till they went up the river and spawned, and then when they came down they lost their oil. They weren't so rich anymore. Those fish you filleted and made what we called *kawas*. You would completely dehydrate that. That fish you could keep for months and months. You'd fillet it very thin, then hang it up in the smokehouse for a few days, bring it in and dry it completely. *Kawas*—that's the Kwakwala language.

The men would go trapping while the women were up the river making *kawas*. I remember my grandfather going out every day, setting his lines, and checking them, and mom and I would stay and work on the fish. This would go on over two or three months. After that, about January, there would be potlatching and dancing all winter till spring.

Every tribe had its own little area, for the halibut season. Ours was a place called White Beach, about a half hour's run from Alert Bay. That was our trolling place. Little cedar shacks for cabins. Our needs were so few—just pack in our feather mattresses and blankets, pots and pans and tubs and we're all set to go. You might bring along a little wood stove. Although a lot of us just built a fire on the dirt floor. By then the weather would be warming up anyway. It was just like a little summer camp. You took just what you needed. A lot of our stuff was made out of cedar—storage boxes, and with the mattresses that's all you needed.

The whole year revolved around the food supply, until the commercial fishing came in. Then most of the women would go to the canneries and work while the men were fishing. A few would stay in the villages and look after things.

Watching and observing so much of everything your mom did, you just picked it up—it was a natural thing built into you, the responsibility of learning to help, from day one. You were responsible for anyone younger than you. It was a natural thing to look after one another.

It was a real shame that they had to leave the villages, because they were such peaceful places to live. I really longed for the village life for three or four years in the school even though I was busy meeting new friends, wrapped up in school work and stuff. I would still get this pang – 'Ah, I wish I was back in the village!' And then the nature of our people was very placid, too, and I think our diet had something to do with that. But there was no rush. You worked through the seasons and nobody was screaming at you all the time because it's nearly four o'clock or something. You moved with the time and it wasn't a lazy moving. You were in harmony with nature.

You never had to worry if you got sick. You always had an uncle or an aunt, or the grandparents were there to lend a helping hand. I can remember waking up, and hearing, 'Oh, there's someone sawing wood. You better go help him after breakfast.' It was an insult to think of paying for help. You just helped and shared everything in the village life. I think this is what we miss.

We grew up in an area where things were really changing and yet when I look back, I can pick out the good that happened too. It can't all be negative. Sure, all those injustices were done to us. It's unfortunate they thought we didn't have any brains to think for ourselves. They thought they were doing good. And they did do a lot of good. I never want to be a product of people that can hold on to bitterness, because it's us that suffer the most when we do.

I haven't been successful at all times for my children not be bitter. For they experience prejudice where I didn't. And I would find it so difficult when they came home and told me things. I hadn't known those problems. But they did. My girl who was quite dark and has long hair – even in restaurants they would ignore her and serve non-Indian people. She ran into those things. It's not easy teaching them to cope with it, and they're always going to be running into it. You have to live the best way you can.

As children we didn't need money to buy fancy toys. We'd just go down to the beach and say, 'Hey, let's play cannery,' or 'Let's play house.' You'd drag all the kelp up the beach, find shells to use for knives and cut it all up and in no time you'd have a big store going – your imagination running wild. You didn't worry about toys. Our beaches were so clean – most of ours had the white shells and that's where we'd play. Oh, we had a good time. There were so many berries out, and wild fruit – you just helped yourself when you were hungry, and kept on playing. Your dogs were running around with you and there was never any harm. We didn't have any desire to go anywhere else. We used to go into Alert Bay on weekends or special occasions, but we couldn't wait to get out of there and back to our villages. That was where my heart always was.

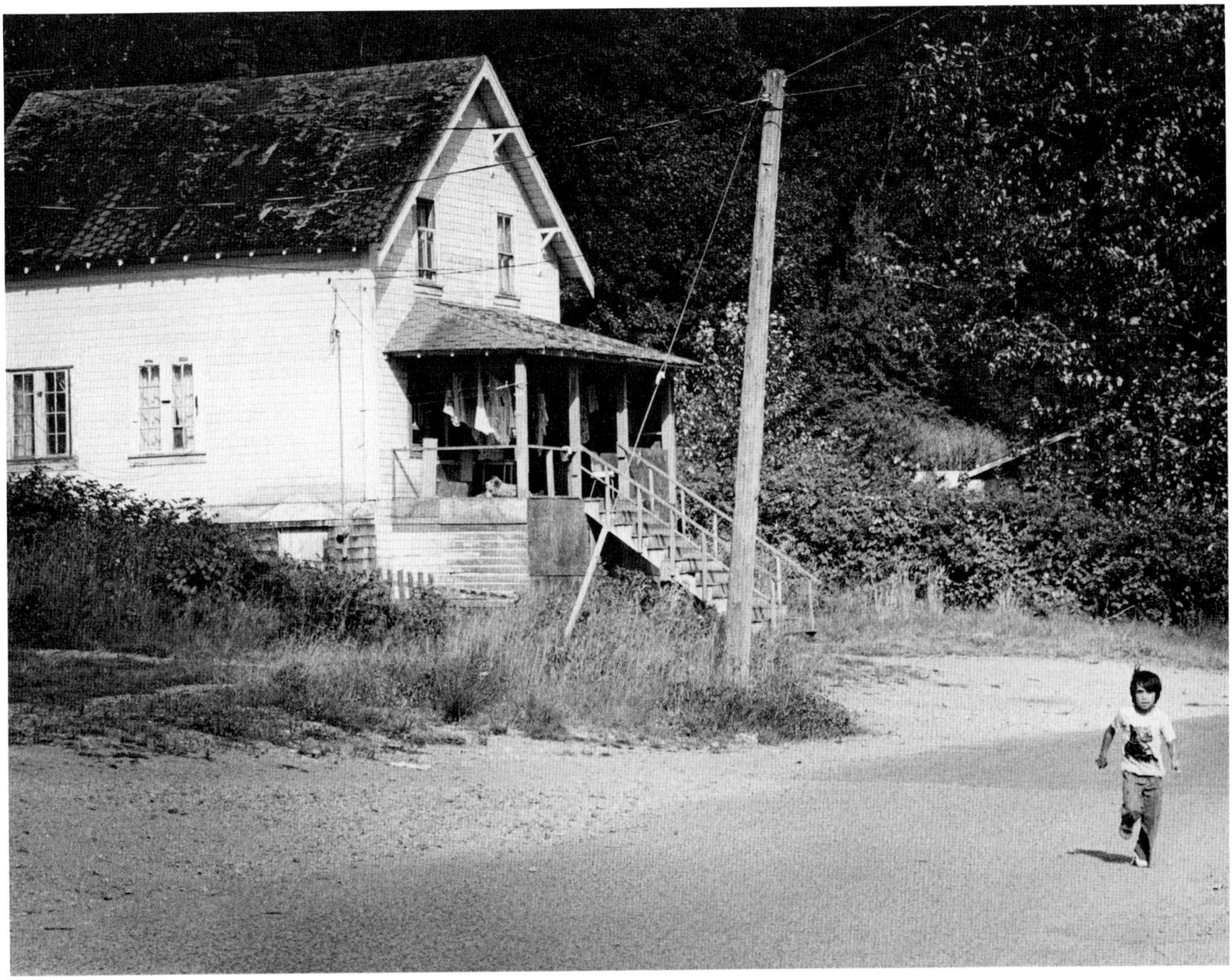

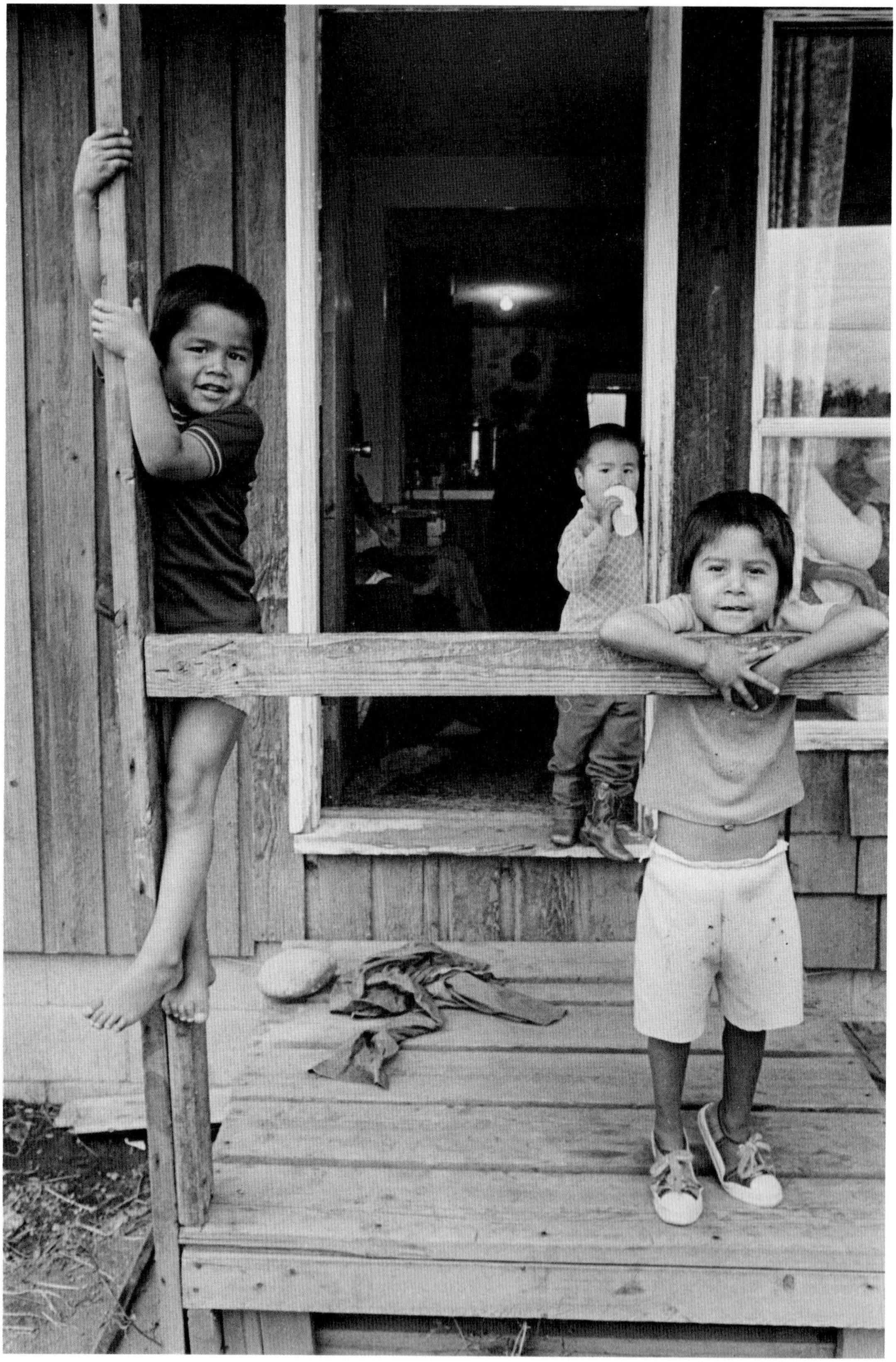

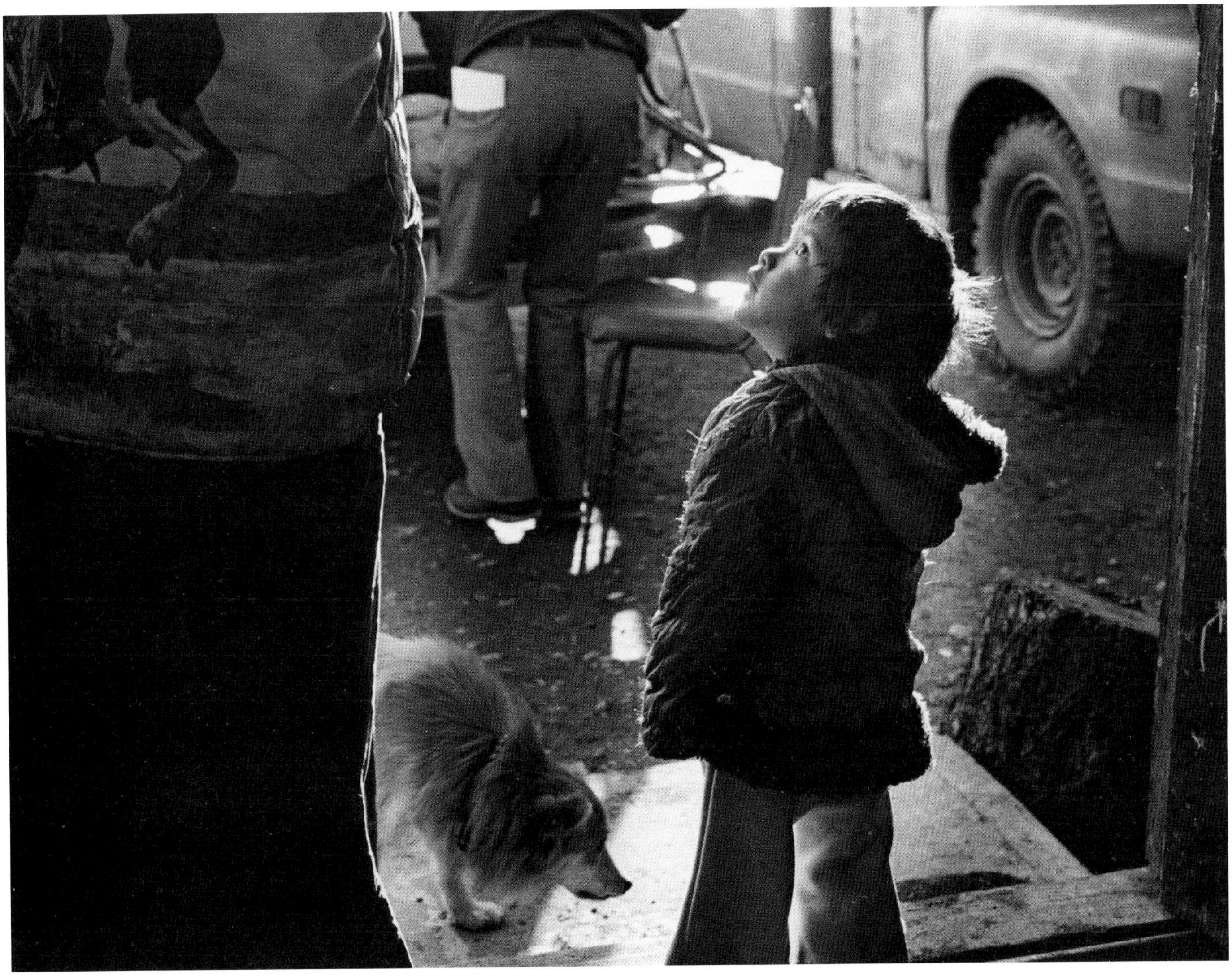

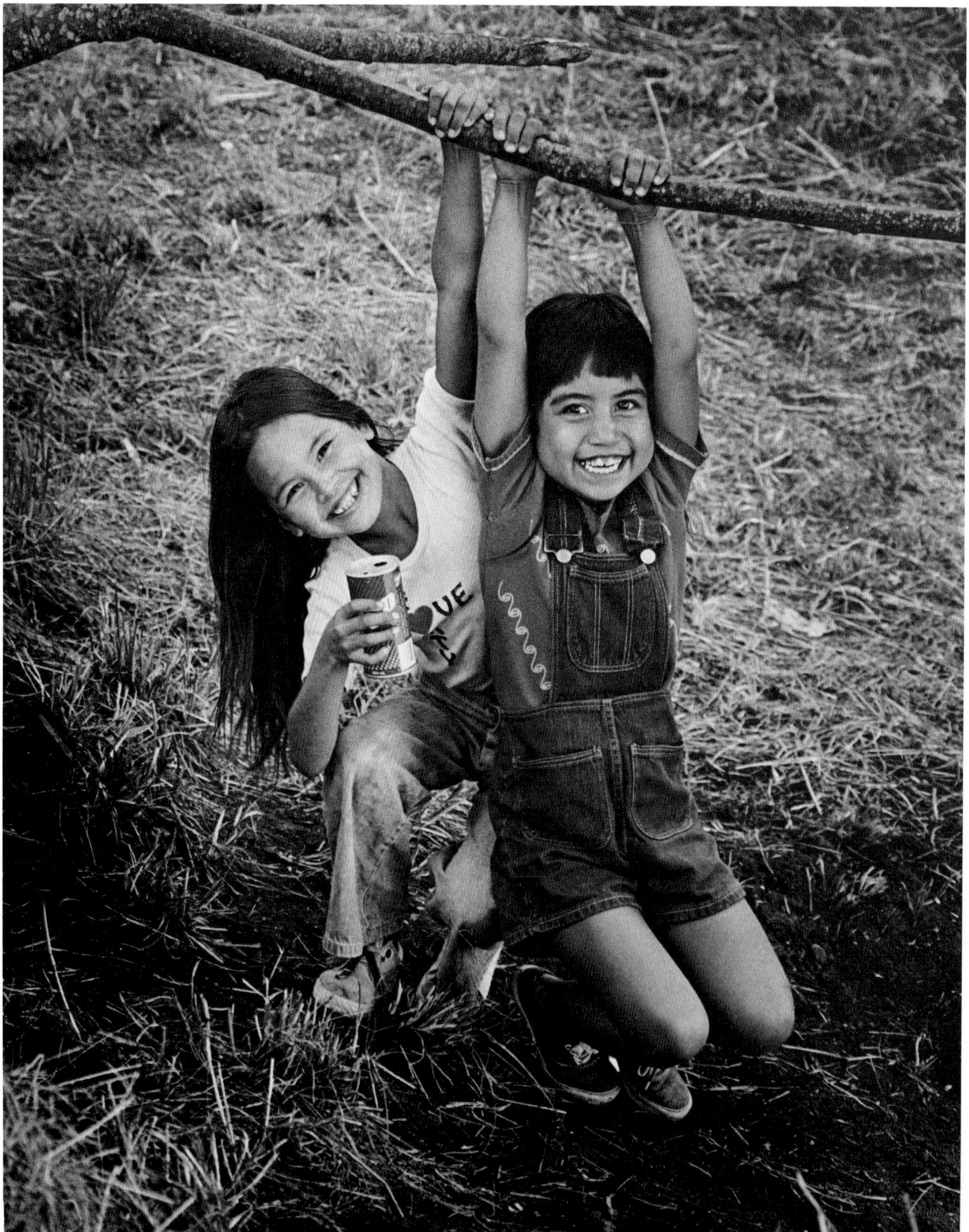

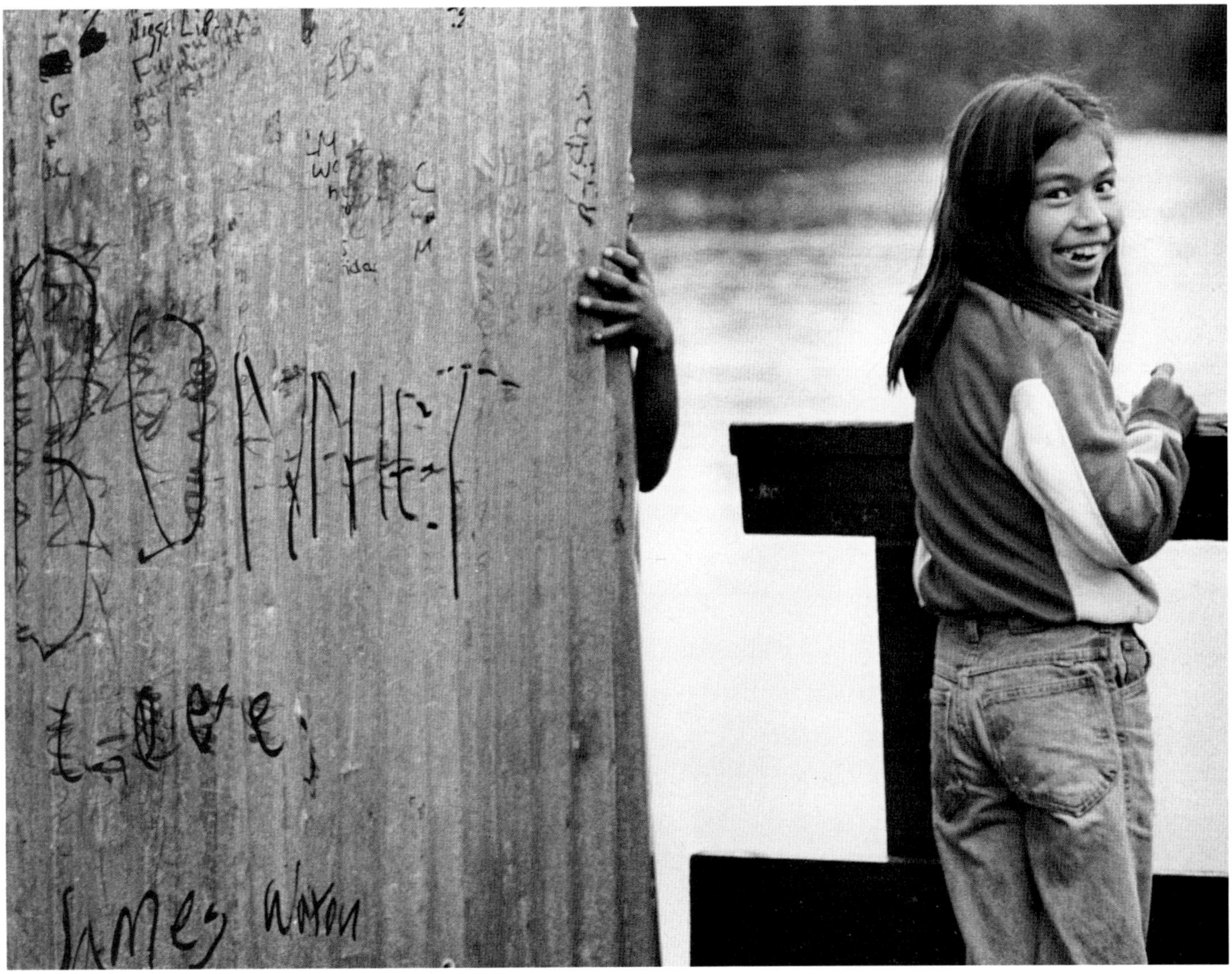

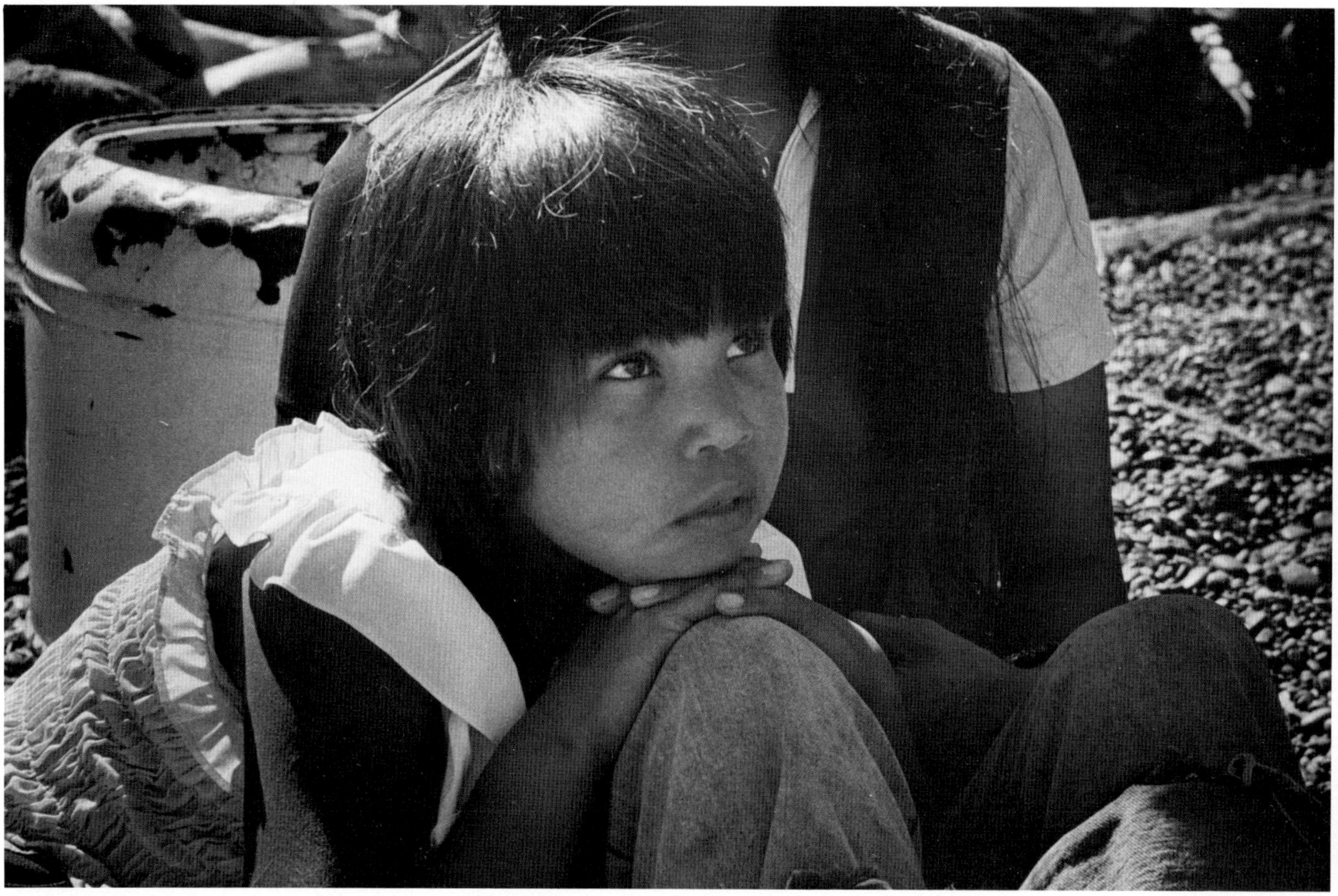

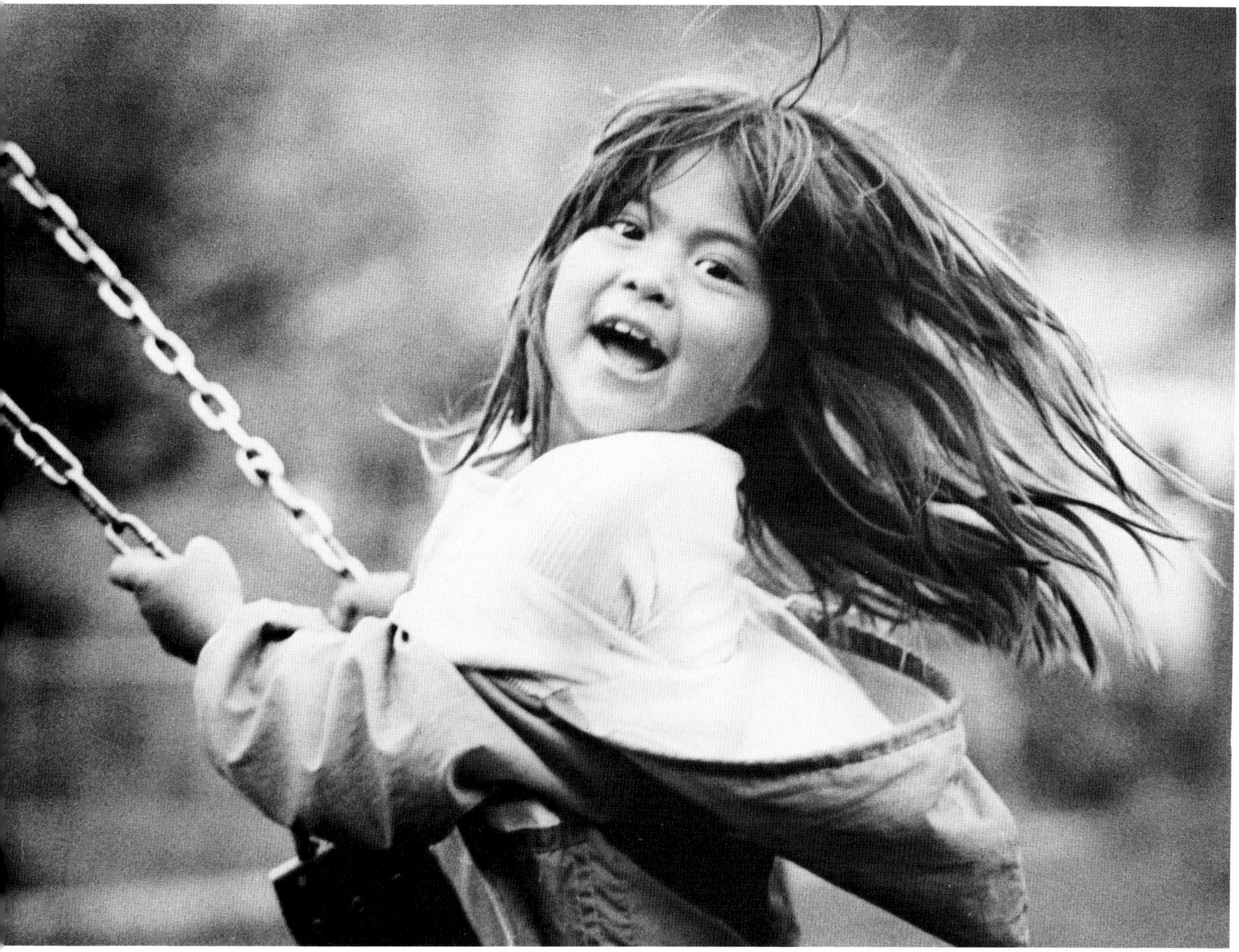

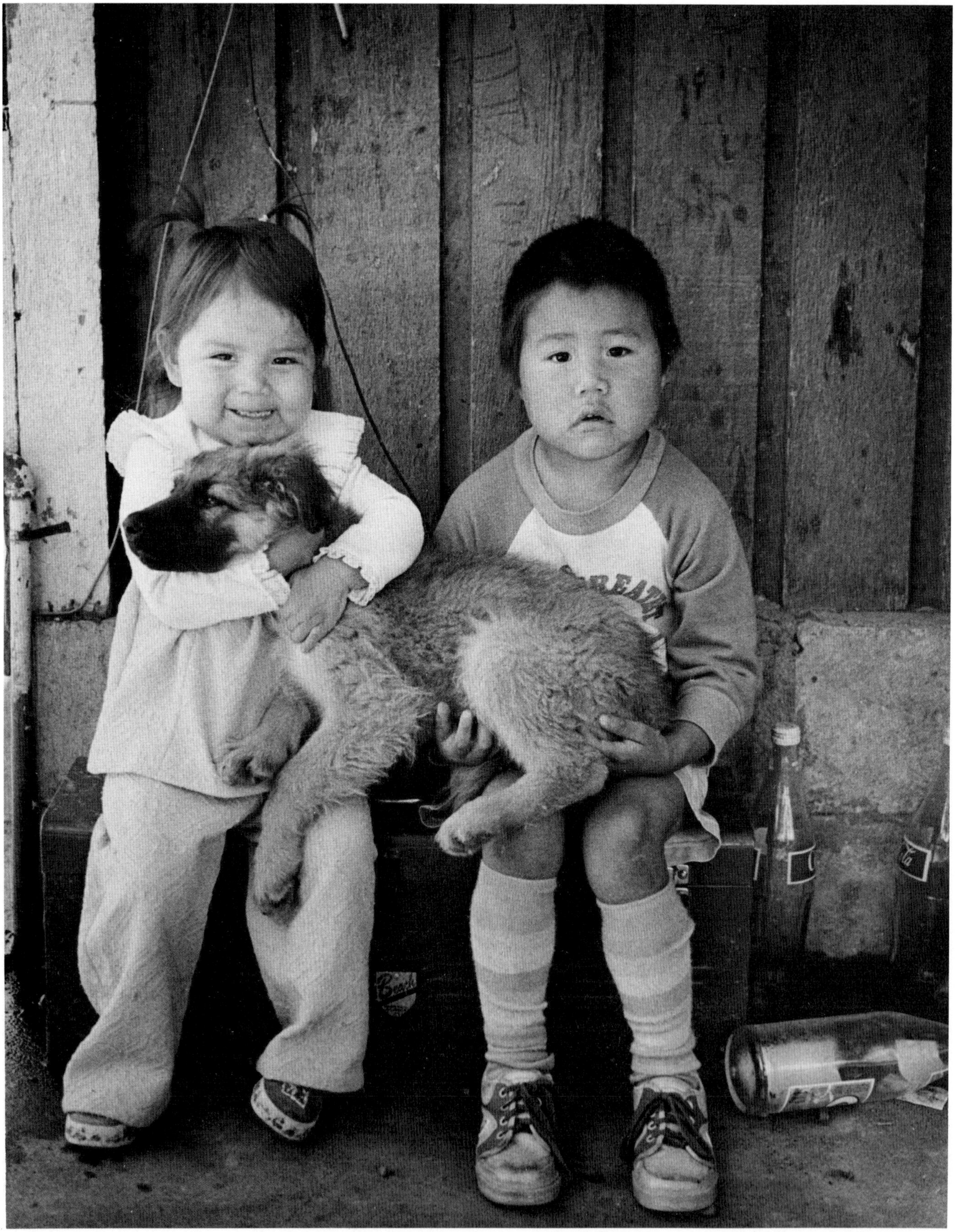

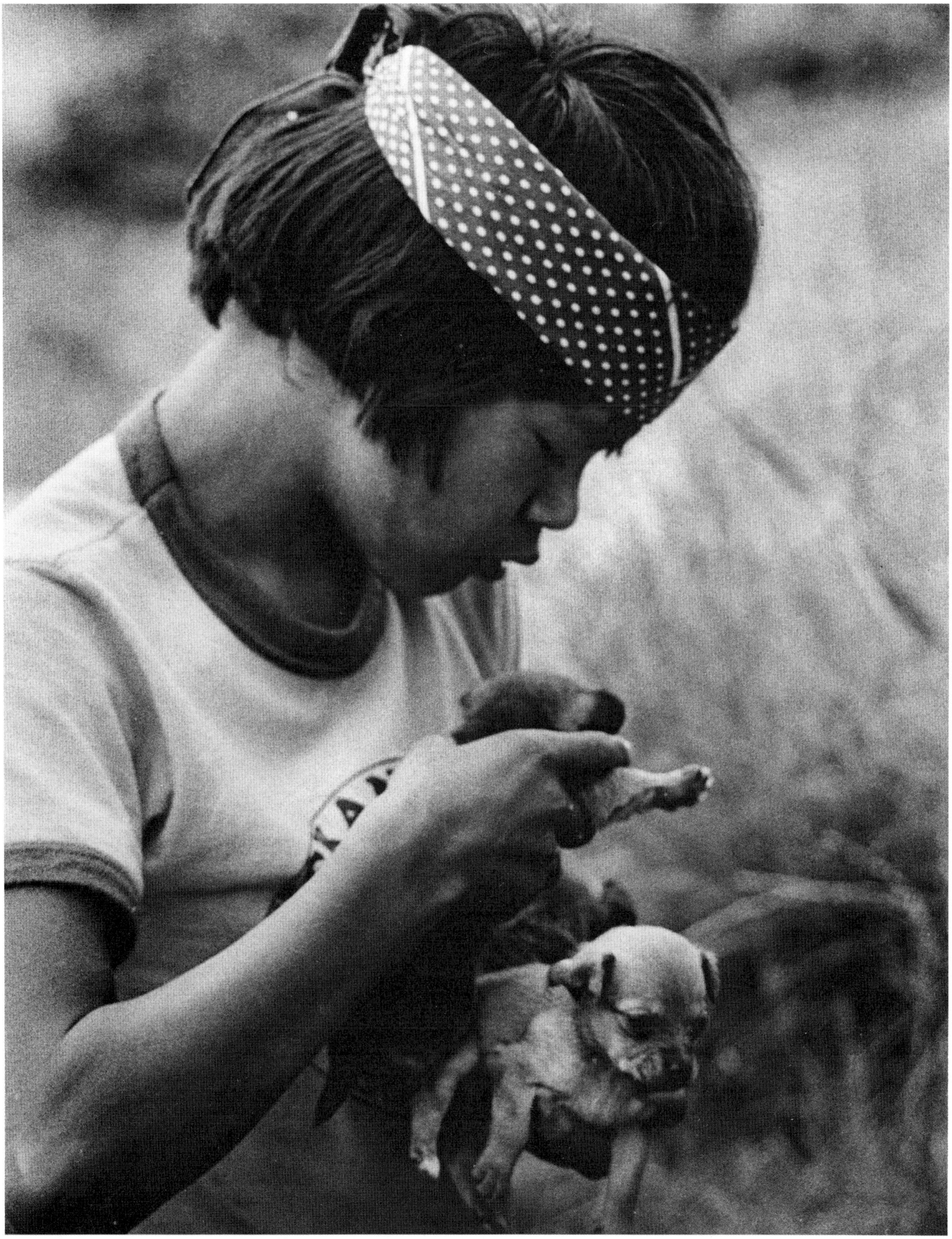

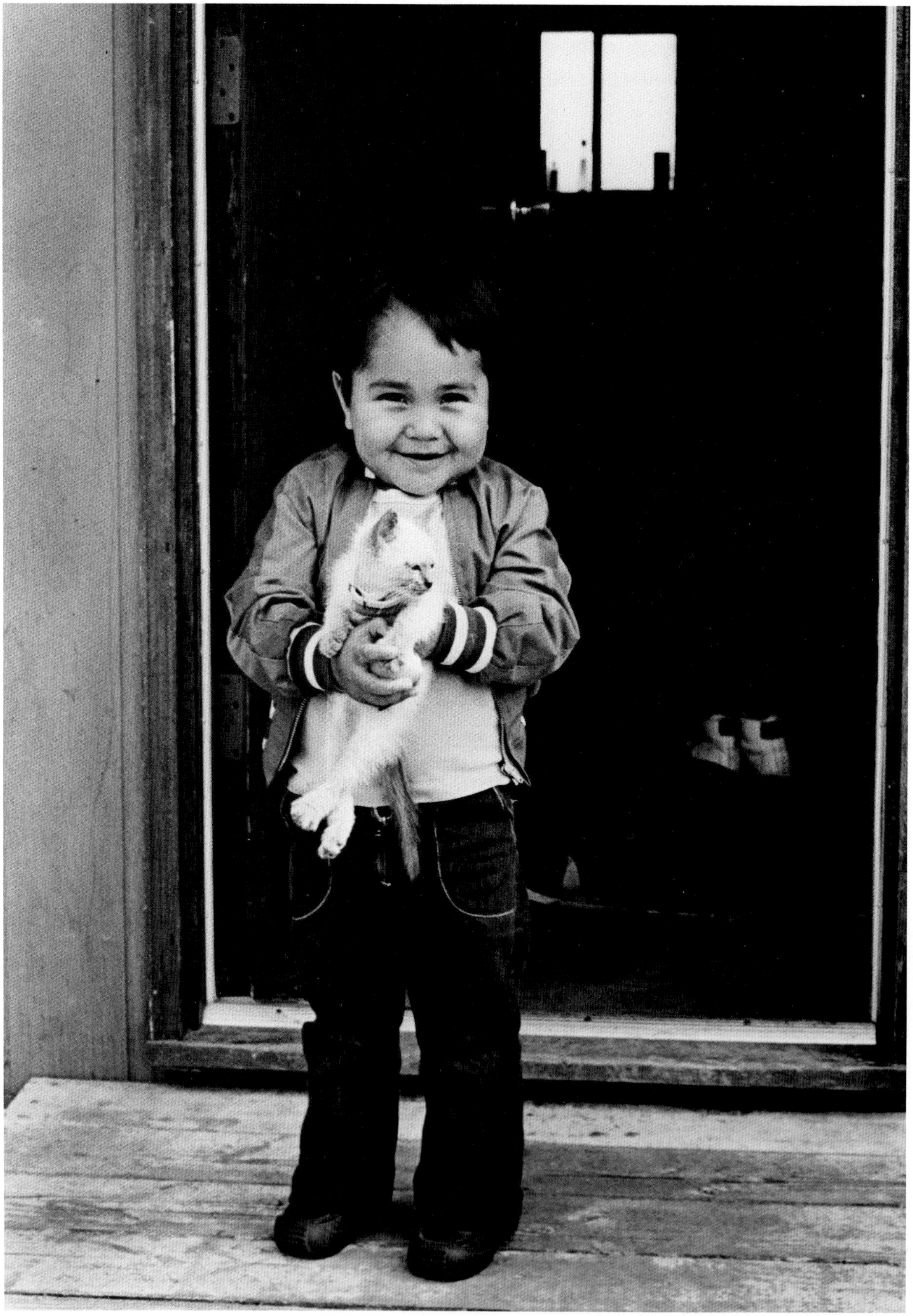

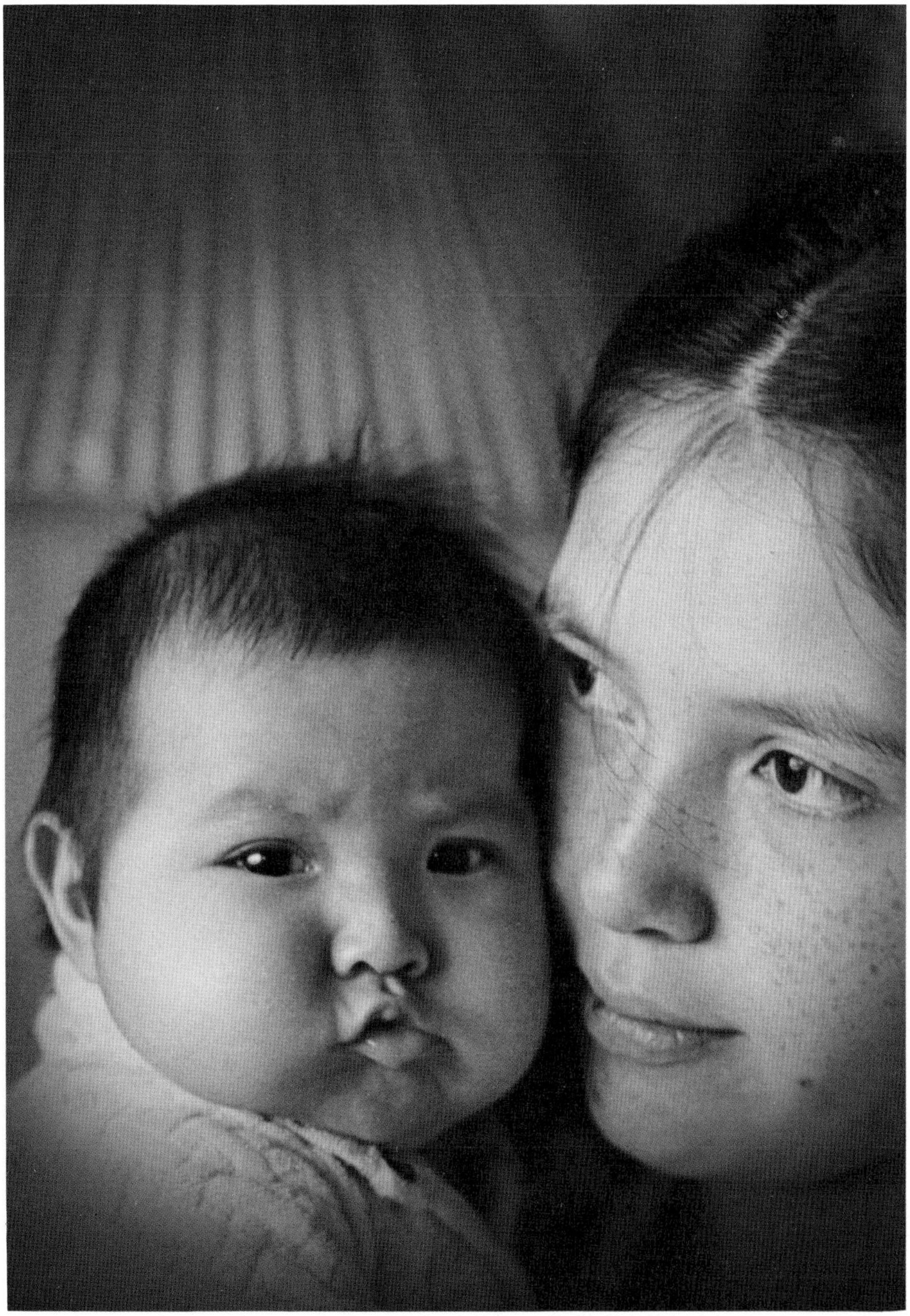

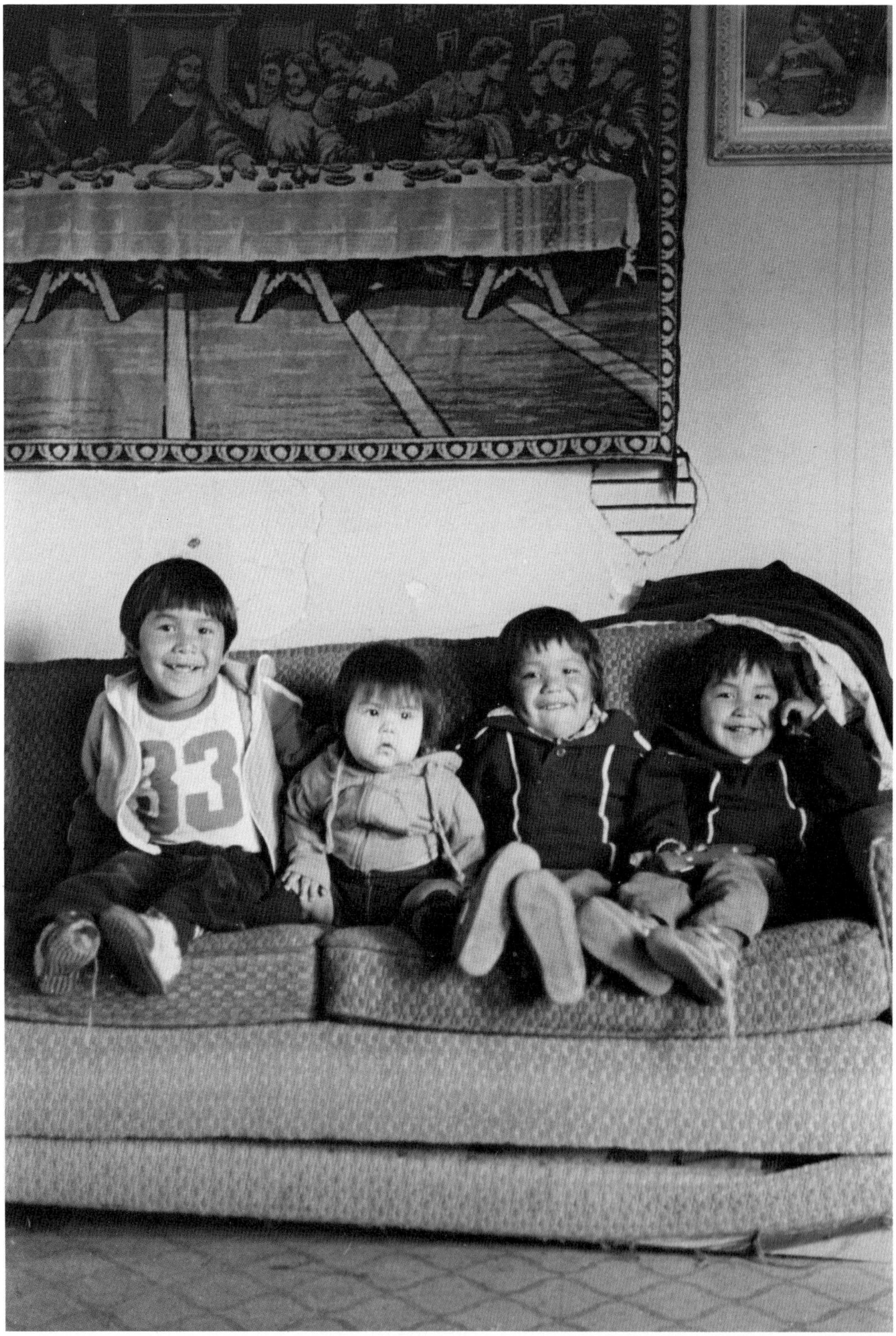

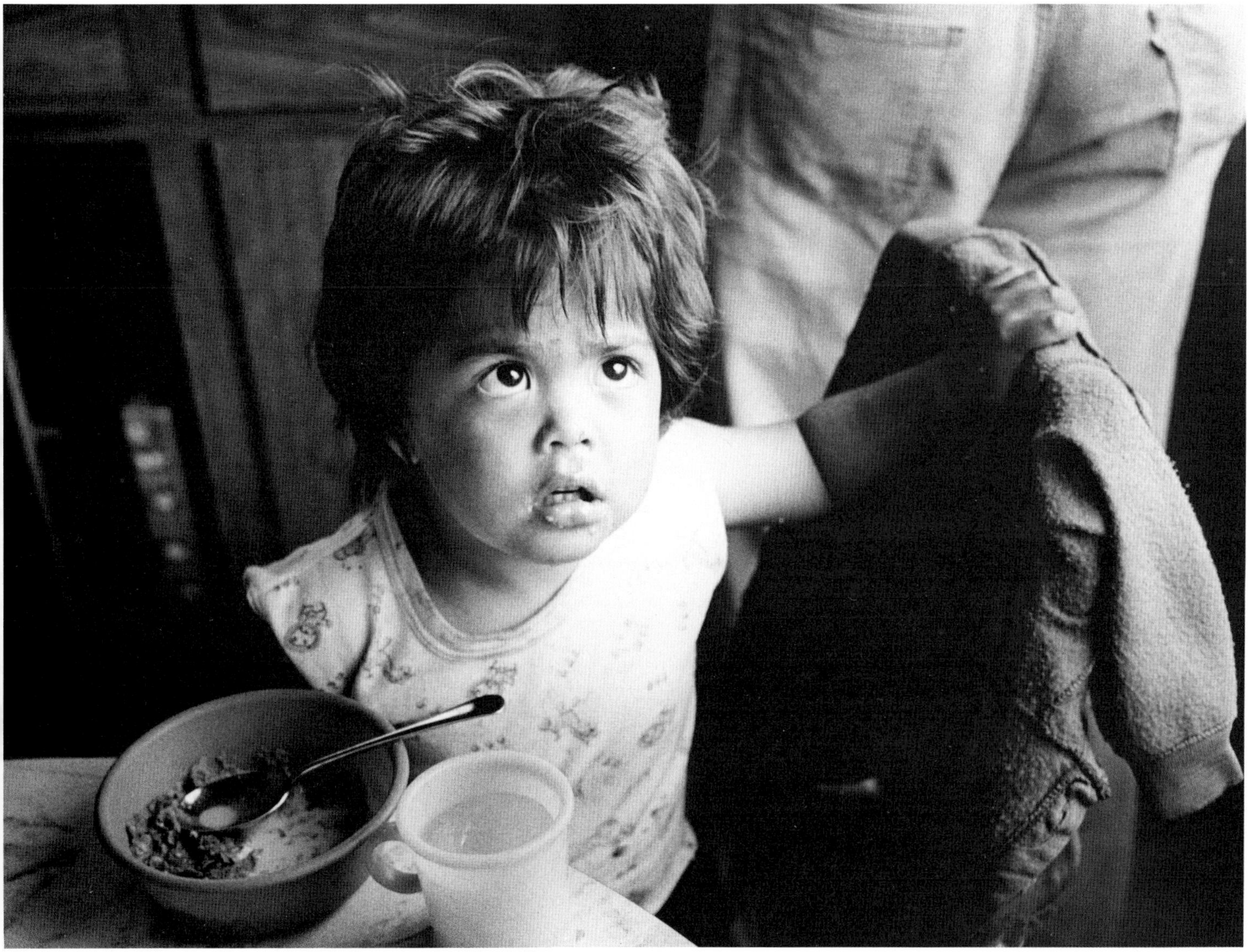

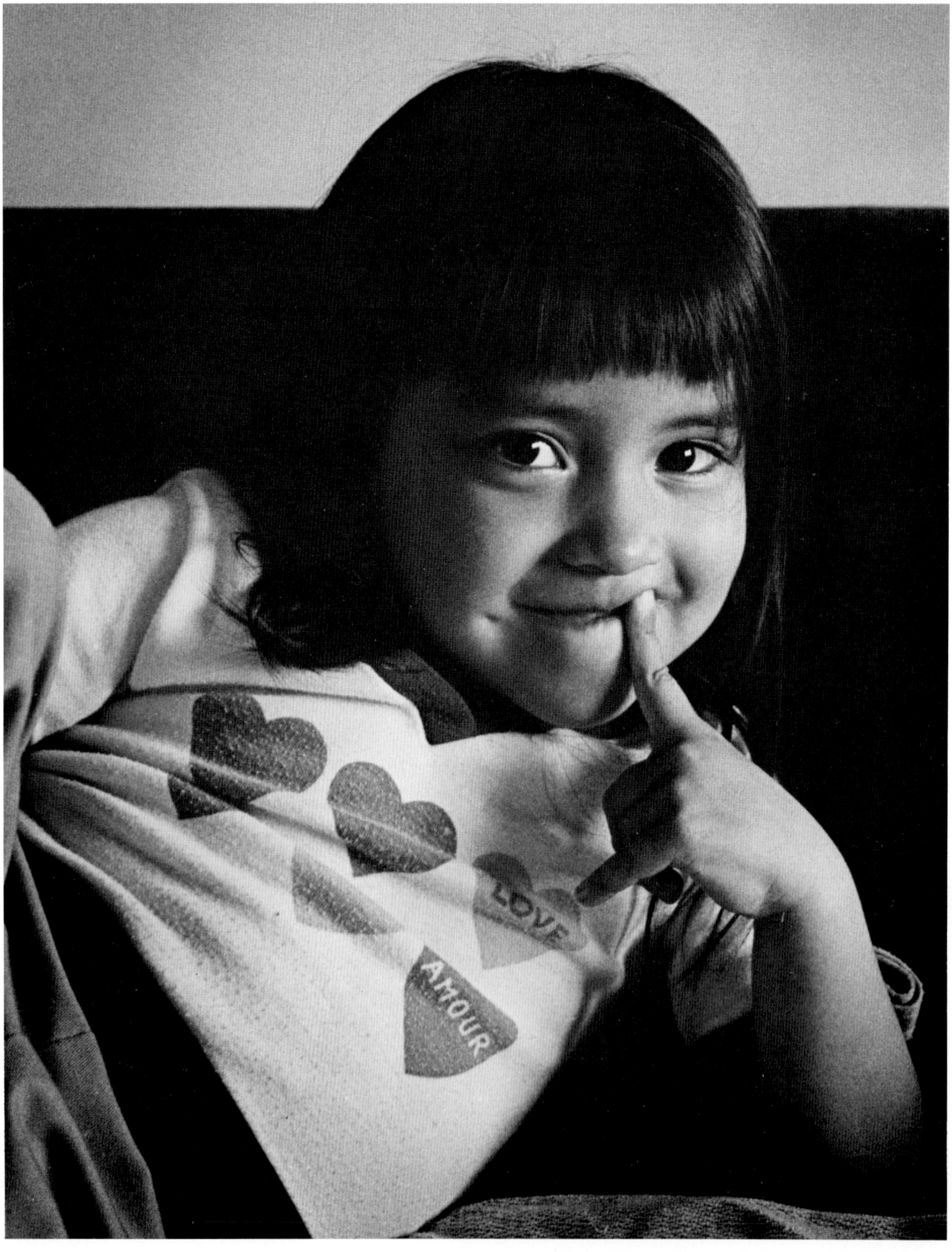
LOVE
AMOUR

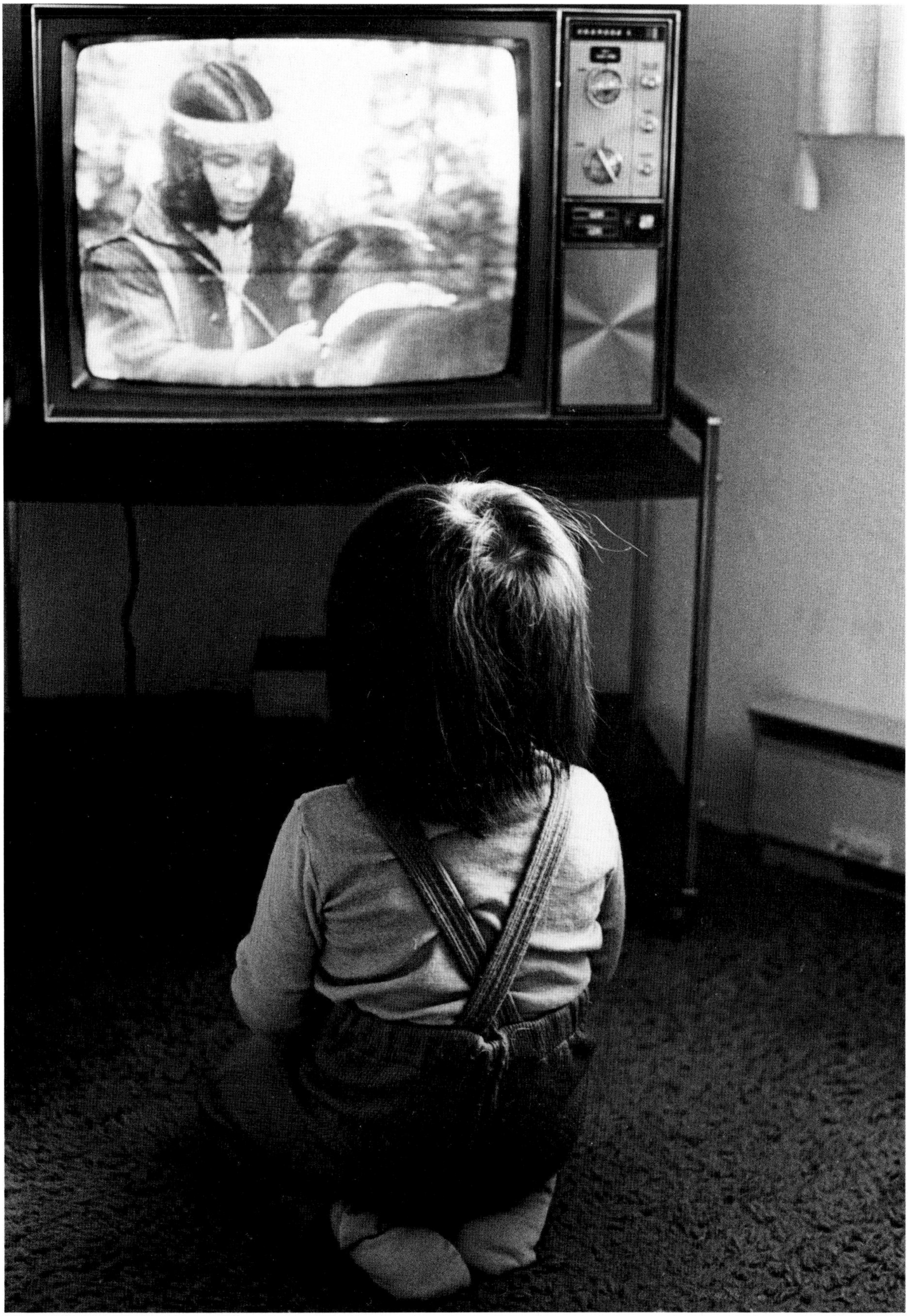

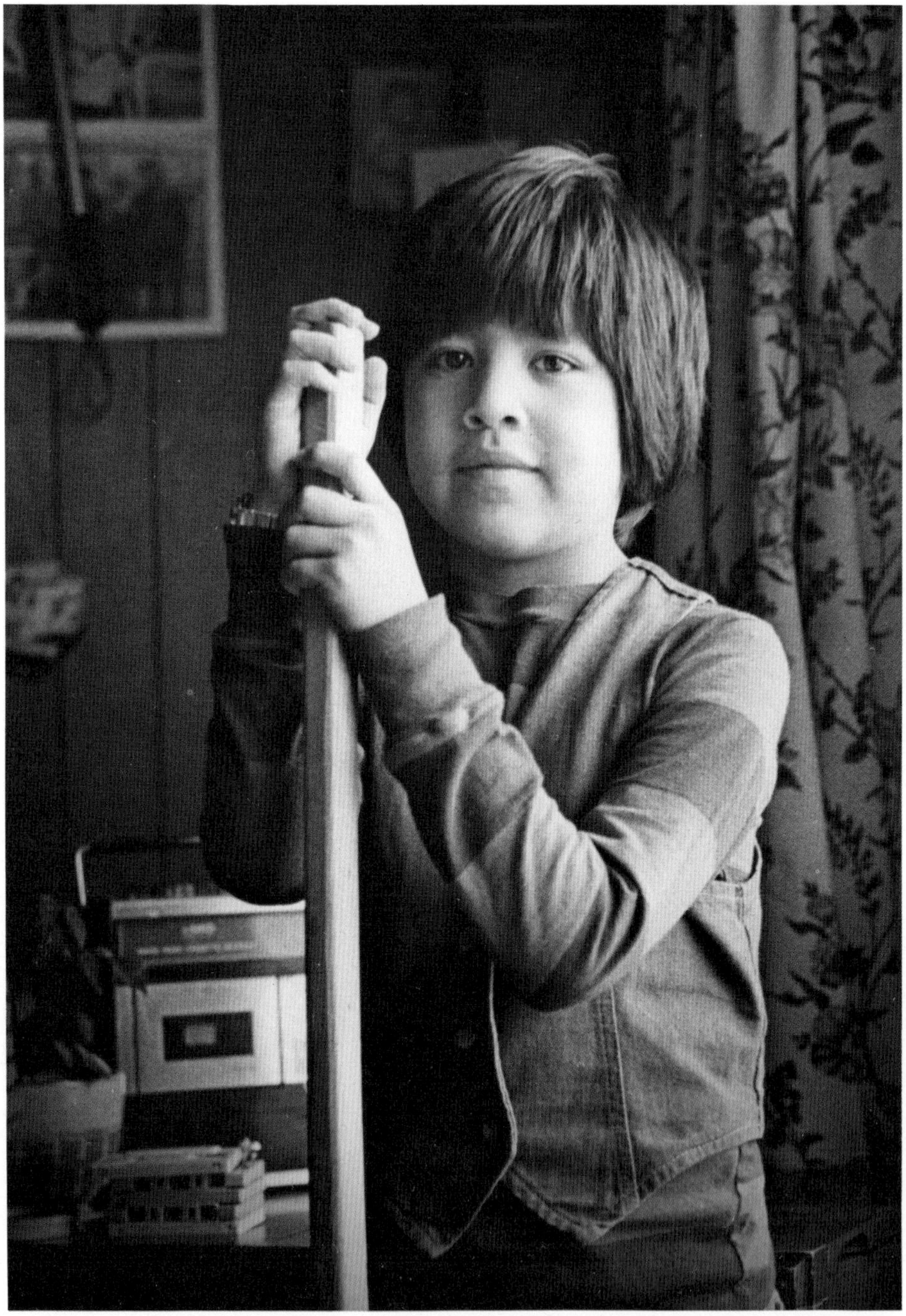

DOROTHY SANVIDGE
Mowachaht

When I was a little girl I lived in Friendly Cove most of the time. When we were going to get the fish we lived in Sand Point. There's a reserve there. Or in a place called Hisnitt – that's where we went for our fish. It's on your left hand as you're going into Head Bay, on a reserve there. We actually have twenty-three reserves to our name – the Nootka Band. That's a lot of reserves they're not using.

In the summer Friendly Cove is nice but in the winter it's wicked. There were daisies there every springtime and summer. Oh, it was very nice when I was a little girl because those flowers used to come out every springtime and there was a man who kept everything blooming and clean. No, there were no berry bushes there. The berries were in the gardens each one had and weren't allowed to grow outside. That's the way it was. And the ball field was nothing but bushes and they cleared that off by hand. They did it all by hand – real big trees they felled. They uprooted the roots. And now it's nothing. And all those totem poles fell down. They just let them go. My sister Terry says she'll never move from there.

Children then were like any others only they didn't wear what we wear today. They wore cedar bark capes and things. It would be nice to show them. I know how to make those capes, but I haven't been doing it for some time now. I've been busy knitting and I've started this bead work. I need grasses to do my shopping baskets, too.

But it seems sometimes that they were happier than some children are now. They were running free, not held back from anything. And they learned quick. I learned how to do things when I was five years old. I could do the work my grandmother taught me. Today girls can't learn until they're teenagers. I'd like somebody to learn the basket work because I'm about the last one from our reserve – I'm the last one doing basket work.

I learned how to help with the fish, smoking fish. I learned early to fix fish, smoke meat, everything. I'd be about nine or ten when I started helping with the fish. That was young. These kids don't know how yet.

The children had a ball game they used to play, and games with arrows and spears. Even little girls played. Boys and girls all played together. The older people played indoor games. The played with bones – whale bones with markings on them, like dice – the white people call them dice. When I was about twelve I couldn't understand what they were playing. But they really enjoyed that game.

There used to be all kinds of games. The men were in one place, the women were

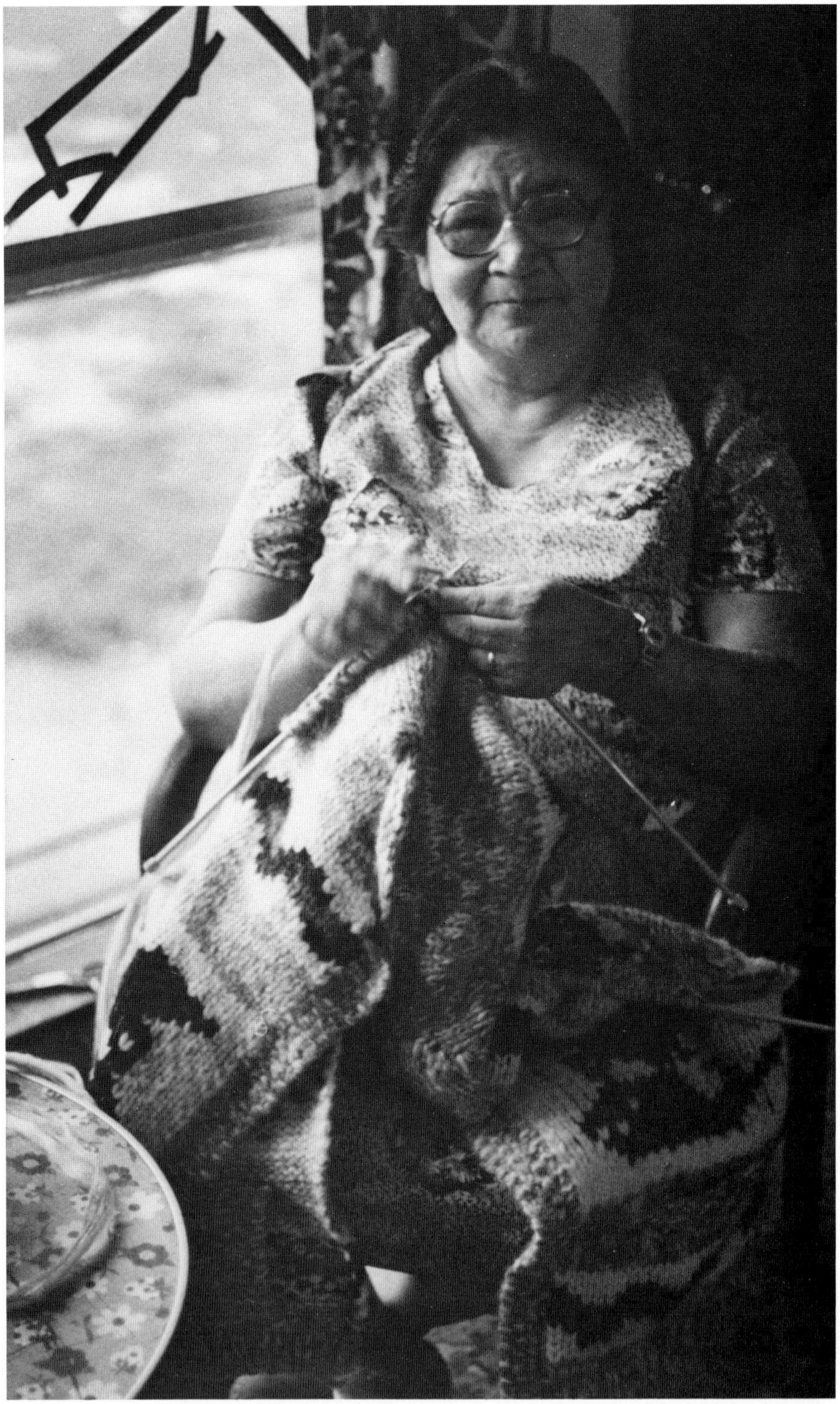

out in another place, and the younger generation was in a different place. They were all separated – all in different houses. In the winter evenings everyone gathered together. There was somebody watching the children, but the little ones, they had grandmothers at home to take care of them.

It wasn't hard to learn things because we listened and from that we learned. We learned at an early age. That's the way it was. That's what I always tell my grandchildren – when I get after them, you know. I have to scold them once in a while. But they have to be told, 'If I didn't care for you, I'd let you do it. In a few years, you'd dislike me, you'd hate me, because I never got after you. Today you think I don't like you because I get after you, but I do it because our grandparents got after us.' That's the way we were taught. They were pretty strict with us, in certain ways. The girls weren't allowed to go out at a certain age. They had to be with their older sisters, or someone who could take care of them. The boys were kind of free, some of them. Some of them couldn't go anyplace after they were older. My dad didn't allow them to go anyplace much. They had to learn to work. Different families had different ways of teaching their children but my dad was pretty strict with us. I'm thankful to him that I learned a lot.

Girls were pretty young when they got married. Some got married soon after they became a woman – to keep them out of trouble, I think. That was before my time, because my mother got married pretty young. Some of them were a little older before they became a woman, about fifteen. But they were always kept in. They couldn't go anyplace unless their family went with them. It seemed kind of cruel that you couldn't go to a dance unless you were with someone. But it's something when you look back on it – we've learned something from it.

Long ago, girls were forced to marry their husbands. The boy's parents would choose the wife, so it was between the parents. I had a parent marriage like that. I didn't want to get married, I said. I wanted to go to a high school and become a nurse. But my dad said, 'If you don't want to get married now, you can go your own way.' So I didn't want to go my own way – I was too young. But my marriage was okay. It was chosen by them but we got along. I lived with my husband for thirty-two years. No divorce or anything. I see a lot of divorce these days. They choose their own husbands, or the other way around. Long ago if a girl left her husband, her hair was shaved right off. They were outcasts in the tribe. Anyone could take them and do what they liked with them and once they did that the tribe had no more use for them. They were pretty rough on the girls in the early years. We had to get married like that.

Children learned when they were very small that they couldn't make any noise at dances—at Indian dances. Especially the wild man dance—with his face all black. The dancers from Alert Bay used to go into the woods for six months or so to become a wild man. And if he was from a different reserve, the children couldn't even chew gum, or drink anything until he had finished dancing. We learned to sit still when we were at a dance. Nobody could move. When they were dancing like that, if they saw someone playing around—they bit them. Because that's what they were—kind of wild. There'd be three or four men watching him so he wouldn't get near the people too much. They'd take him out when he finished dancing. It was something to watch.

There were all kinds of dances that aren't done anymore. Dances to give the kids names—Indian names. They lasted about four days. The kids were kept in a room and couldn't be seen until they got their names.

The houses were decorated with ferns for the dances—all over the place. It used to smell nice. They used to do that in Chief Maquinna's house. He had a real big Thunder Bird, and a man could sit in there and make a rattling noise like thunder. It was very nice. I was about five or six years old when they had that Thunder Bird. They put it away when Maquinna died. It was a whale with a thunderbird sitting on it.

Some of the children can dance. It goes according to the people who own the dances. We all have—well, most of us have our own songs for dancing and the little ones can do these dances if we teach them. I know my own songs from my grandmother. She taught me when I was young, and I'm trying to teach my son. He's going to tape it so he'll remember it. My father knows some songs from his side. He's got different songs from my grandmother's side. Her father was a chief, and that's where they came from. If Chief Maquinna was invited, my great grandfather had to be there. Even if there were ten other chiefs invited, he had to be there, because it was the rule.

We all had our own seats. My grandmother gave me that seat. At a big party they'd call our names and we had our own places to go to. We couldn't sit with our families. When I got married, they gave a party and they gave my seat to Wilfred, my brother. Because I married into a different tribe. It's something to know about because it was something great to them at the time. We had respect.

Children were taught to respect. They learned everything at an early age because they were told things every evening before bedtime. The elders sat and told the children about things. And if they weren't teaching them anything, they were singing the songs which the children had to learn. That's how I learned all the songs we were supposed to have—our own songs.

I'm used to having children around. You have to understand children. If you scold them too much, it's not good for them. I know—I have grandchildren. They're all grown up now. I always tell them, 'Never look back, you look ahead. Look at the people who are raising you.' And I say to them, 'I tried to teach you the right way. I never hit you or anything.' You've got to be pretty good, because they need correcting, you know. You have to understand them.

I think in some ways it is harder for a child today. A lot of them aren't with their parents. I have some of these kids who haven't been with their parents for years now.

I tell the children every day, every time we're together, 'Make use of your education, because I didn't get much education. I just went to grade eight—never got a chance for high school. You kids have a chance. I want you to go through that.' One of my grandchildren is thinking of going to university.

There's a lot of children that are going the right way, after their schooling. Sure, there's some that aren't, like every different nationality. There's always somebody going the wrong way. We're not all the same. I was raised and I was taught how to do things and I'm so used to doing those things that I love children and I want to help them. That's why I want to make this a bigger place where I can have more children to take care of. That's all I've always wanted—to help the little kids.

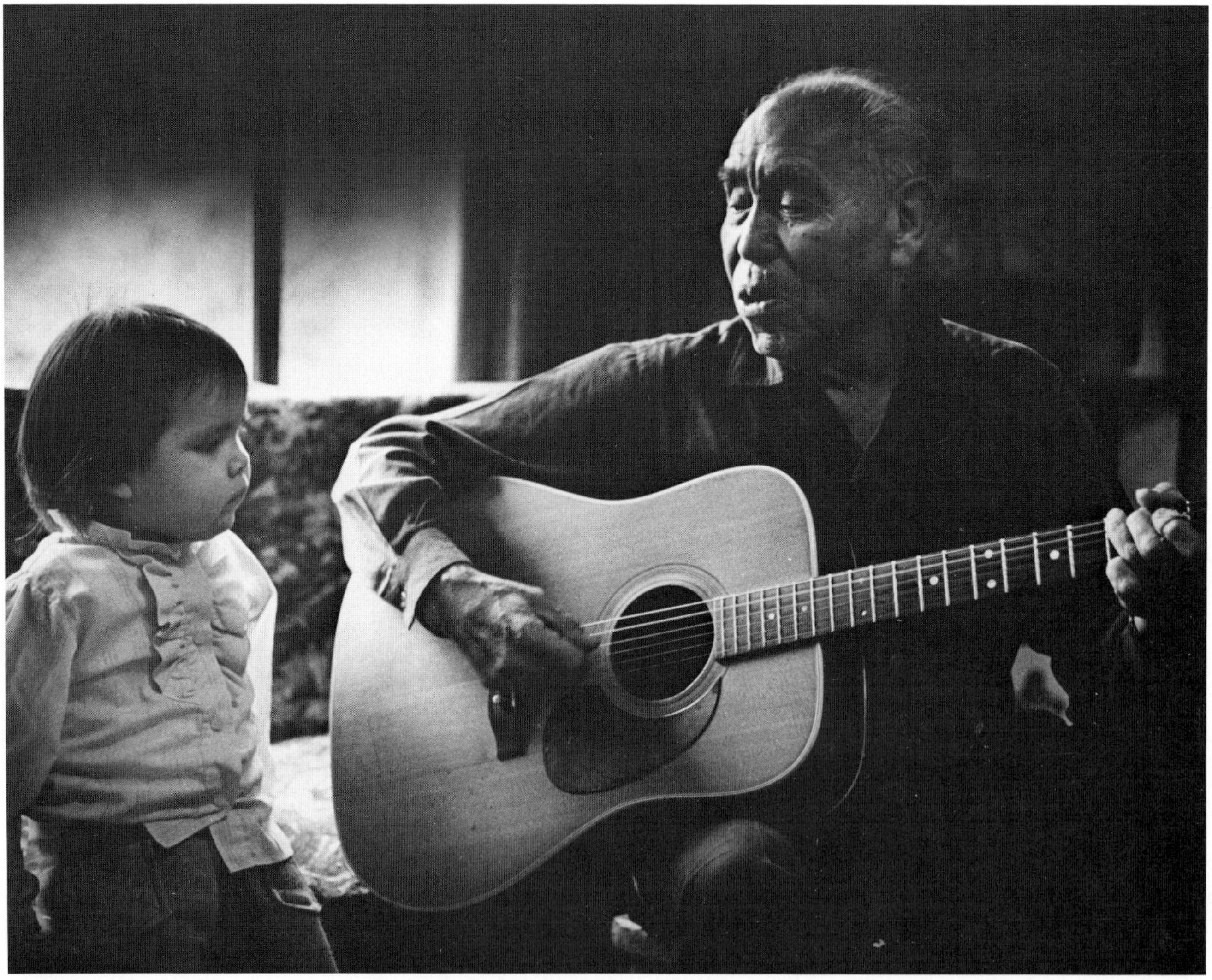

STAN JAMES
Nanaimo

I was born in Nanaimo and I can't remember what year, but my dad died when I was one, and my mom had a real hard time. She couldn't keep me. She sent me to a boarding school when I was seven and I stayed there. It was hard because I longed for home and my dad. I had no dad, no land, no nothing. My mom didn't write me any letters. I never got any Christmas gifts. The other kids got them—the kids from home. So I was pretty despondent all the time. I'd be found down by the river, crying. So the teacher told me, 'You better yourself as best you can, and think you can do better than those that got a dad.' So I did my best. Kids who carved—from Prince Rupert, Masset, Skidegate—they liked me. So I learned to carve.

The school got to be my regular home—I had a lot of buddies there. In fact, I cried when I left that school. I had to leave there when I was eighteen. I didn't go very high—grade five. When I got home I didn't know anyone. I had to start over again.

I came out of school and went to Eli Sampson's dad in Chemanus Bay. They kept me very well. They didn't speak English, and their life was the horse and buggy days. They're the ones who taught me a few things. Like, when they got something kind of rare to eat, the young kids had to go without, and keep a cheerful attitude. And when they fed the children, the mother took the bread—it was homemade bread, bannock—and she'd measure the chest of the child and that's how much they could have. She says, 'Don't worry, that'll keep you going. We don't want you to be fat.' The children were taught not to lie and not to steal.

They had clams and dried fish. I remember the mother used to dry lots of salal berries. Oh, I loved that. Just like prunes—soak them, and they come up fresh. I just couldn't wait, couldn't help myself.

My grandparents used to take me along when they picked the salal berries. They taught me to make buckets from cedar, showed me how to go and get it, the right time of year. Just peeled it off in the spring.

There were many different powers, different spirits in the longhouse. When the little boys are about seven, they're told not to go out in the bush or the mountains when they're hungry. Not with an empty stomach. That's when they get that evil spirit.

We always had to be up before sunrise, and not be caught napping when the sun went down. That way you'd live a long life—that's what they taught me. If you're not awake early in the morning, they'll grab you and throw you in the river. Not as a punishment – it's for your own good. Lots of our people will tell you the same thing. They take them and put them in cold water. It'll be good for them. It will keep you strong and you will live long. Those things I remember.

A boy, eating at table, he's got to finish it off. Got to finish it all off, or don't touch it at all. That's what the old people said.

When girls are small, between the age of just beginning to talk and the age of twelve, they've got to be real careful. Keep their backs straight, don't slouch, don't lie, don't worry, keep a happy attitude and that will set the rest of their life for the future. It's quite critical between the time they start talking and up to twelve. That's when they change. Those years they have to be real careful.

I remember horse and buggy days then –
we go out to sell clams, just horse and buggy –
the horse knows when he smells cougar.
He went wild, and boy I had to hang on.
The old people, they know what it was –
they know it was cougar that scared the horse.
I had to hold on tight under the seat.
My grandpa was driving the horse.
I had to sit at the back.
I was about eight years old.

And I'll tell you one thing – when children lose their teeth,
when their teeth drop out –
Got to go and look for a river where there are those big real strong
smooth black rocks.
When they lose their teeth, don't just throw them away.
Take them to that river
and throw them in with those strong rocks
and they'll have strong teeth all their life, till they're old.
Make a wish that they'll have good teeth
from those big strong black rocks.

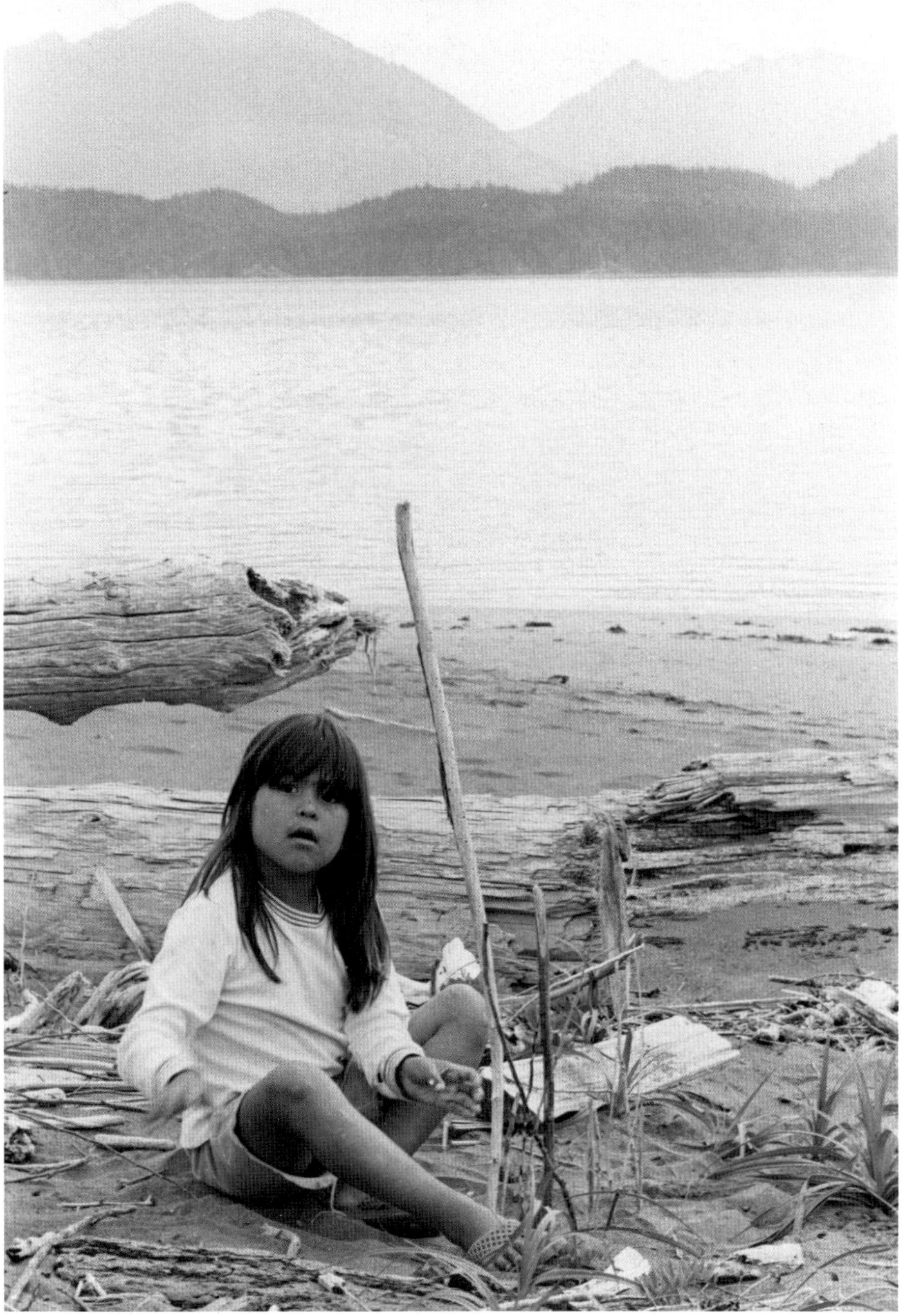

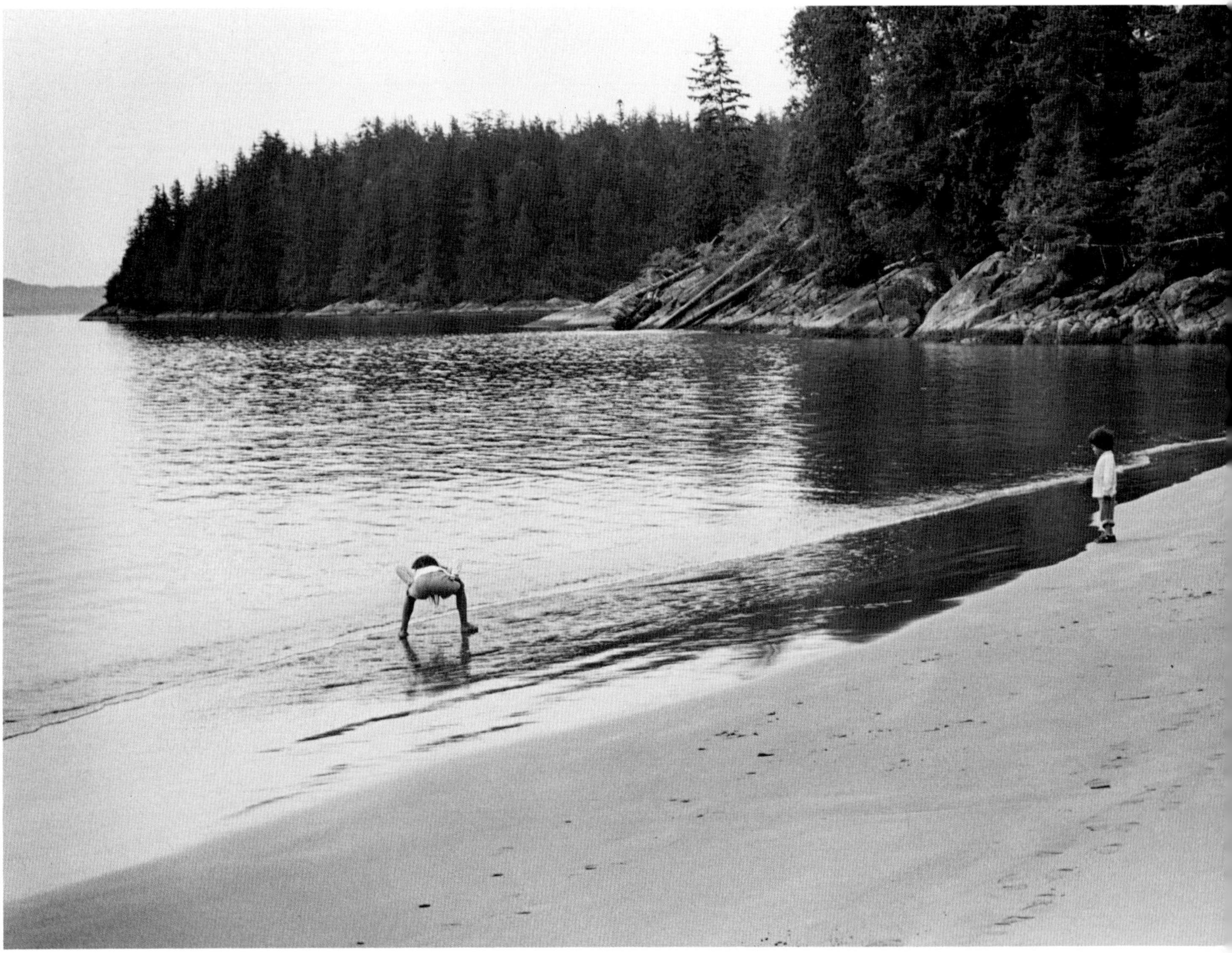

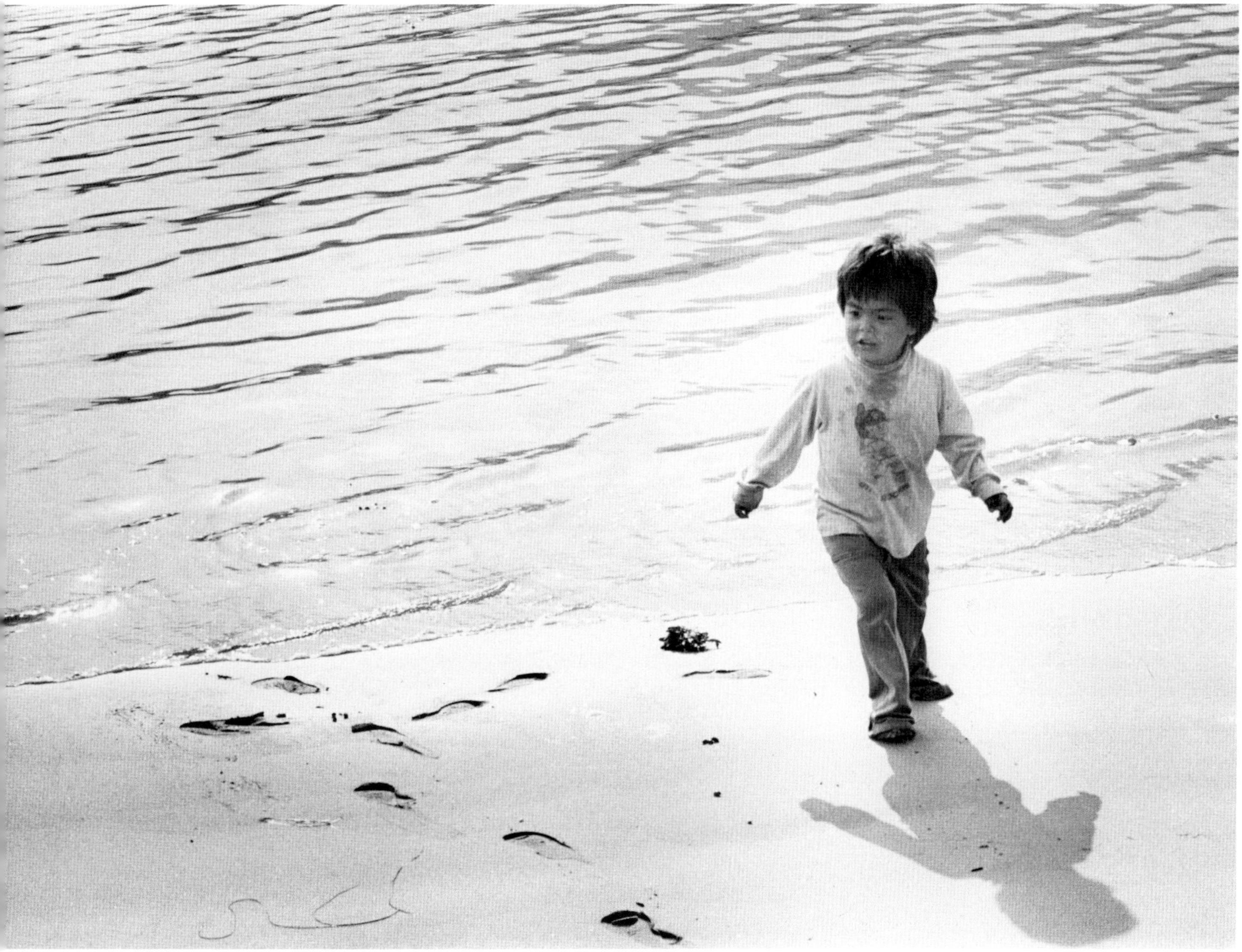

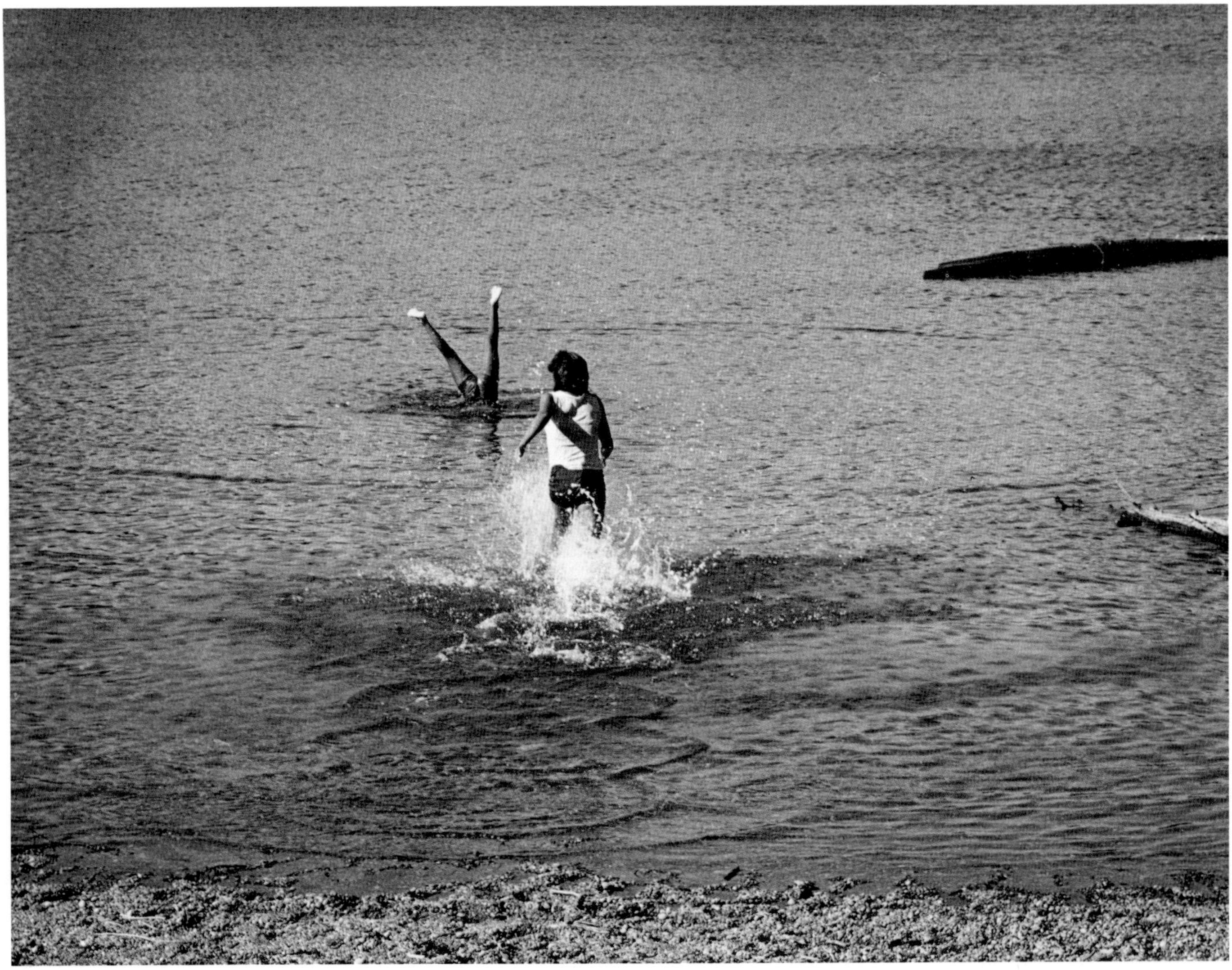

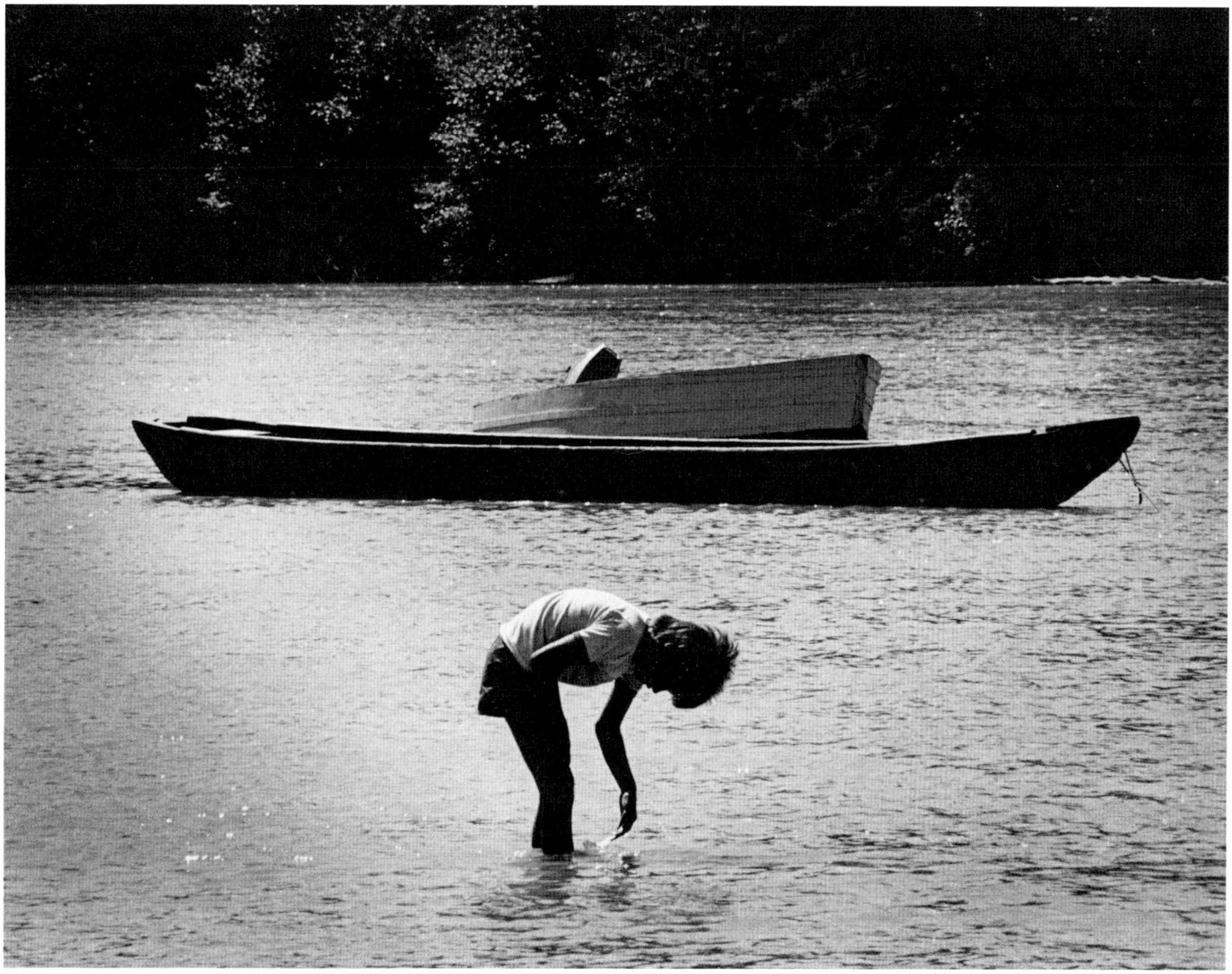

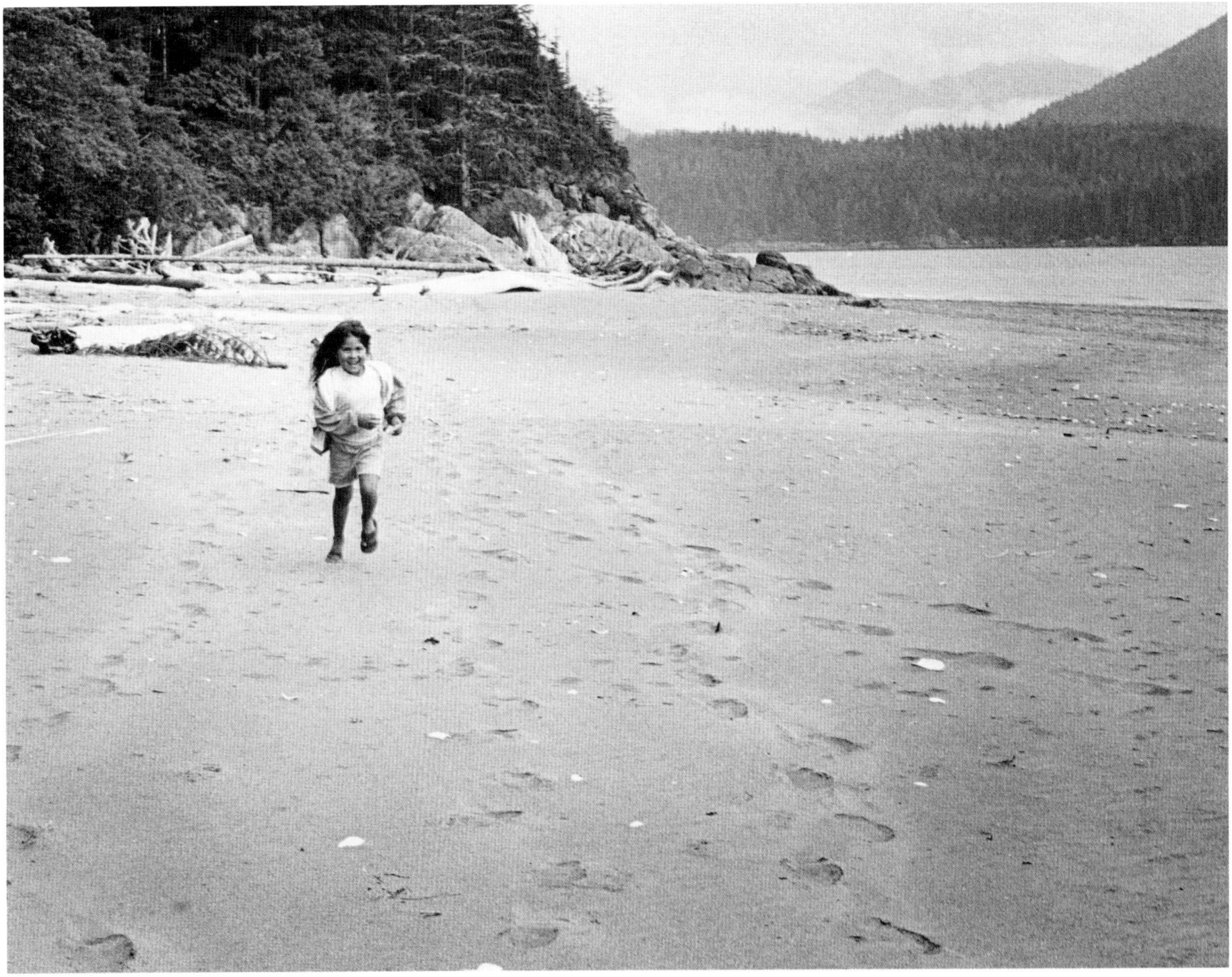

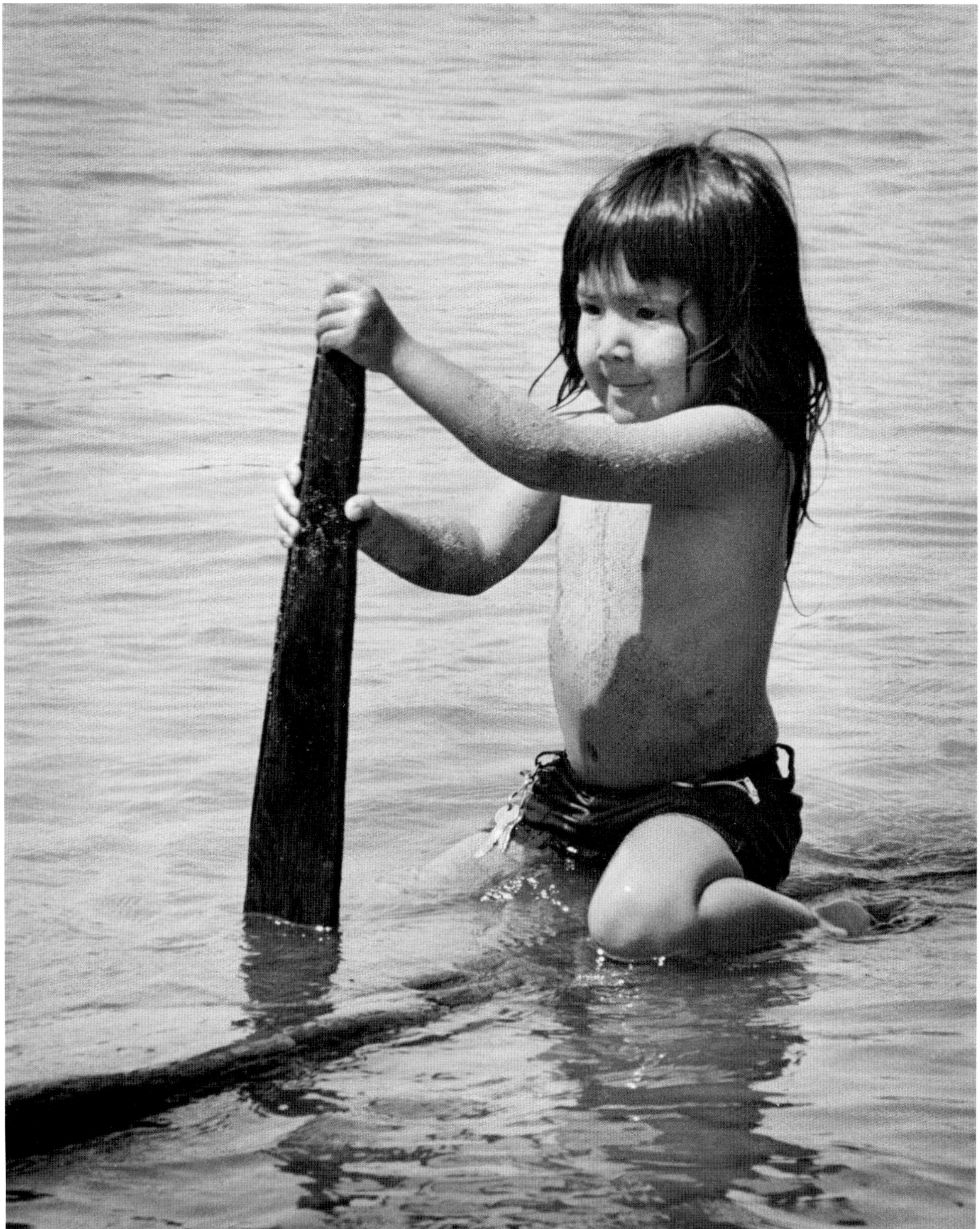

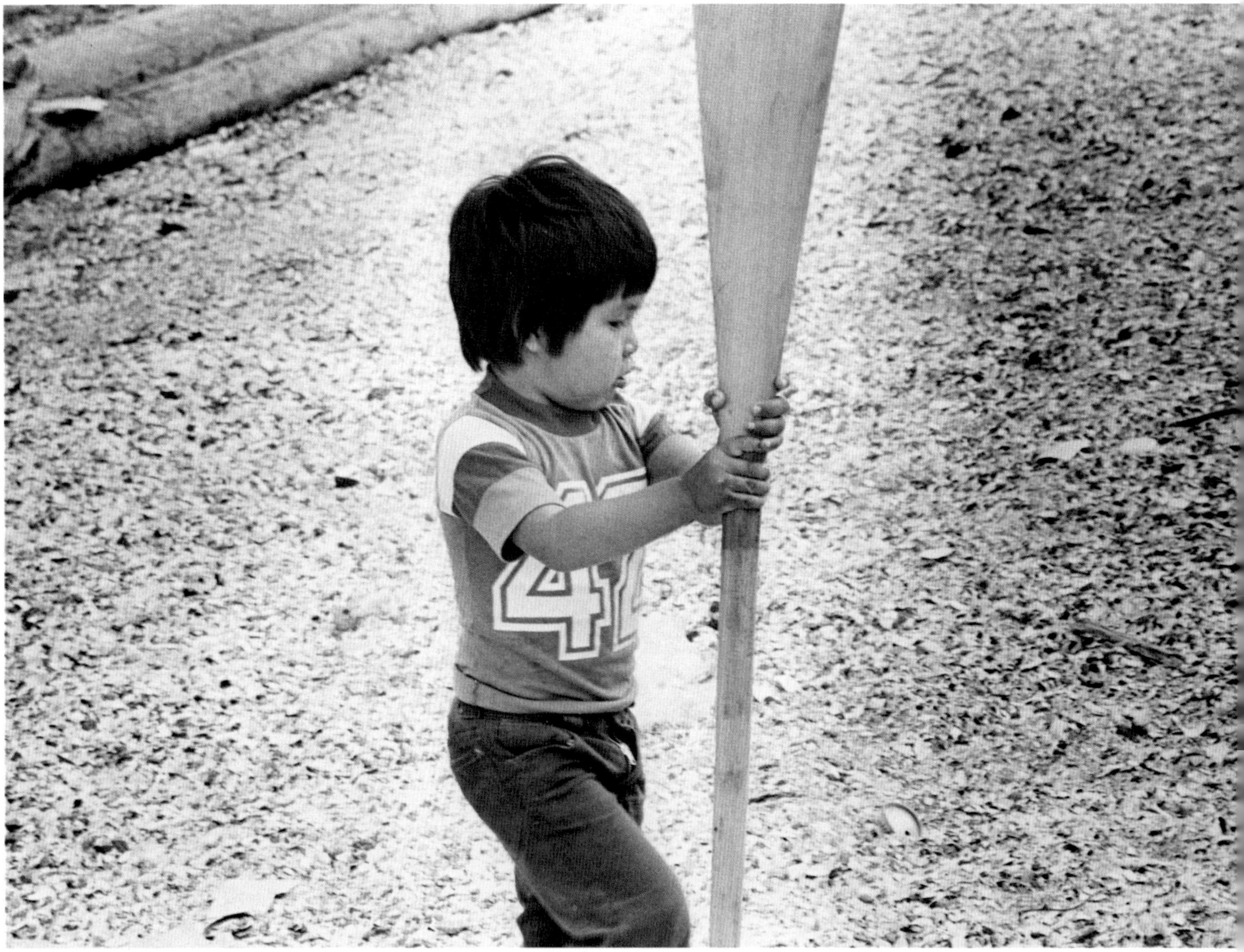

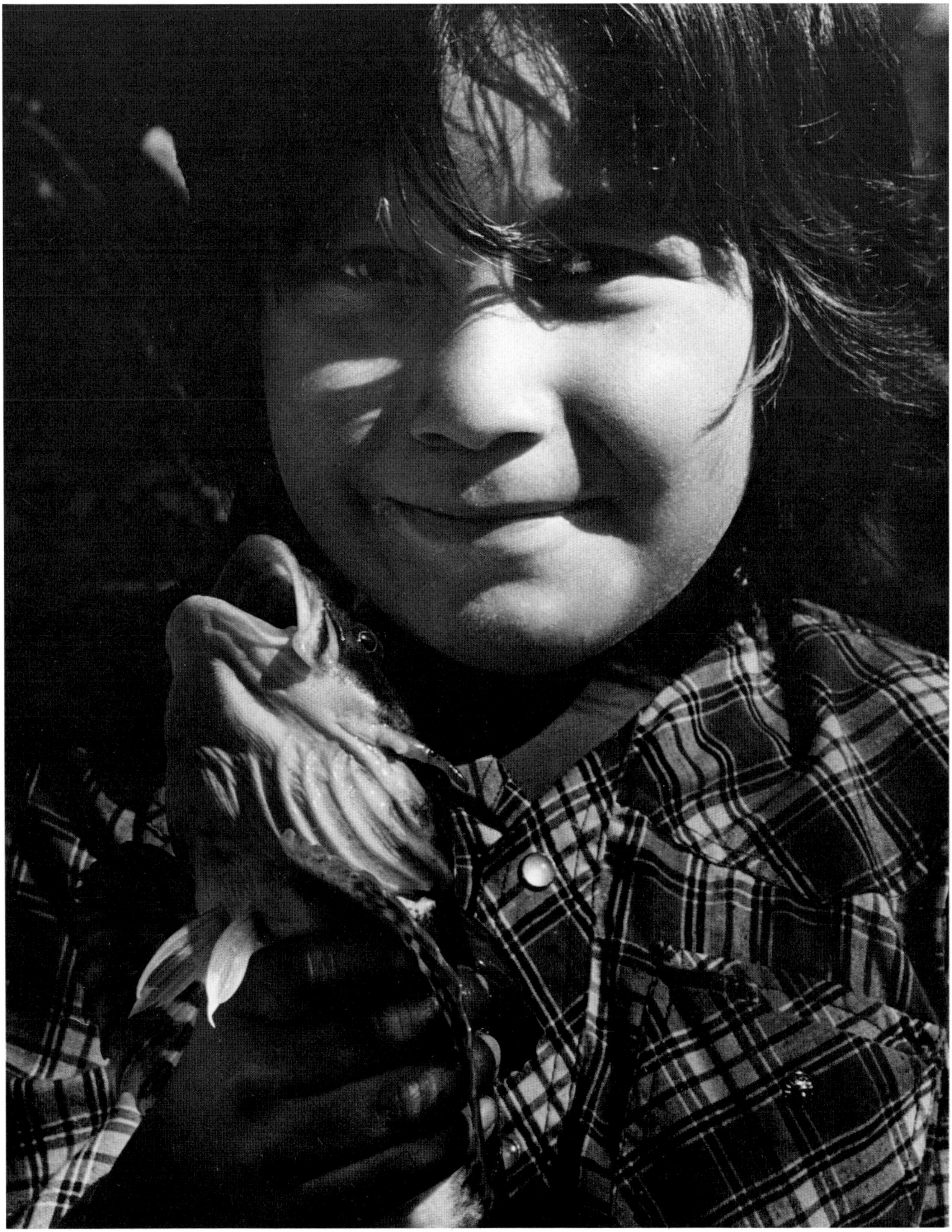

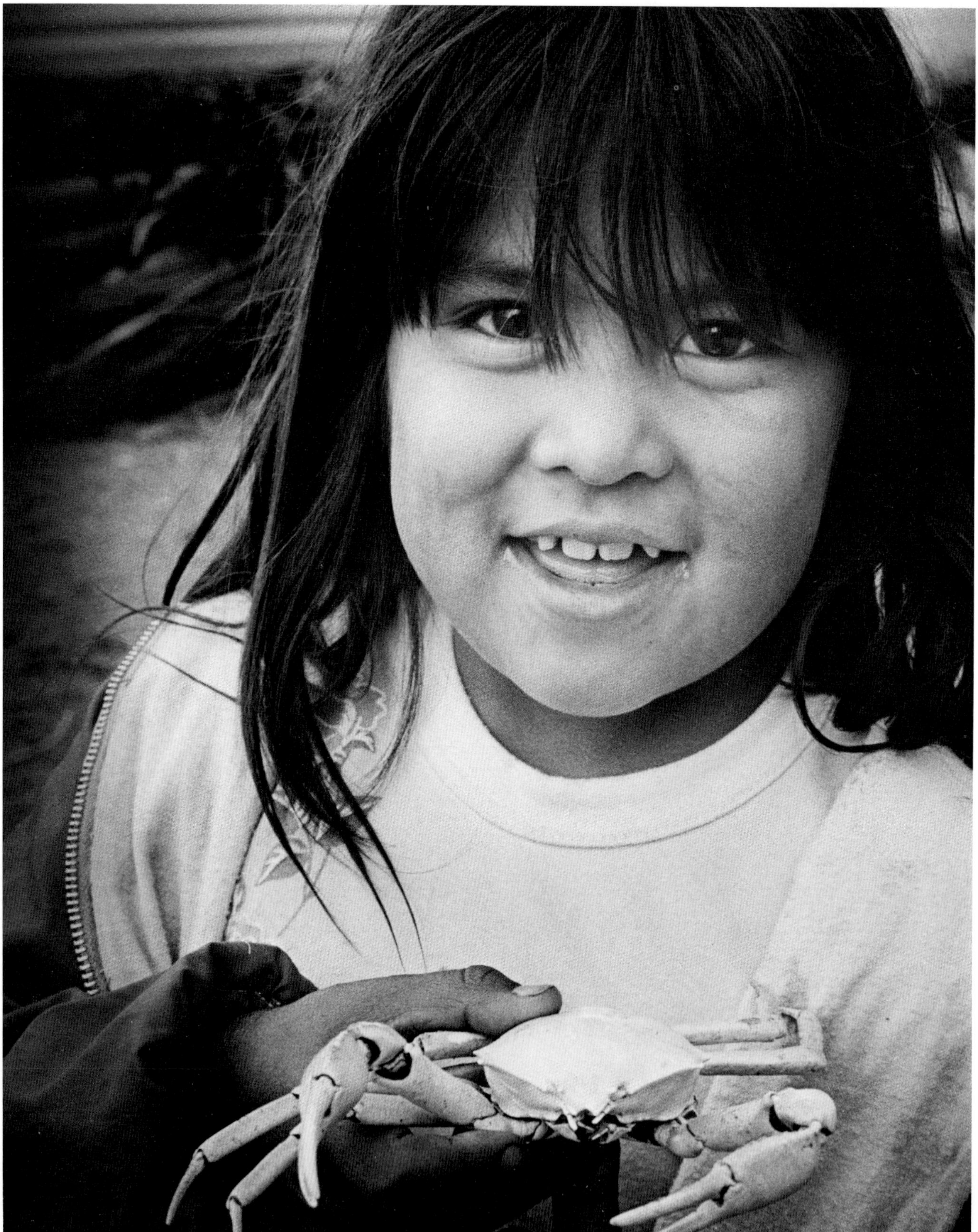

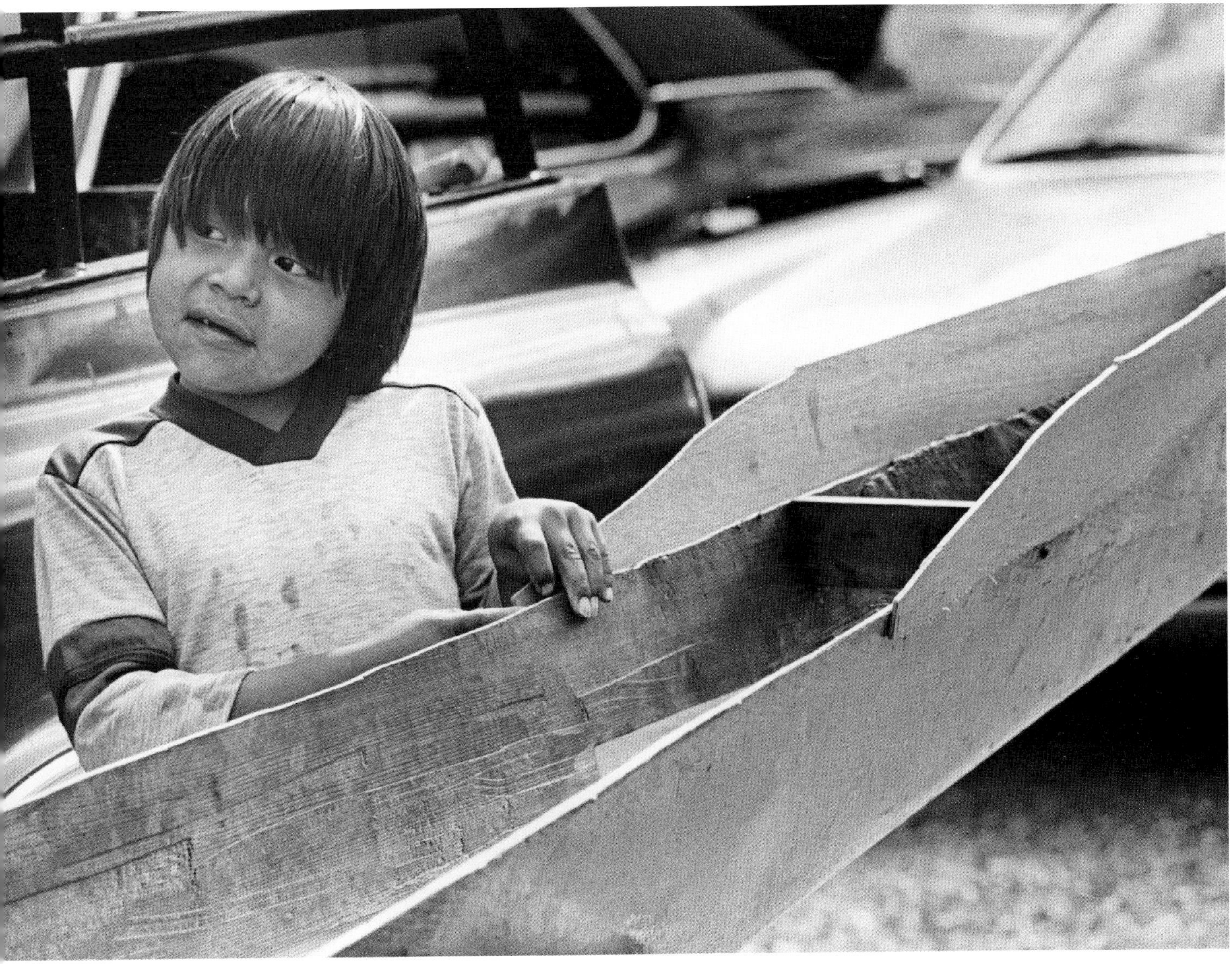

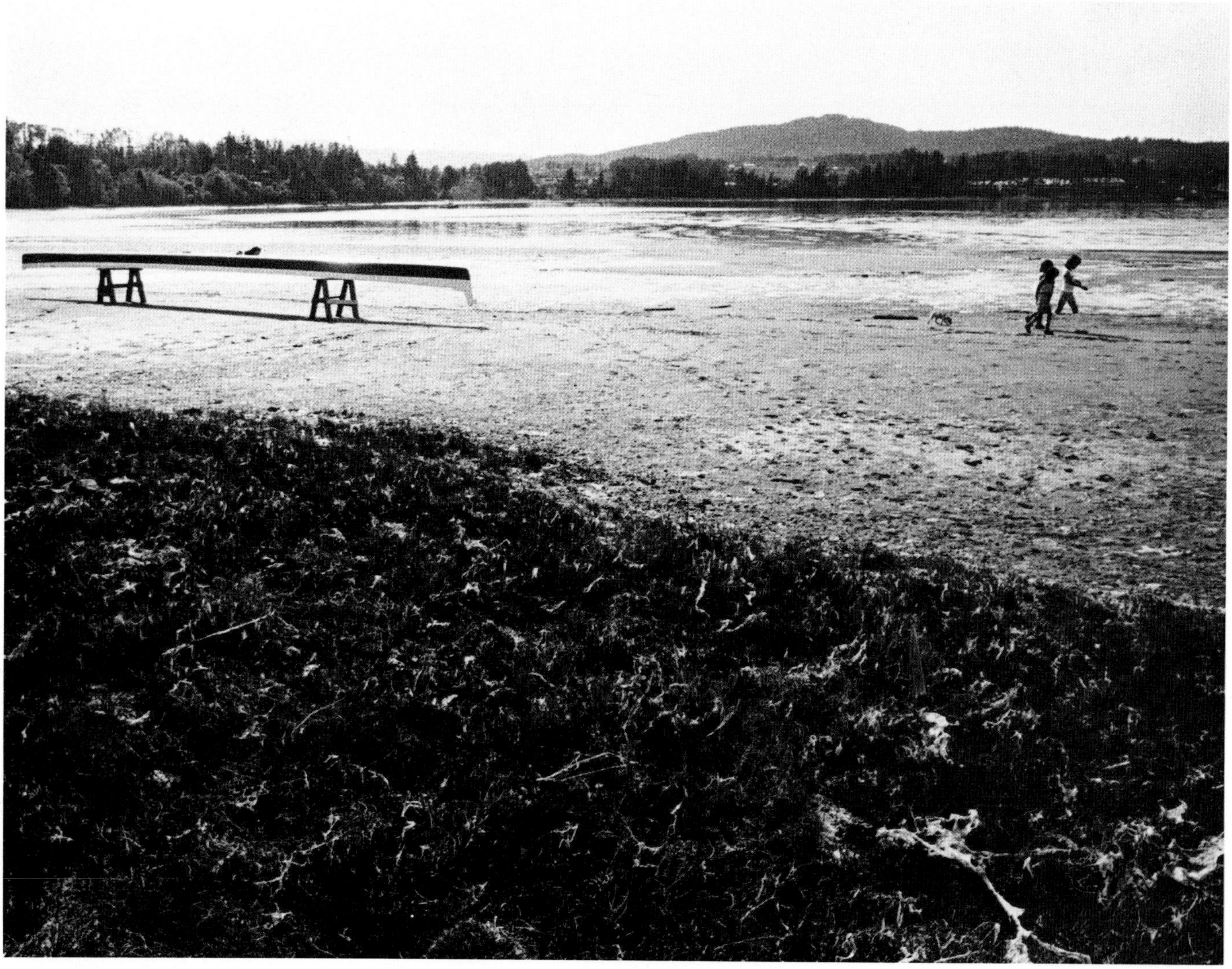

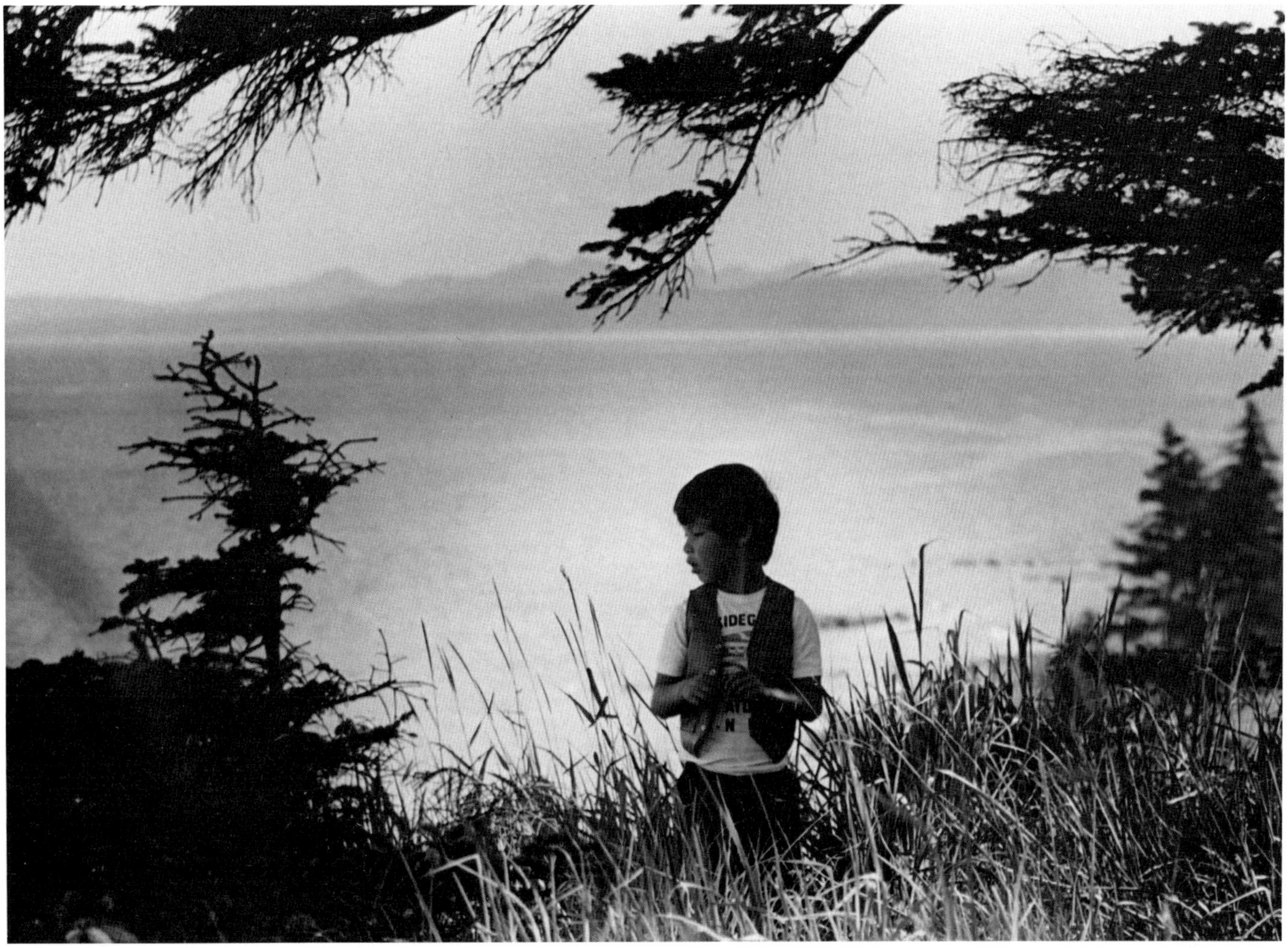

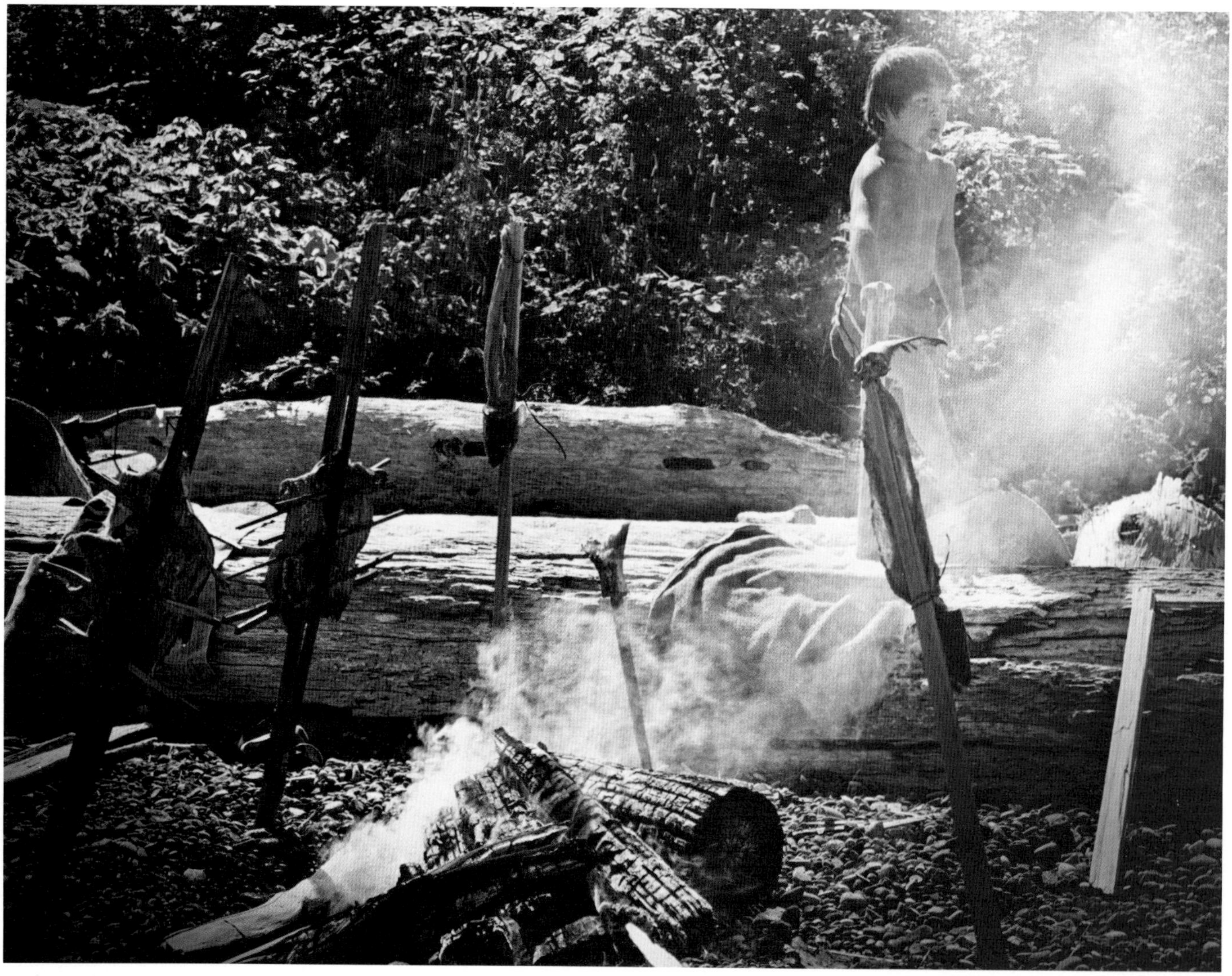

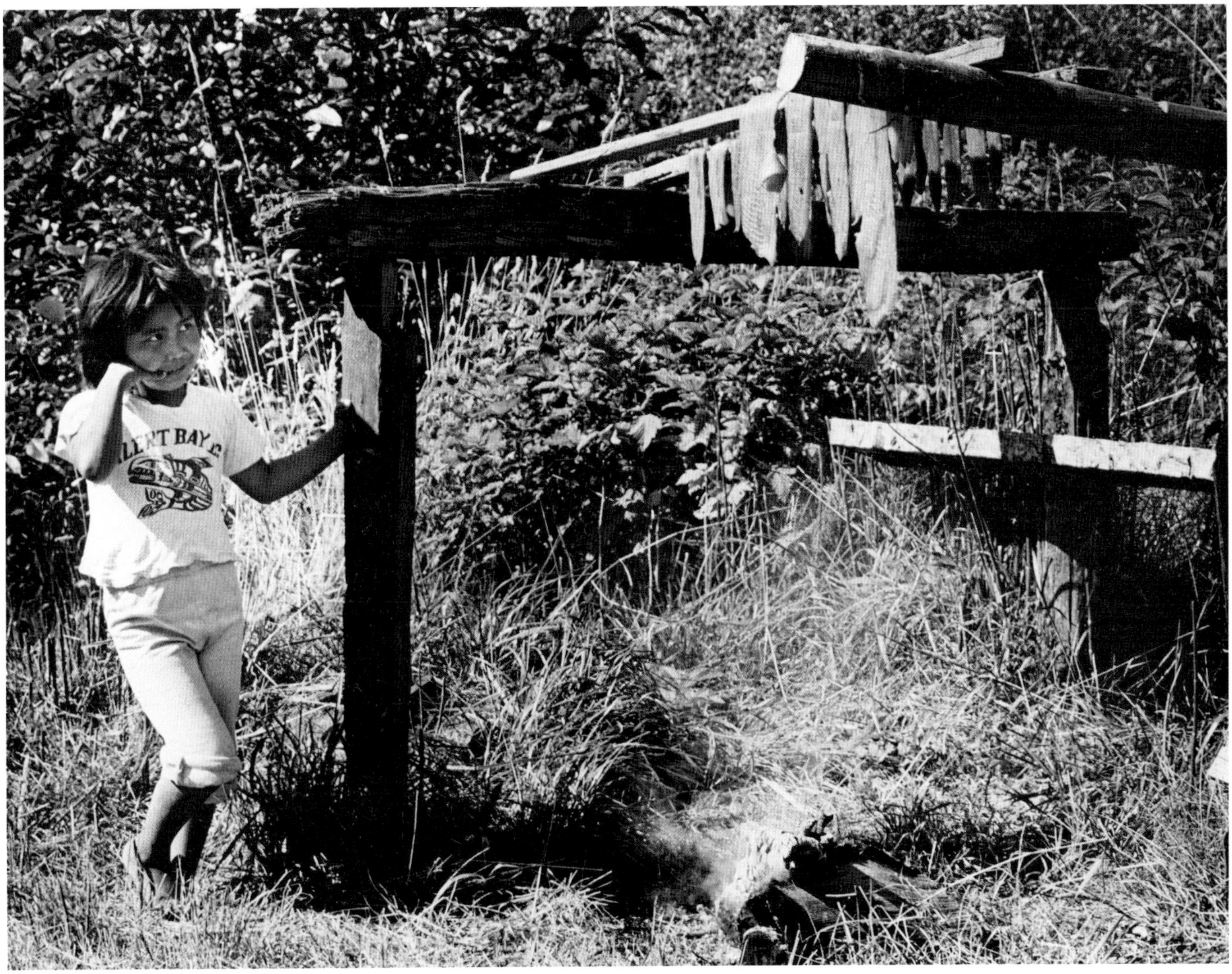

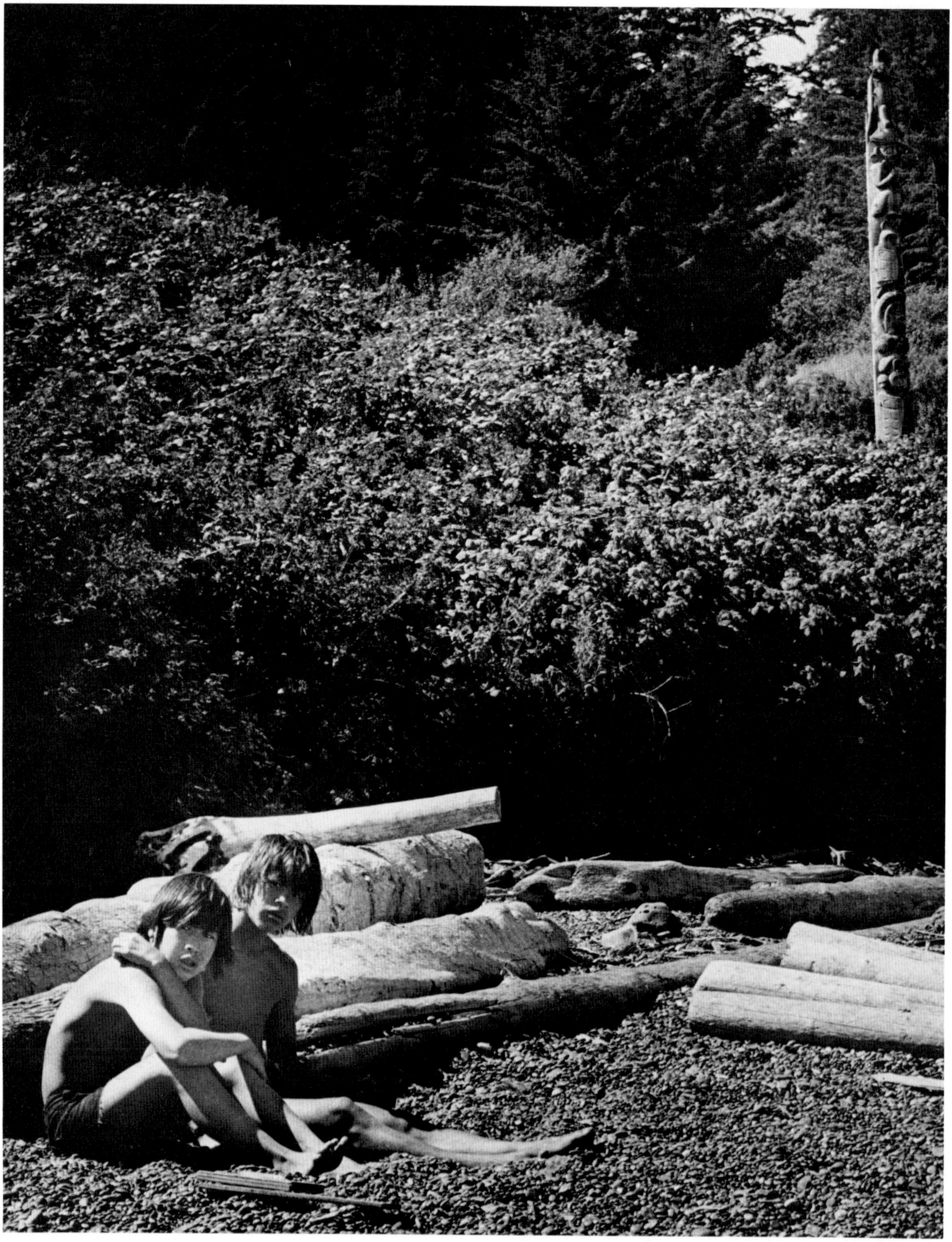

ALEX AMOS

Hesquiaht

In the first place, my grandfather was in Neah Bay when he was a young boy. He was a slave there, like there used to be years ago – taking young fellas or girls for slaves. So my grandfather was raised in Neah Bay. No fault of his at all. As a young man he helped bury the dead in Neah Bay. And then they let him free. 'Okay, young fella, you're free now – you're free. Go anywhere you want. You're no more tied to us, you're free.' So he went on a ship at Neah Bay, and he went around and away. But he wouldn't know where they went. All he remembers is that they got into India. That ship went in there. He could see the people swimming and diving a long time under the water. That's what he saw. I guess he came back on the same ship. And when his people heard that he was free, they went over to Neah Bay. 'Okay, you have to come home now.' So my grandfather went home. He was grown up then, a young man.

He didn't wait too long to look for a wife. He got a wife from Mah-ha-pie. Her name was Toub-paut. She was the daughter of a chief of that place, Hesquiaht Harbour. Used to be a big place there, lots of people. So he got that girl from Mah-ha-pie to Homais. A sister was born, and then my father was born. John was my grandfather's name, he had the two kids. One day they were invited over to Hesquiaht – that's the town where things were going to happen. He said to my grandmother, 'We'll walk to Hesquiaht.' They started walking from Homais, on their back was a little boy, my father, in a basket. He's too young to walk. When they get close to Hesquiaht, my grandmother says, 'Hey, I've dropped my cape.' She had a nice otter cape, that's what they used back then. 'I've dropped it out of my basket, you'll have to go back. I can't afford to lose that.' My grandfather says, 'Okay, I'll go back.' And so he walked back.

And while he was going back, he found a woman drifting in the sea – a young lady, a white lady. I guess there was a ship wrecked somewhere off Estevan. My grandfather thought he could just pull that lady above the high water mark so she wouldn't be drifting around on the rocks when the tide comes up. So he just dragged her up above the high water mark – way up. Okay, he was getting in trouble. Maybe he told the people he picked up a woman. And this one chief, this mean chief, he got his Hesquiaht people together and he said, 'Now listen, listen you people. I don't want any of you to get in trouble. I want John, I want him to get the blame that he killed this woman.' No evidence, no evidence at all. And this chief says, 'When the authorities come in here from Victoria, everybody says John

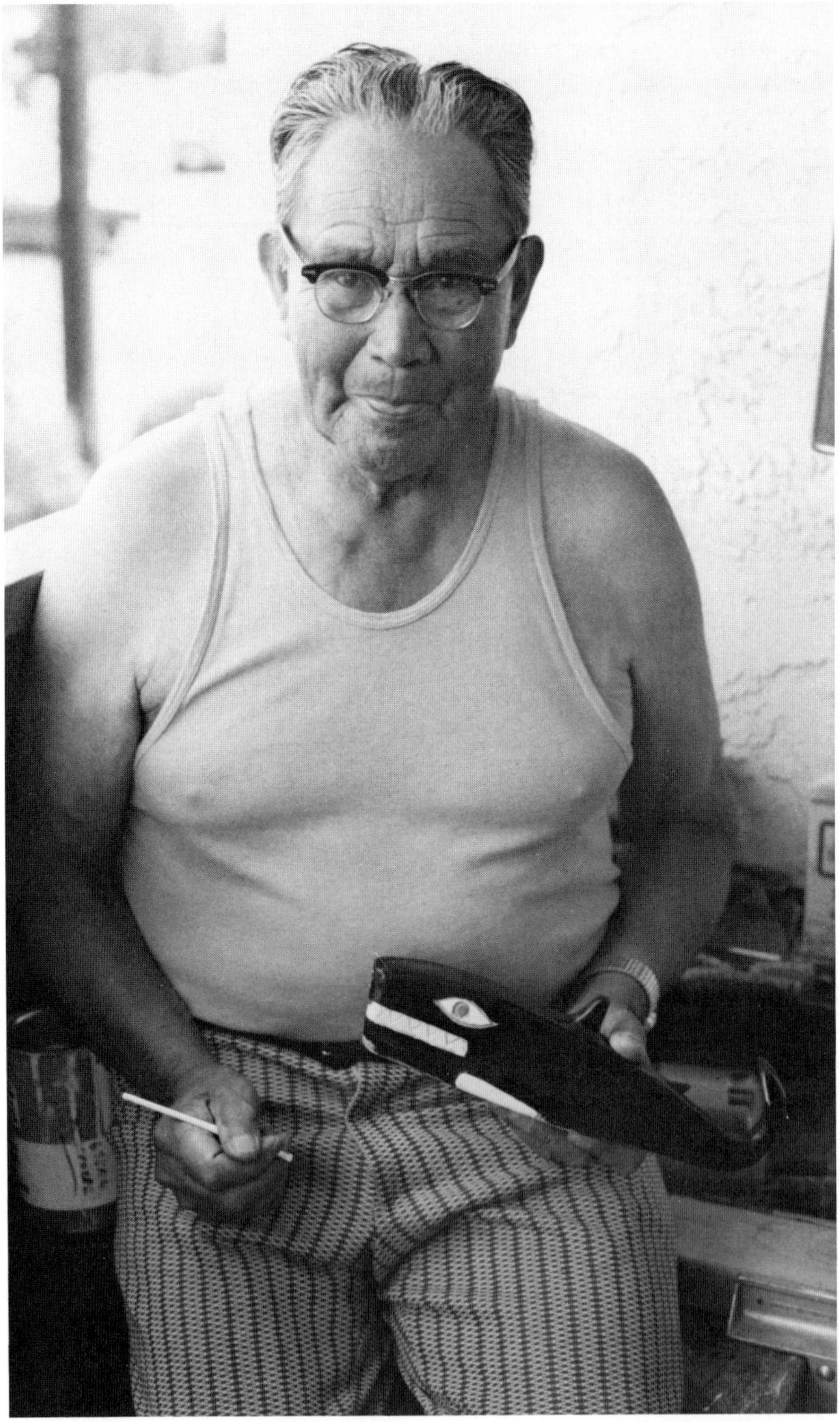

killed the woman. Everyone of you. You promise?' And the people say, 'Yes, okay, yeah.' So they were told by the chief, you see. And when the battleship came in to check the wrecked ship off Estevan, they came and the Hesquiaht people say, 'John killed that woman. He's killed her, he's killed her – that woman was alive when she got on shore.' But she couldn't be. No, it was too rough, fifteen footers – breakers – and the rocks. She couldn't survive it, no.

Now John was pulled in – my grandfather. And my father was just a little boy. My grandfather had to go to Nanaimo – pulled in, no evidence, no witnesses. All we know is that it was that chief's idea. Just like the Americas today, killing their head man just like that, all jealous. So my grandfather was going to be hanged, you see, and he sang a song when he was going to be hanged. He was a nice man, very kind, just like us, the Amoses. That's where we come from, real nice. The song – he's telling the world, 'I'm going to be killed.' That's what he was singing about. So he was hanged, and my father was orphaned.

We went barefoot all through summer until the cold weather started setting in, in November, and then our shoes that were put away for the winter came out. They bought me a big size, you see, so they would last me many years. I remember they lasted me maybe five years because I was growing.

We never had a regular meal during the afternoon – the kids before me too, you see. They just took a piece of smoked fish or something and go play and when it's lunchtime, just sit down and eat. In my time, we'd go home and get a piece of bannock. Not many yeast breads in those years. My mother used to make some once in a while, not everyday. So it's most of the time bannock. And then we'd just go right through the day, playing, swimming in summertime. We had a nice pool there, right in the village behind the houses. Just deep enough for those children. Used to go in there, dry up on the hot part, lay down, and back again after an hour or so. All day like that. When we wanted a change we'd go in the salt water and swim in there.

We used our language when we were kids until we went to school, and then we weren't allowed to use Indian language. Not one word, no. In my father's time, Father Brabant taught them in school in Hesquiaht. My father picked up a few English, very few English. He was called Amy then, not Amos. When the schooners, sealing schooners, came up the coast, my father got a job on them and they changed his name to Amos instead of Amy. Now today we are Amos. My father had that job all his young days until 1911. At that time they closed up the Bering Sea and then my father was out of a job – no more sealing up in the Bering Sea. My father used to get away on the first of July, just the day I was born. He used to tell me that when I was born the schooner was waiting out there in front of Hesquiaht. 'Well, here's a little boy!' He just took me on his lap for a few minutes and then went out to the Bering Sea. He'd be away for four months. July, August, September, October.

One day my brother was asking for ice cream at Hopfield and my parents wouldn't listen to him. That's how strict they were. They weren't poor, but they wanted to keep money for emergency or potlatch. You see, my father invited Ahouset twice in his young days while he was on the schooners. He made good on seals, he used to tell me. Seven hundred dollars he'd make. It would equal two or three thousand dollars today. Then he invited Ahouset. That's why he wouldn't buy that ice cream for my kid brother. Keeping the money for potlatch. My father was a good man but he was too tight. When we had the kettle and we went to town to kill a bull or something, we never had more than one meal. That's the way my father was. They give it out to the people. Only had one meal. He was a good man, but too much potlatch in his head, yeah.

In olden times, in my father's time, when he was a kid, they fed him on potatoes most of the time. Potatoes – spuds. I used to hear him telling about when he was a kid at Homais – that's where he was growing up. Everybody was in Homais. It was our village in my grandfather's time. But my father, when he was old enough, got himself out of Homais to Hesquiaht. So when they played they had potatoes for lunch – potatoes, maybe some smoked fish or halibut. There's halibut out there in Homais, used to be lots of halibut. That was my father's boyhood days. No pants, just blankets.

They had instructions every night when my father was a young boy. Every night an important man talked – a real smart man. He's from Clayoquot. He liked to instruct the kids coming up. He'd say, 'Now listen, here's what you have to be." He used to say, 'Be kind to everybody and don't part with your relations. Never. Because if you do – if you don't like your blood relations – then you'll have to look for a friend who is a stranger to you. You don't know his manners or his character and you won't make a friend out of him or her. It won't last long. Pretty soon they go because it's not your blood, not your relations. Keep your relations together. Be kind to them. Don't part with them. It's no good if you hate your relations. Now be kind to everybody, no matter who. Even if you don't know the person, talk to him, talk to him nice.'

Whenever there was a party, a potlatch, that's when the children got their names. Or some people would be way ahead and before they're born, they would have the names for the kids. My older son was like that. I think it was my father's idea then. He was named Tukha (Francis Amos). After that they had to give a big potlatch to name their children. They can't go without a potlatch to name their kids. That was strictly a rule. The baby is named after his great grandfather, or named after my mother, or named after my father. All that just to get a name. That's the way they did it. If they wanted another name, one of the families gives a potlatch, and they have a chance to get another name. Then they announce to the people, 'He's changing his name. Well, his uncle is giving a big potlatch. You call this boy after him.' Some of them have a lot of names. My first name was Hispaat when I was a little boy. That means 'I came from many families.' And they keep the name in the family, you see. Like Hispaat. If we were still running, we could give that name to my great-grandson, Donna's boy. If we were still on that. But it's fading away. So that's they way they were in olden times. That's how they got their names.

My mother and me, when I was a big boy, used to go out fishing in the canoe for cohos. Lots of cohos in those early years. Today, none, nothing. My mother used to get out there, but I must have gone to sleep because I remember she packed me down to the canoe early in the morning. That's in the summer time.

And then they got ready for smoking salmon at the end of August or September, my mother and my aunt who was my father's sister. They worked together, used to get a lot of driftwood, load up a canoe and take it up the river to the smokehouse. Two or three loads like that and that's enough for the dog salmon season. They were smart, the ladies, you see. Had nothing to worry about for wood. Some big pieces for night time. Night time they don't put out the fire—they put on the big pieces, two together and it's on all night because you got your smokehouse.

Then at the end of Octobor my father would come home and we moved over to the Lake Creek—the Hesquiaht Boat Basin Lake. It's a big creek, big lake and a river coming down. It's the lake creek for dog salmon. We had a nice house there—half smokehouse and half decent. We'd stay there another month and get some more smoked fish. That smoked fish would last us till May—six months. We'd go home in December to Hesquiaht. Oh, it used to be lots of fun, going home to Hesquiaht. And then what the Amoses did was party. Had everything—biscuits, tea, corned beef, soup. Almost every week a party. Someone else would have a party. That's in the winter time.

Now it was different in those days from today. Today there's no fish to be got. Dog salmon gone, spring salmon gone. In those times we fed on the spring salmon. Big ones, in Hesquiaht. Yeah, it was a good life.

Never miss your prayers at nights,
Ask God to give you riches or anything you want—
If you're after fish, if you're after seals, pray for it, ask God.
And ask God to let you run into luck. Every morning, every night, never miss.
Then you will be well off when you grow up.
My father was telling me, you see—he got all that instruction
And he was like that and he turned it on to me when I was young.
Well, I'm old enough to brag. I've been well off in my life,
Really well off. I had seven boats.
And then I bought three speed boats and two cars in Victoria.
That's the end of my life, see.
Good fisherman, real lucky.

That instruction is still in the Amos family.
Today I'm happy to say my grandsons are well off.
You should see my grandson in Gold River—nice cars, beautiful cars, a truck.
We still have the same instructions,
So it will be in the family right through.
Yeah.

HELEN ALPHONSE
Cowichan

We had a neighbour next door, we were real close to each other, Sadie—she's gone, same age as me. Joseph, Charlie, and some more. They just take one week and they're gone, buried. They didn't like doctors, said they poison Indians. And this nice woman, she's a Catholic nurse, middle-aged, comes knocking and trying to help. They lock the door, watching. Now my mother, she never hated those people. She's a longtime Catholic. So we were never scared. She never speaks English but she knows how it is. She's smart.

I think Joseph went fast. They were all small, must be around seven or eight. When I started school they were all gone. I was nine when I went to school. She tried to keep me, too—didn't want me to go—the one who raised me. Sadie was gone, must have been about seven because I can't remember when they buried her. And Joseph was gone fast too. Nice looking little boy, must be only two years—we called him Charlie. I guess he jumped, broke his hip. I never forget him wearing a skirt, just like a girl's dress. Real poor. He suffered, I could see. He was quiet, never got to talking. He was the chubby one in the family, that one, Charlie. I'll never forget that nice looking little boy—gone.

Swimming—that was my real favorite, when I began to get strong. Sneak out to go swim—oh, I loved that.

But I was a farmer when I was real young. I was always in the field and watching the cows. Lots of fun, and my little friends sneak in. Jumping in the barn, in the hay—

Went to the States, picking hops—
I hate that smell.
Can't go out and play with the kids—just like in jail.
Awful. Two of us, I'm always working hard.
One time I'll never forget—it hurts too much.
Those hops are sharp. So I think I better do something.
I've got a big basket like you put laundry in—
I'm small, pretty skinny at that time.
So I went under that basket.
And she's just busy picking hops—I'm in there, hiding in there.

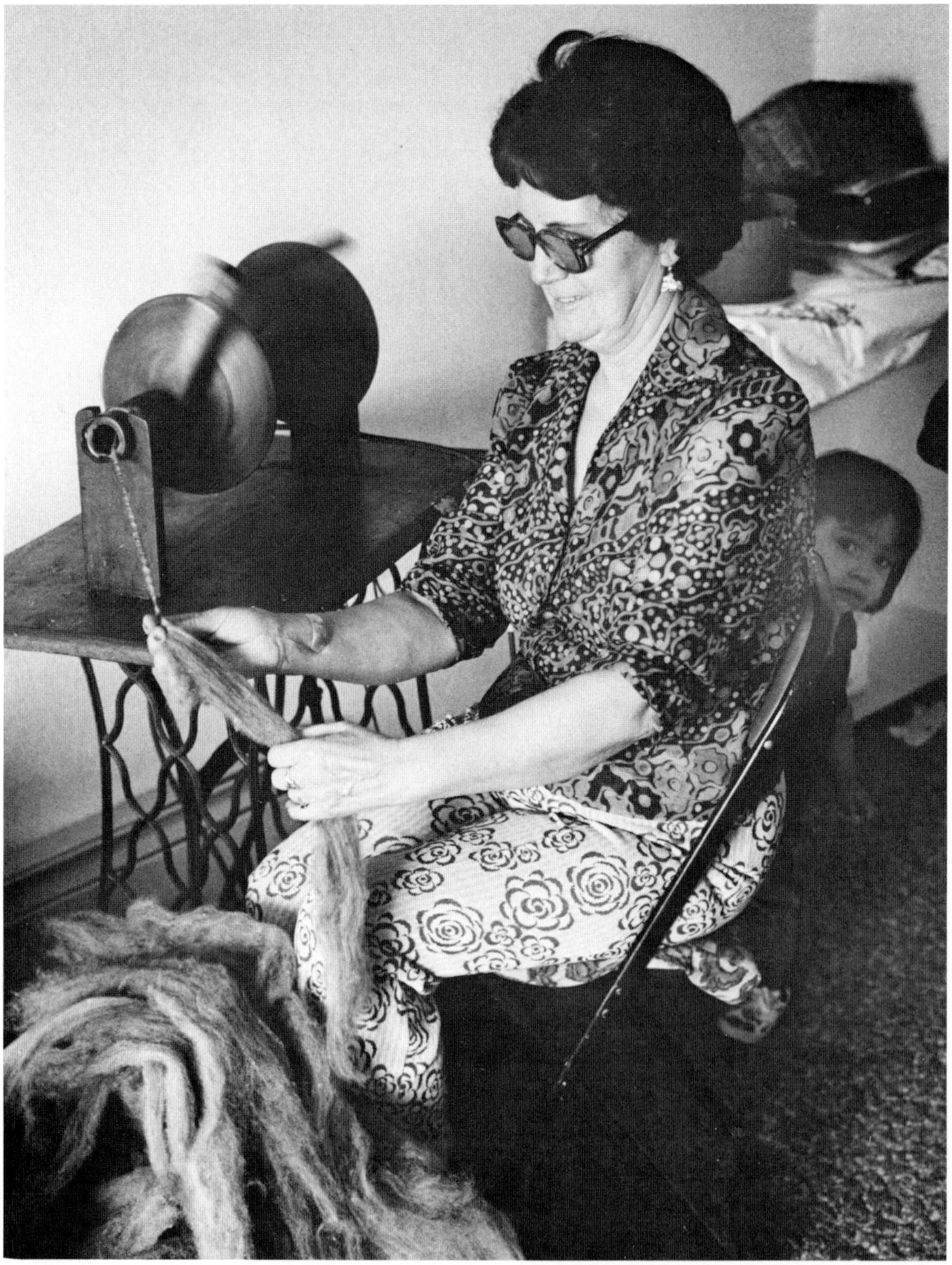

She's gone asking where I went.
I don't know what happened—I guess I got scared and finally got out.
Lots of hops, you know.

I just started knitting in my own mind. I started on dolls. I found what I called a Jimmy Little—a doll somebody threw away and I start fixing him. My mother never knit too much at that time. I was watching an old lady like I am now, who always knit socks. And a neighbour, she's got no family. Her husband's always out fishing or hunting and she's knitting all day. Maybe I got it from her. I just watch and I start a little vest and a little hat just like a man's hat. I don't know what I'm doing. I put a chain in here for a pocket watch. All the men got a chain for a watch and I copy that. I'm real small, only eight.

At nine I start spinning. My mother never taught me. She was kind of sick and kind of slow. She was always going out to sell fish, spring salmon. She put a net in the river, close by. Lots of springs at that time. Sometimes I'm alone and I spin. Try my best because I was there when this lady wanted to trade an Indian sweater for a fur coat. I'll never forget that fur—white, grey. I did baskets too, and little jars covered with weaving. I got that from two people—my auntie and an old lady next door. We never buy from the store, just trade with stuff. The woman next door knows everything—the one who lost her family. She was a nice person.

I start going to the dances when I'm older, maybe eleven. Little bit of dancing, not too many people. You always get a little something, like apples, different kinds of food, Indian fixed. Tulip bulbs you peel like a banana, peel it when it's cooked. They put them on hot stones before putting it on top and cooking with branches—that makes it have a nice smell. It's got an Indian name—*spanah*. Not too many people making it at that time. They were getting low on everything, I guess.

Old people fixed everything a long time ago—
you know—smoked fish, root-like potatoes.
That's what I heard.
In the mountains or dry parts—women going up there to dig the root.
Husbands go far away—just walk to the mountains and get some moose.
They dry it like fish, smoked fish.
I'm small at that time eating that dried smoked moose.
Real thin they cut it, boiled it with potatoes.
And deer, they smoked that, and everything from the fish.
I have to try and copy the old ladies—hang it in there and smoke it too.

Even the fish head, salt it, never throw it or the tail.
Never throw anything away. You got everything.
Just soak that salt fish – I like fish head when it's salted.
Taste it – different.

He's my grandmother's brother but I call him grandfather.
He's coming in, he always talks nice, never shouting.
'Granddaughter, clean up in the morning,' he says.
I'm real young. He's helping us with the hay, you know –
puts it in the barn for the winter.
Just four words – I never forget, never.
I start smelling the big house, the old house, all the smoke
– little bit up your nose. And I start to clean up.
And I start washing in the big tub – always white sheets, never coloured.
And old ladies, I tell you, they never throw out a flour sack.
They wash it and make sheets, yes.
And they buy old man's pants – my auntie opens them up and makes a skirt.
All the time real busy people, never lazy – cooking, you know.
That father never chopped wood, never brought water.
I go across to get two buckets of water for cooking and washing.

A friend, a relation from Queen Point, always comes to see my mother.
Must be eighty-five years old, no shoes. Real thick feet, I'll never forget.
I'm a little girl, all small with my friend Sadie.
He's got an overcoat, big thick one when it's cold wintertime.
I'm sorry for him. Always has a cup of tea at my mom's.
That's why he visits – lonesome.
Thick coat and real old hat. Old, short, and kind of chubby, you know.
Going home again, got a cane.
Never talks too much, quiet, and the other kids kind of bad,
pulling his coat in front of him.
My mother says, 'Don't be like them.' – I guess she's watching.
'When you get old, you might be worse than him –
you're going to get old too.'
Nobody, just him alone, no wife, no brother, just him.
I'm so small – he's the one I want to tell you about.

JOHN THOMAS
Nitinaht

As far back as I remember, we were still practising the old way of being with our mothers for the first six years of our life. At that time women had equal standing in the band – very important because they were the first teachers in our lives. In the life of an Indian growing up, she was considered to be the first teacher of mankind. So her position was as important, maybe more so, than the men. She taught us everything that a young child should know, even helped us to start walking and start talking. We learned our language from her. This took about six years of our lives and then we were turned over to our uncles for training. It was never the father who trained you because they're too personal. This was traditional in certain families. I come from a whale hunter's family, so I'll talk about that kind of training. If I was a fisherman's son or a hunter's son, I would have been initiated differently and trained differently. My uncle trained me in getting along in life so it would be easier to survive. At that time we had no supermarkets or places where you could go to buy meat and things. We had to live off the land. In order to do this, we had to be trained. My uncle and my grandfather taught me the physical and spiritual sides of life. They taught us at equal rates. So we were taught to pray while building up our physical strength.

For about four years I went through the training with my uncle. He was real impersonal. He wouldn't think anything of shoving me into the river. My father would never do that. Many of these things were harsh and hard to take. For instance, I was hit with a switch, a spruce limb, while I was standing there naked. He told me to look across the river and not to holler whatever happens – don't cry out. He gave me a piece of stick to put between my teeth – if it fell out, I failed. You were never to cry out, no matter how much the pain or how uncomfortable you were. There were about eleven kids in our group, and just seven of us got through because the others dropped the sticks out of their mouths and cried out. When he hit me with the switch on my back I jumped, and I'm not ashamed to say that I pretty near swallowed the stick. But I didn't make a noise. Next thing I knew I was being lifted up bodily and thrown into the river. My uncle came in after me to see that I didn't stay under. Then he told me what to say – the first words for when you come out. You have to face the east where the sun comes up, and pray, pray for a successful life and pray that you're not going to fail. These words are secrets within families and among families and nobody else repeats it because that's your own personal kind of prayer. We were taught to pray and to keep

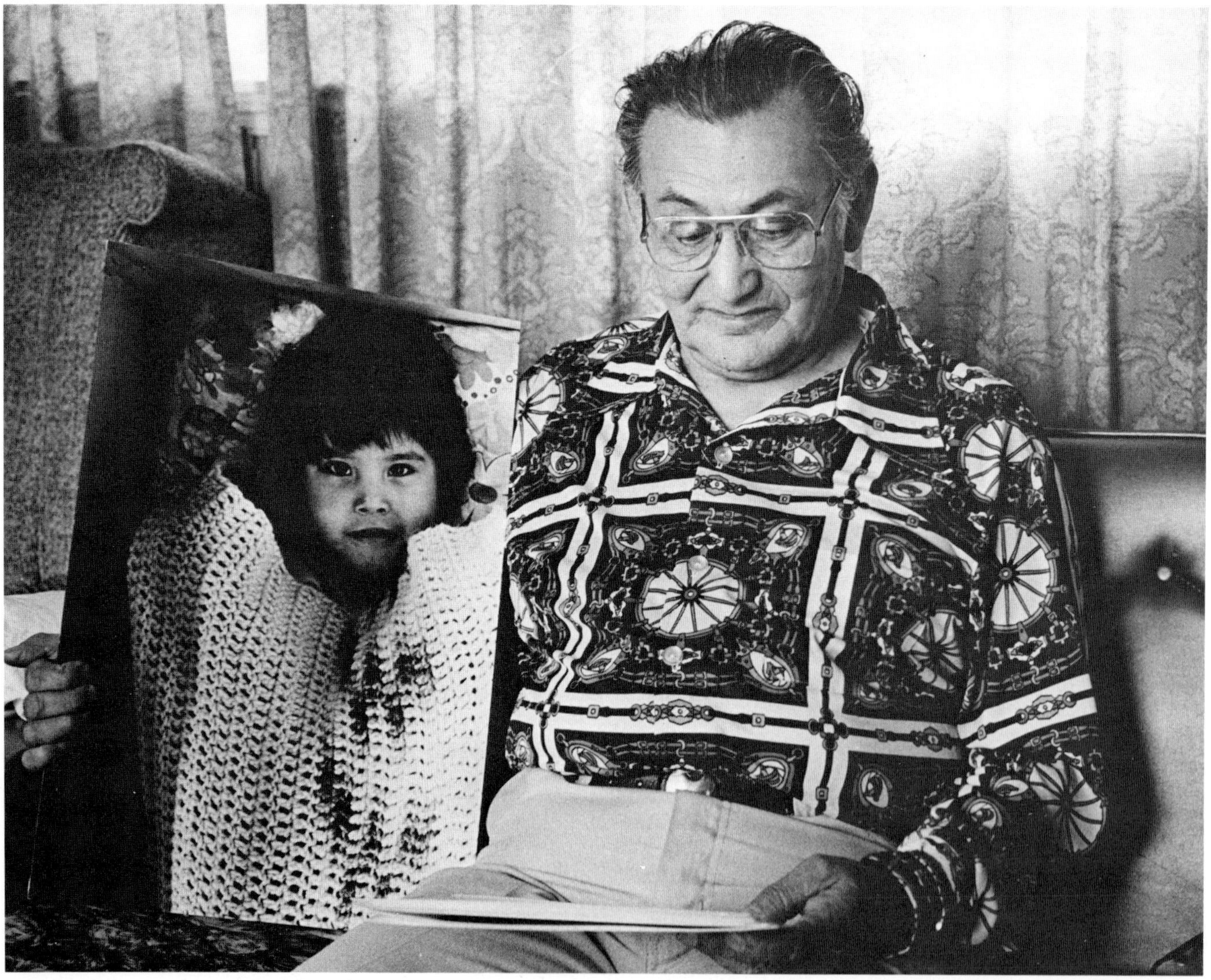

ourselves clean – to sort of purify our bodies and minds at the same time, and not to think different thoughts. Certain thoughts in your mind were forbidden. We were separated from our sisters who went to their aunts and their grandmothers where they had their own way of learning how to get along in this world.

I was sent to school when I was ten years old, so I didn't complete the training. I was learning to make tools, hunting implements, bows and arrows, different spears – especially the whale spear which is part of our ancestral heritage. There is a lot to whale hunting. You don't just go out and catch a whale. You had to be physically and spiritually fit. You had to know what you were doing. One mistake could be your last, so you were told over and over again how to perform certain rituals to get the power to go out and hunt the whales. To this end we were taught how to make the tools, even pieces of rope. We learned what to say to the tree before cutting it down, which way to fall it. You didn't just cut it down. It took four days just to cut down a tree for a whale spear. You had to fall it toward the sun, just when the sun was coming up over the mountain. You treated it like a person coming home. You talked to it and you continued to talk to it even when you were using it to spear a whale. So things like this were part of it all. Every little piece of equipment was spoken to. You were old enough to go hunting when you finished the training. You had to go through a lot of things before you touched the whale gear. You had to wait till you had twenty-odd years of training. If you failed – like some of the kids in our group – then it took longer. It wasn't a disgrace or a shame to fail because of the harsh things you go through, but if you failed two, three times, then you weren't good enough.

The initiation took ten days. They waited till the full moon was just starting to wax. You never had any ceremony after it started waning – it just won't keep. So we used to keep doing things for about ten days of each new moon, then we were sent home and warned not to talk about it to anyone – not even our mothers or sisters.

I remember making a bow. I was real proud of my workmanship. I showed it to my father and he said, 'What are you going to do with that?' He didn't tell me what I was supposed to do with it. He said, 'Go get a bird. If you get one, bring it to me.' So I went down and snuck up on a bird. There were lots of birds there at the beach. Snipes – those little sand snipes. If you get real close to one you can knock it over with no trouble at all. But I couldn't get the heart to kill one, just to prove that I could use that bow. I didn't and I just couldn't – and I was sure I had failed.

So I went and picked up a feather the bird had dropped. I brought that to my father and said, 'I pretty near hit him when I knocked a feather off.' He said, 'Okay.' He never asked another thing about it, although he must have told my uncle, because my uncle asked me, 'Now, why didn't you kill that bird?' I said, 'I couldn't. I didn't want to kill it for nothing.' He said, 'That's all right, don't feel bad about it.' So I didn't.

We used to talk about it when we were eating. We'd sit at a little platform on the floor in the longhouse. About five different families. We had bark mats for place mats. The old man of the family would be talking—talking about history, talking about our traditional songs and dances, and telling us the old stories. Generally giving advice on how to get along and behave. He used to say that people will single you out. You're going to stand out in the crowd if you behave like this, and there'll be those who point you out, saying 'He's from a whale hunter's family.' People would recognize you. He used to say, 'Don't kill for nothing. If you need to eat, okay. Go and get a duck or something. But not for nothing.'

In the meantime when we weren't training we played games. There was a beach about three miles long where we could play at low tide. We played a kind of sand hockey, with sticks that looked like a cross between a golf club and a hockey stick. We made balls out of a certain kind of kelp. No goals, no goal posts. We started off at a mark in the middle of the beach and chose up sides. The team closest to their end lost when the tide came in after about four or five hours. So it was back and forth along the beach all afternoon. We'd race on the beach too, jumping and wrestling contests. That's the kind of games we played every day. We never saw any girls. They were learning how to make baskets and how to cook and things.

When I first left the reserve I didn't know a word of English. They sent me to school up the Fraser Valley. It was four or five hundred miles away. Before that I'd never been outside our village, let alone have to speak another language. We got there at midnight and were given pajamas and put to bed. I didn't know why we had to put different clothes on to go to bed. It was all new to me. They gave us clothes that didn't fit. That wasn't too important because I didn't notice till years later that our clothes weren't right.

There were twenty-seven of us from Nitinaht and Port Renfrew and we were separated and weren't allowed to be together. That was so we wouldn't talk our language. That was forbidden. If we got caught talking, we got punished for it. We learned to speak English pretty quick. I could speak a little Chinook that I'd learned from my grandfather. I used to listen to him talking to a white man in Chinook. So the kids used me to communicate with the principal. He was the only one who could understand Chinook. Anyway, I became a one-man grievance committee. Every time something went wrong, I had to go and tell the principal in Chinook.

The thing I remember best about the school is the bell. Even today when I hear one, I look around to see what's going on. The bell rang early in the morning, and then the matron came in—real loud, you know. I wasn't used to people talking loudly. In our culture people raise their voices when they're angry. So, on my first morning, there was this loud-mouthed matron charging in there, pulling the covers off the kids, getting them up. I was already up. She told me with sign language to go to the washroom and wash up, and gave me a towel and soap. I knew what that was for because I had already learned that at home. So I washed up, scrubbed my teeth and everything else and went back to my bed and was made to stand there. This is when they issued the clothes and socks and shoes. I had never had a pair of shoes before. They used to really bother me. I took them off every chance I got and was always getting into trouble for it. Then the bell would ring again and we'd be driven into the chapel for morning service. Another bell and we were marched downstairs and lined up military fashion. We were made to count out loud and take roll call. I didn't know how to count. Somebody said, 'Seven—that's your number. You say seven.' We started all over again and I was bright enough to know my number was seven. We got together later on the playing field to discuss what was happening to us. We figured that the numbers they'd given us were our new names. My name was seven and my cousin's name was fourteen.

After the first four or five months of confusion, we started to make the best of the situation. I remember going into classrooms, sitting down, someone writing on the blackboard—never could figure out why it was a blackboard when it was green. So we worked out how to write down numbers, how to spell and how to read from pictures. How to say man, moon, cow and all that. Other than the fact that we were homesick, I think we became used to the place and were relatively happy over there, away from home. As a child, I was really curious and I liked to find out things and this kept me from being bored. I had to find things out myself, investigate and learn things that way.

Today, things are a bit different. Children growing up in isolated areas are still a bit happier than those in the urban areas. If they move closer to a large city, that's when they get into trouble. When the kids were still going to residential schools—that's when the family separation did its damage to our culture and language. Being away from home as I was, I slowly lost the language. After six years, I forgot it. I had to learn it all over again after I left school. I'd sit with the old people and listen to them talk—learning all over again. When I tried to speak I couldn't, because my tongue was oriented to English. Today I'm teaching the language at the University of Victoria—it's turned around. I'm teaching them my language and they're learning my language. The same as the teacher who taught us English. I think it is good that we are beginning to communicate at last.

Those residential schools caused problems in families because what the kids learned was no good in the village. When a person is lucky enough to get educated he moves away, moves off to an urban area and then he gets a job there. He's not doing his home village any good because there's nothing to keep him. There's nothing there for him to make use of his knowledge. And that's another separation for our culture. But it seems to me that the children of these people that go out to earn their livings off the reserve—that they go to public school and don't seem to have as many problems. It's these kids that are directly from the reserve and who are adopted into a family or staying with people, who have these misunderstandings and cultural differences and linguistic differences. This is why most of the kids are a year or two behind their age group. But most of our kids don't have this problem because they're away from the reserve and wise to what's going on outside the reserve. We're hoping now to have a say. We're moving into the school system and moving into the administration part of it. We have people on the school board now and we have people working on the curriculum in schools to fit our native kids. I think in the future things will turn in our favour for a change.

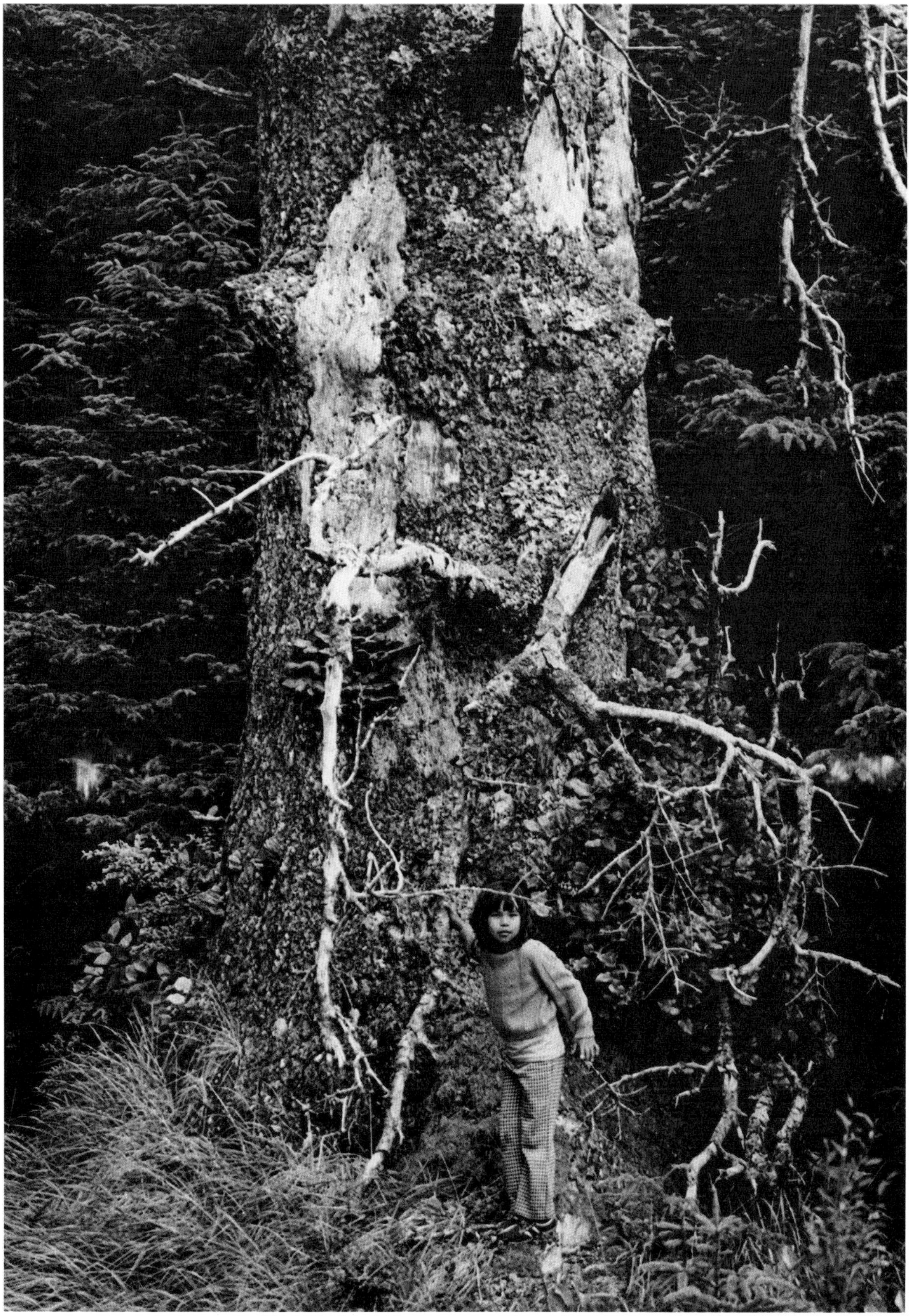

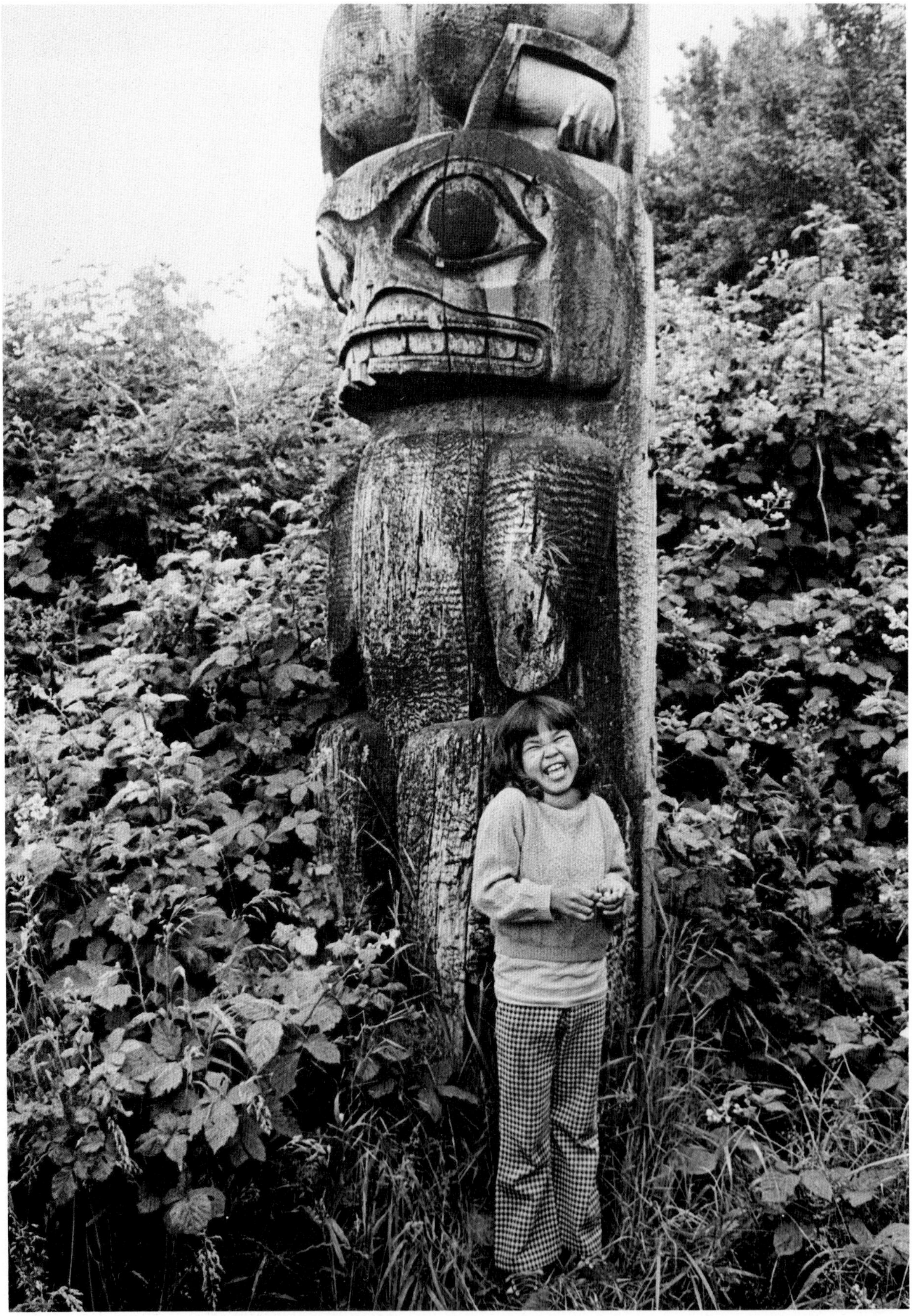

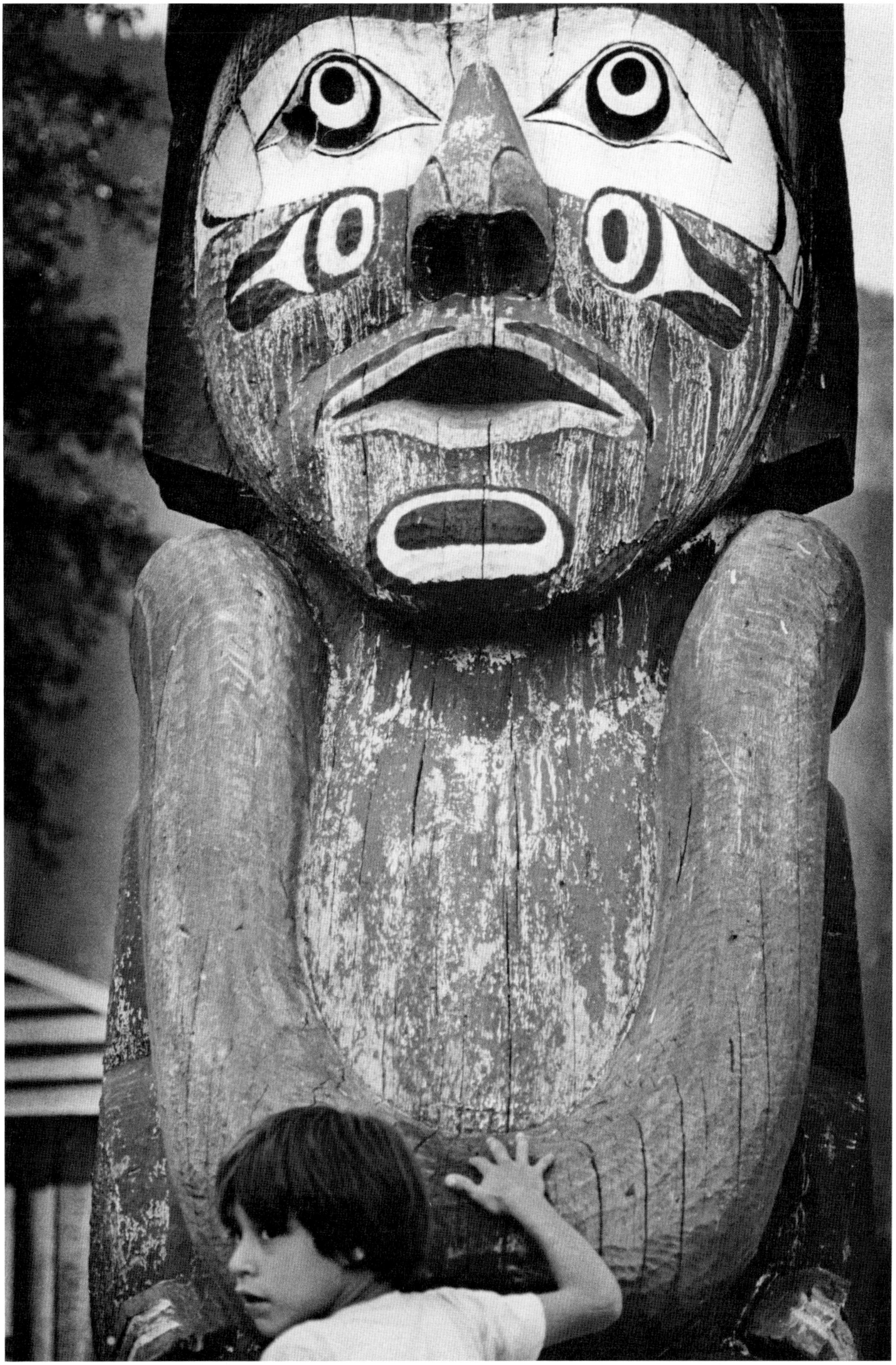

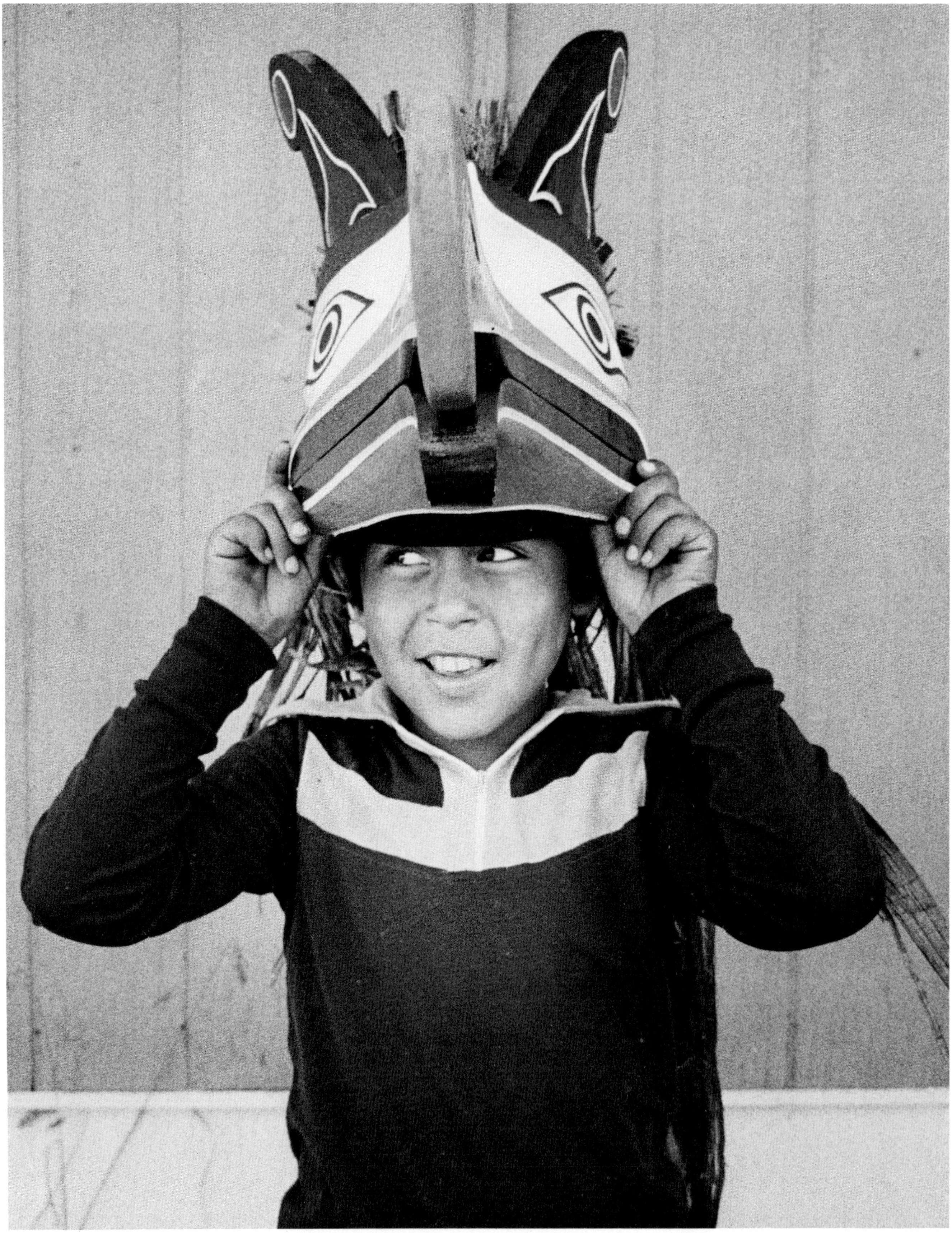

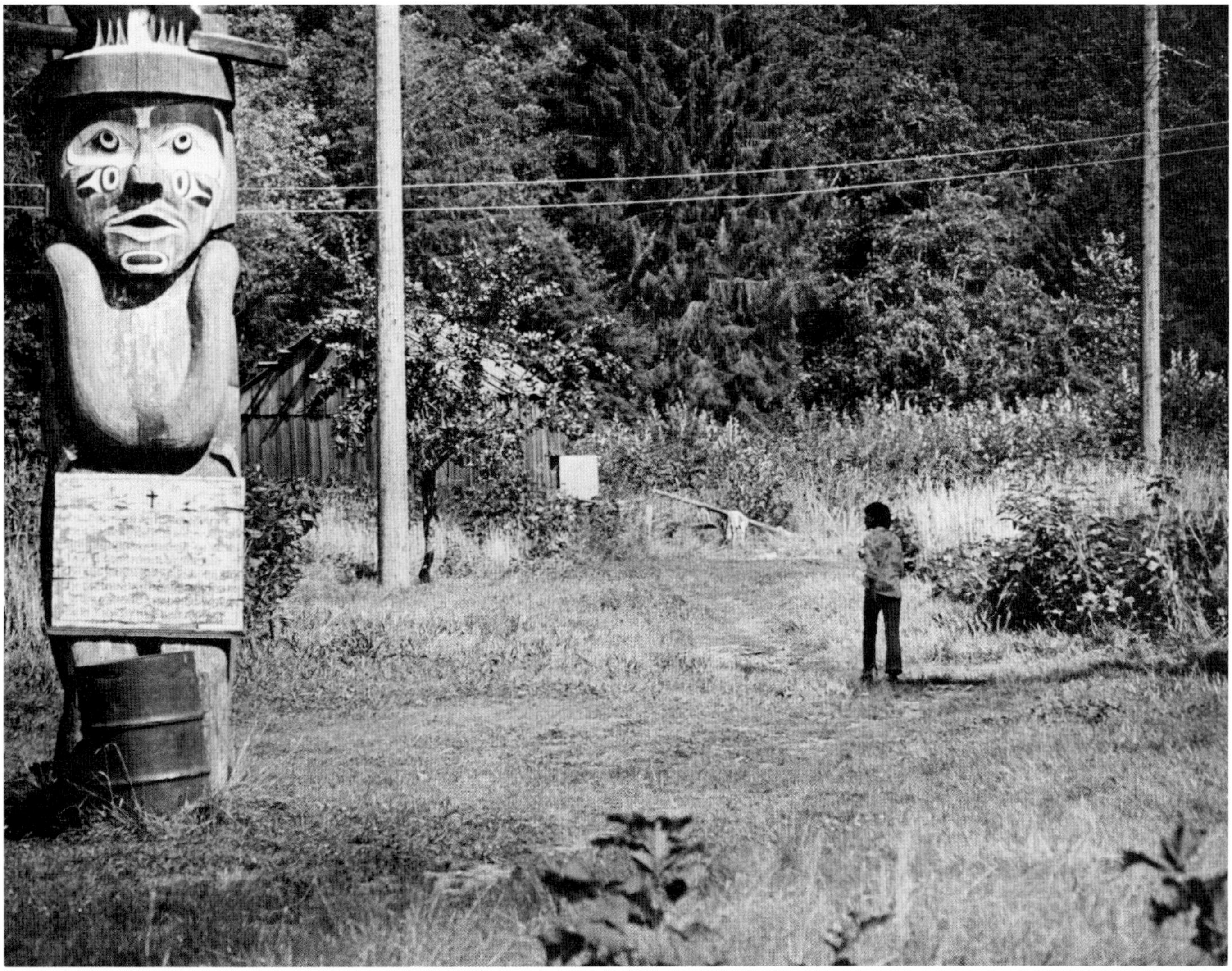

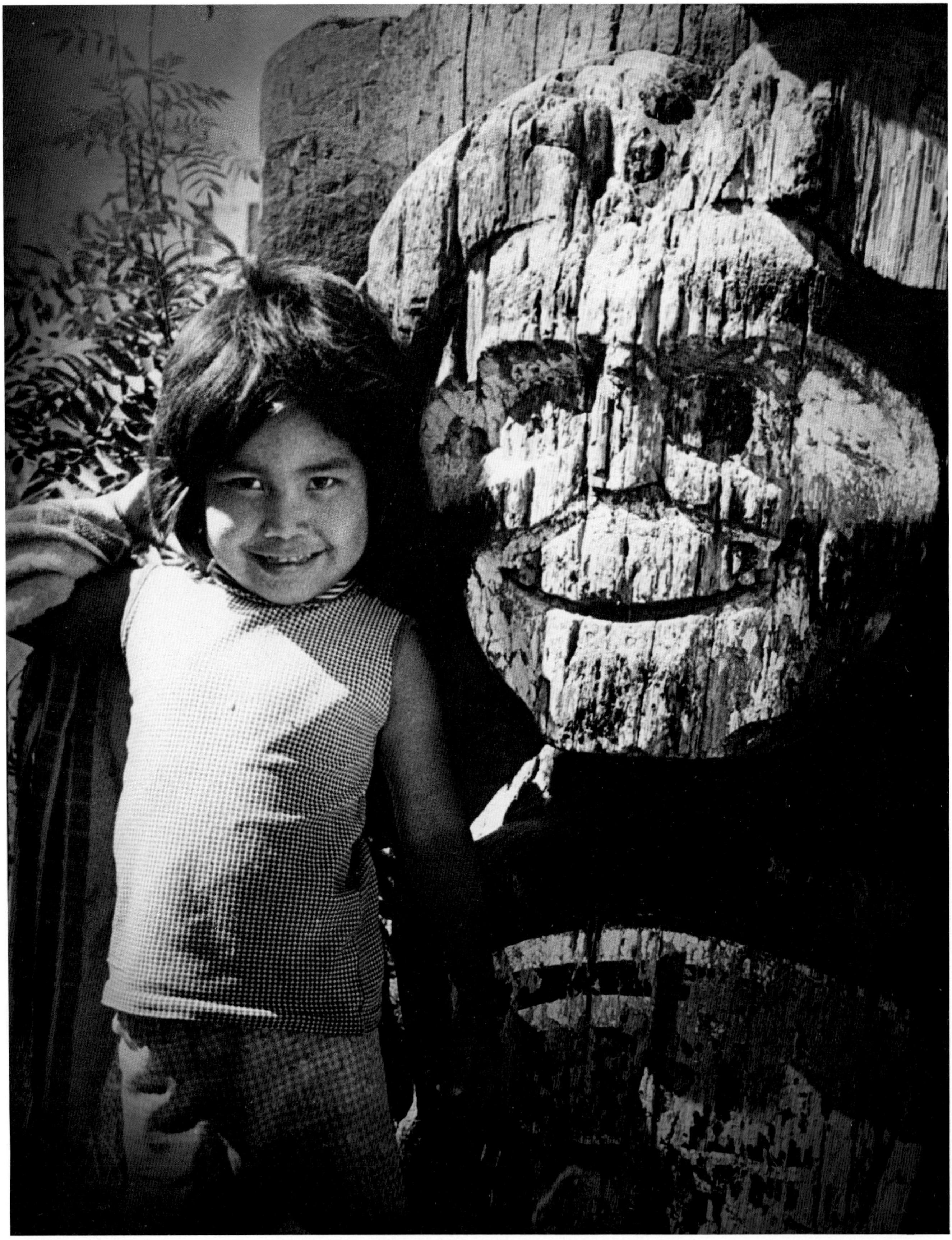

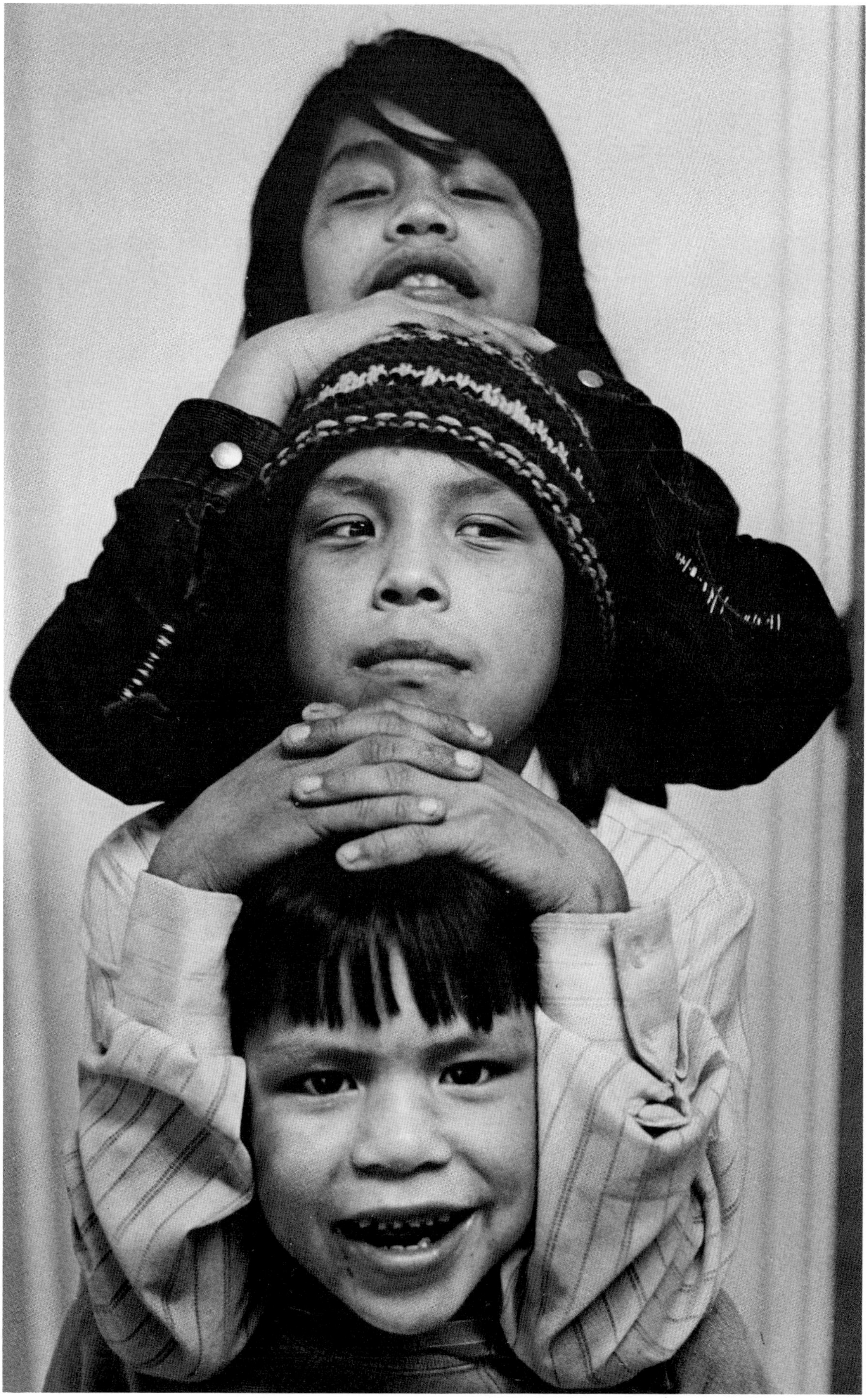

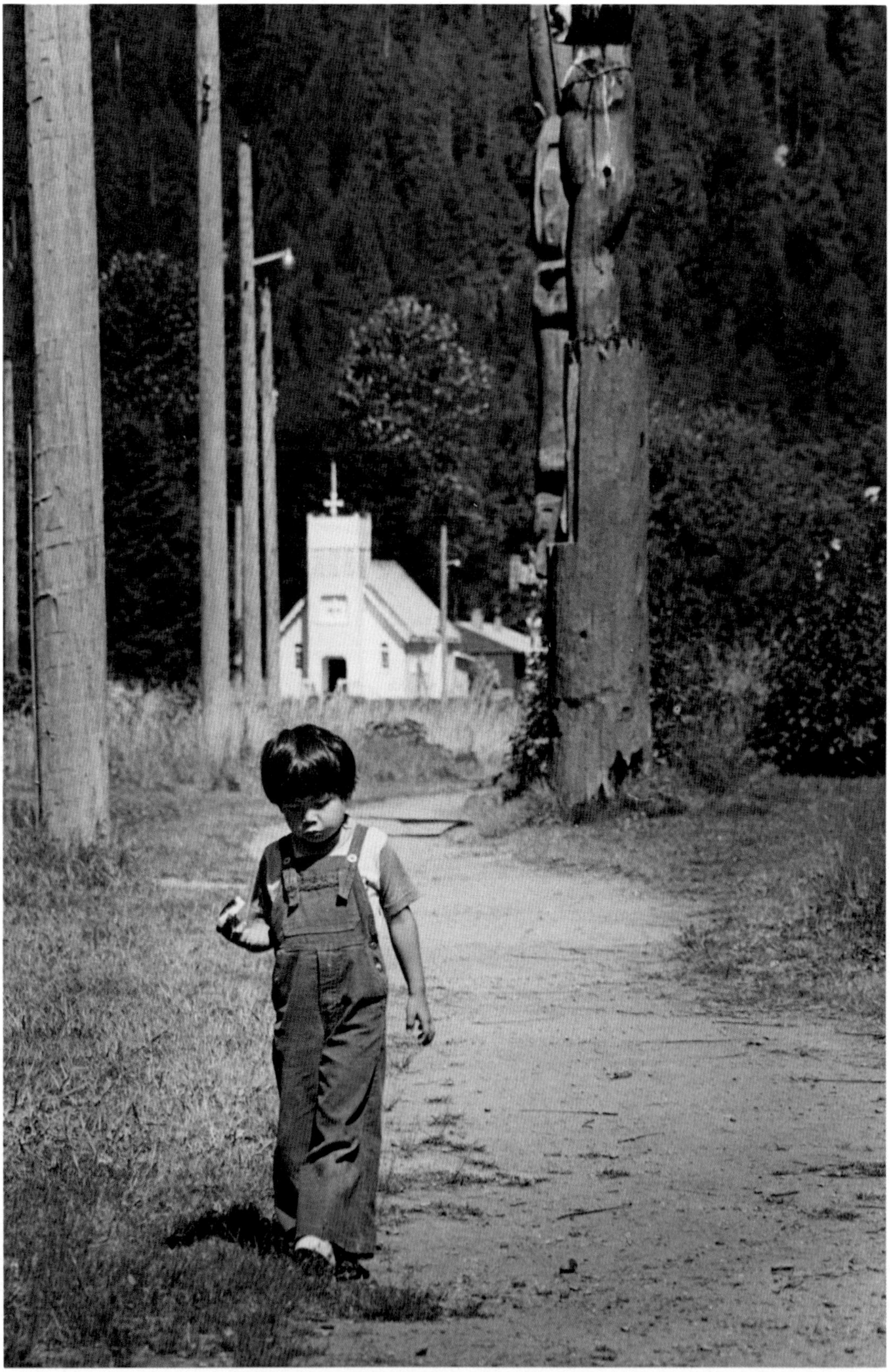

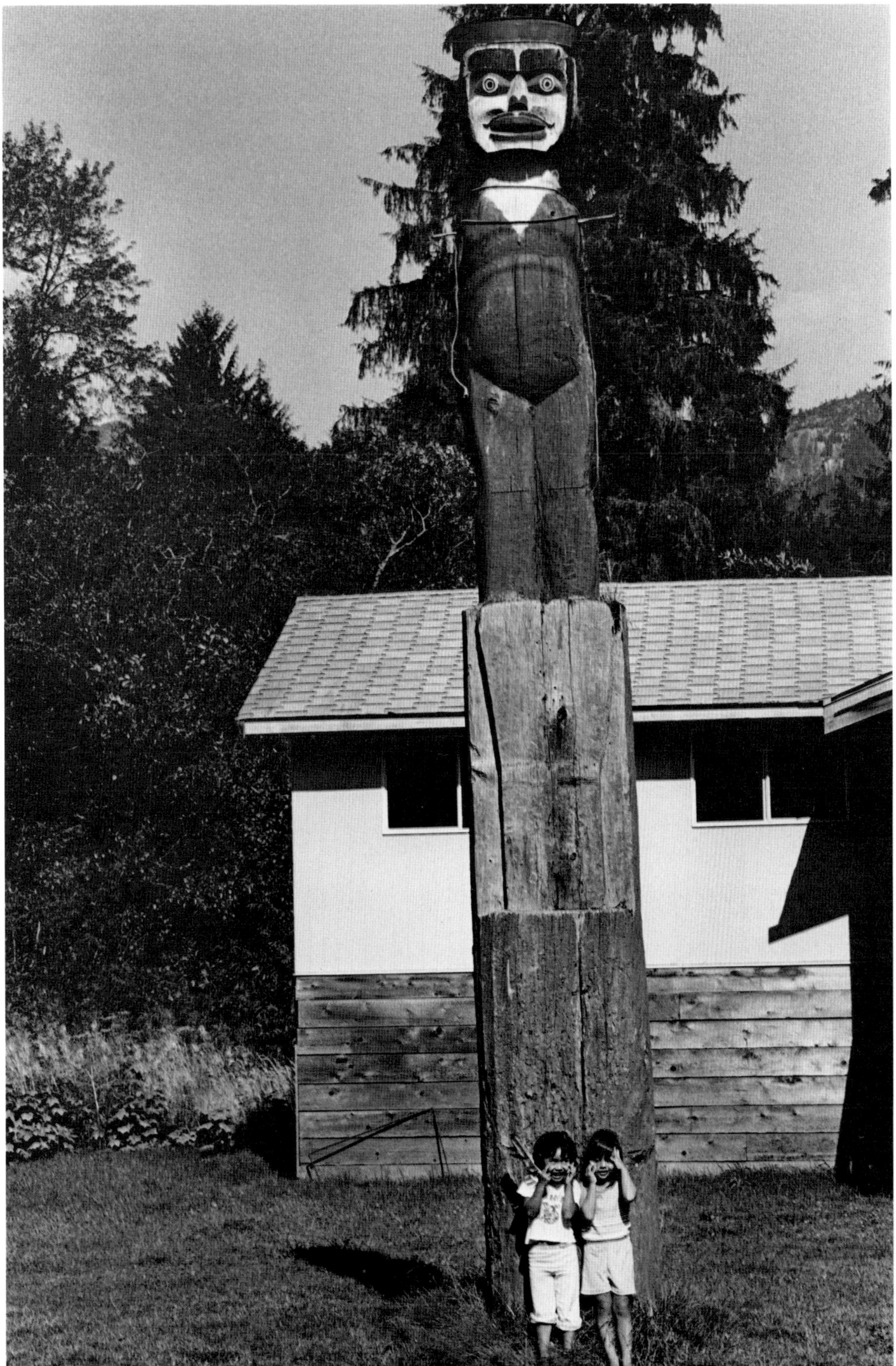

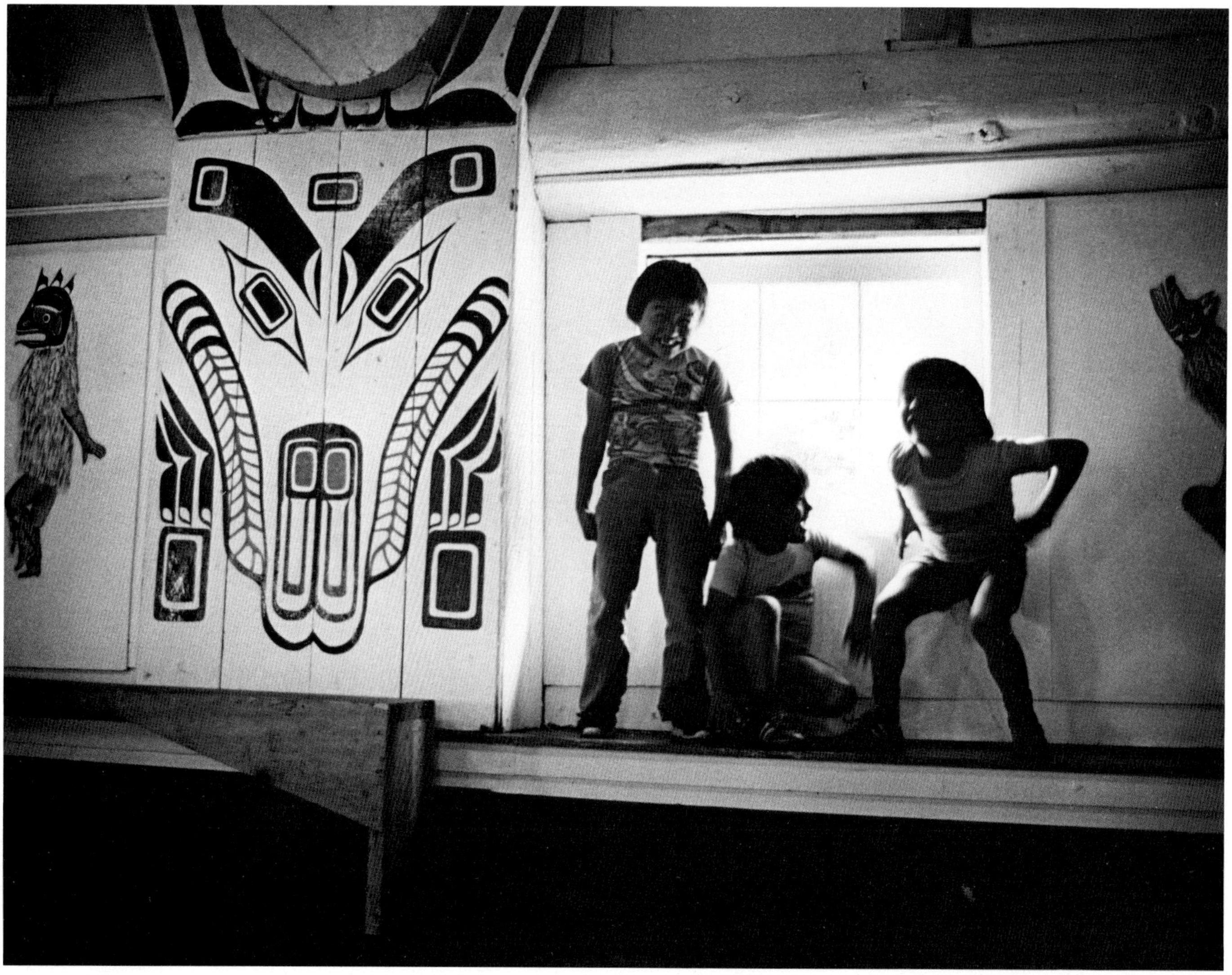

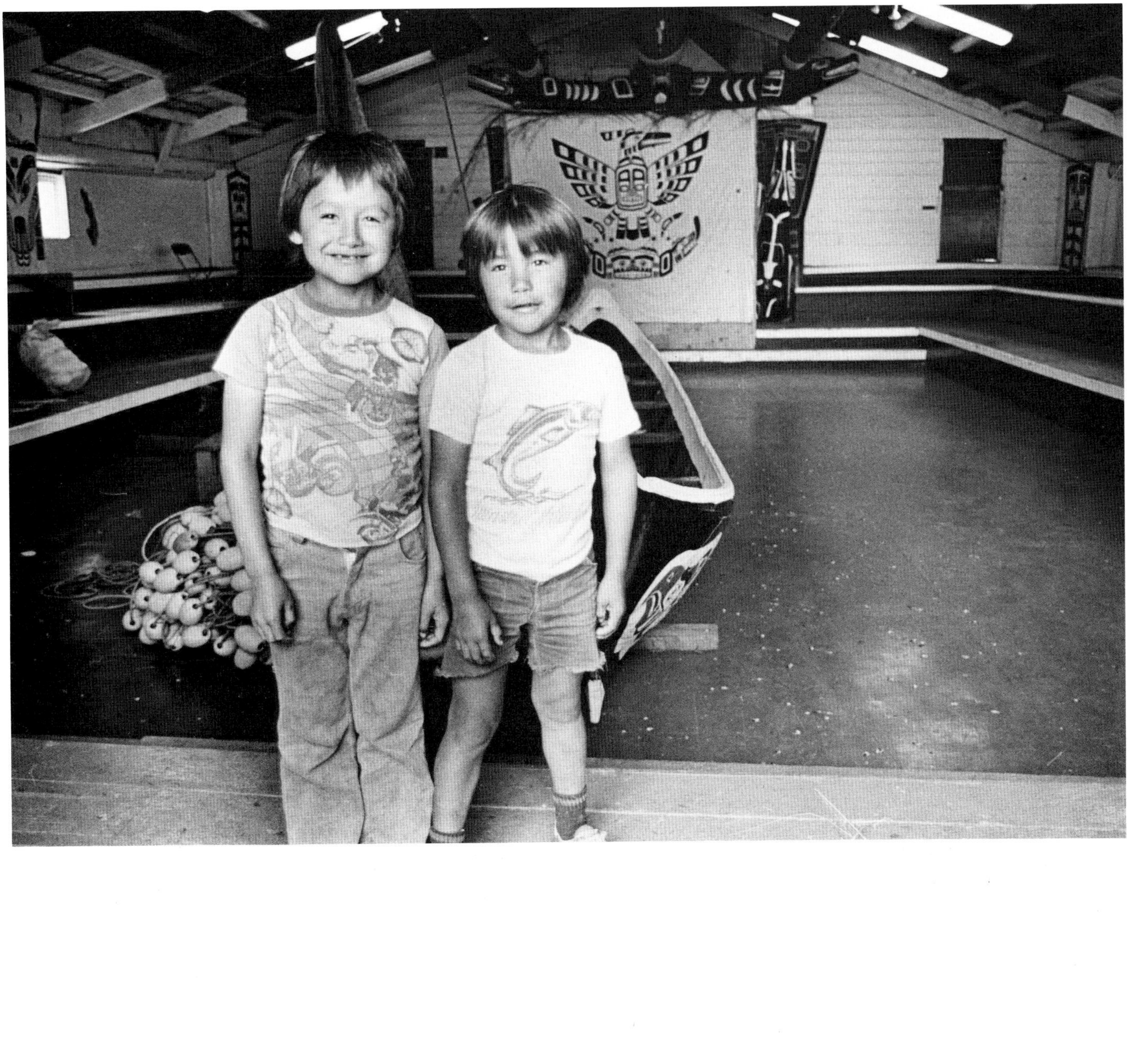

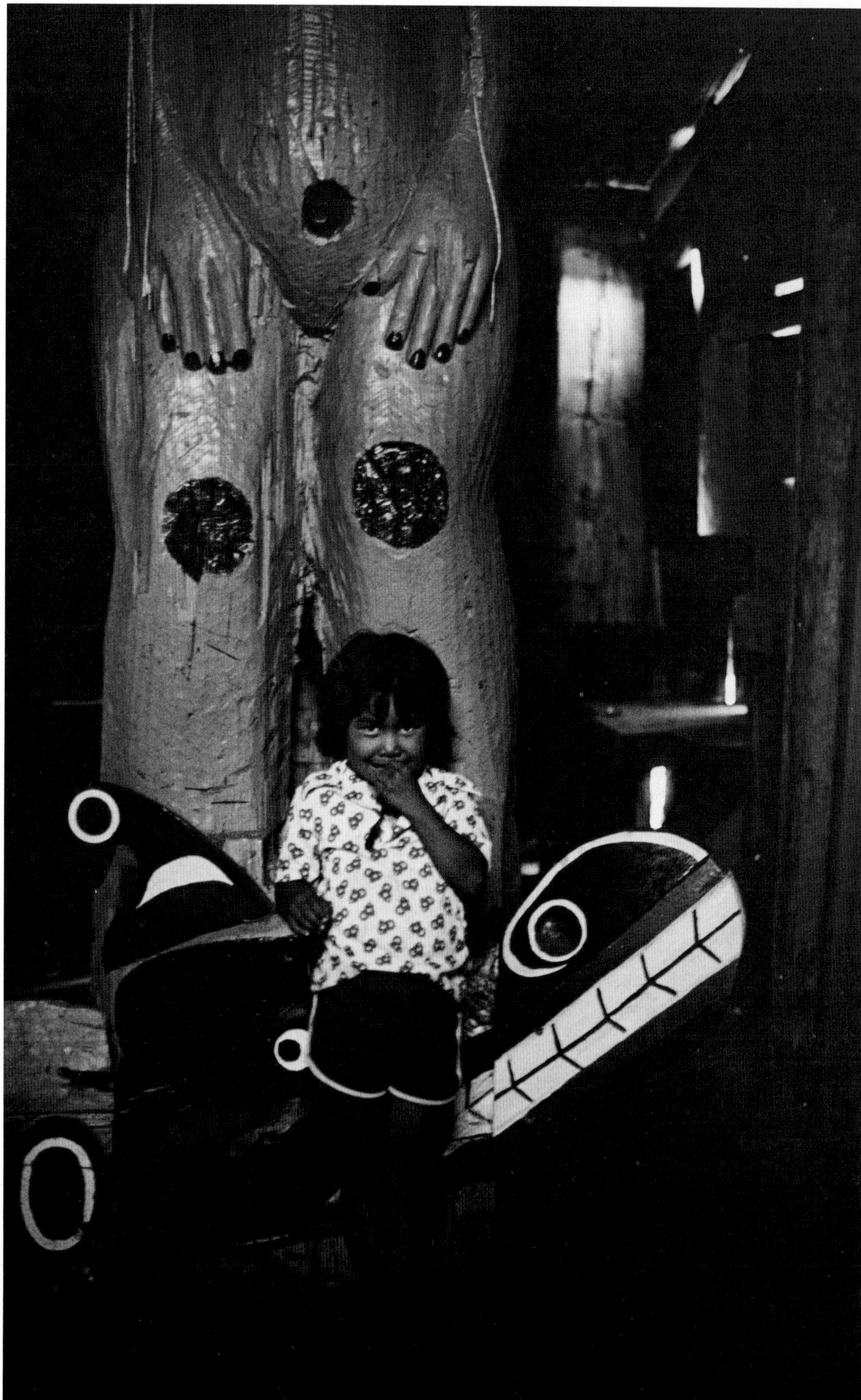

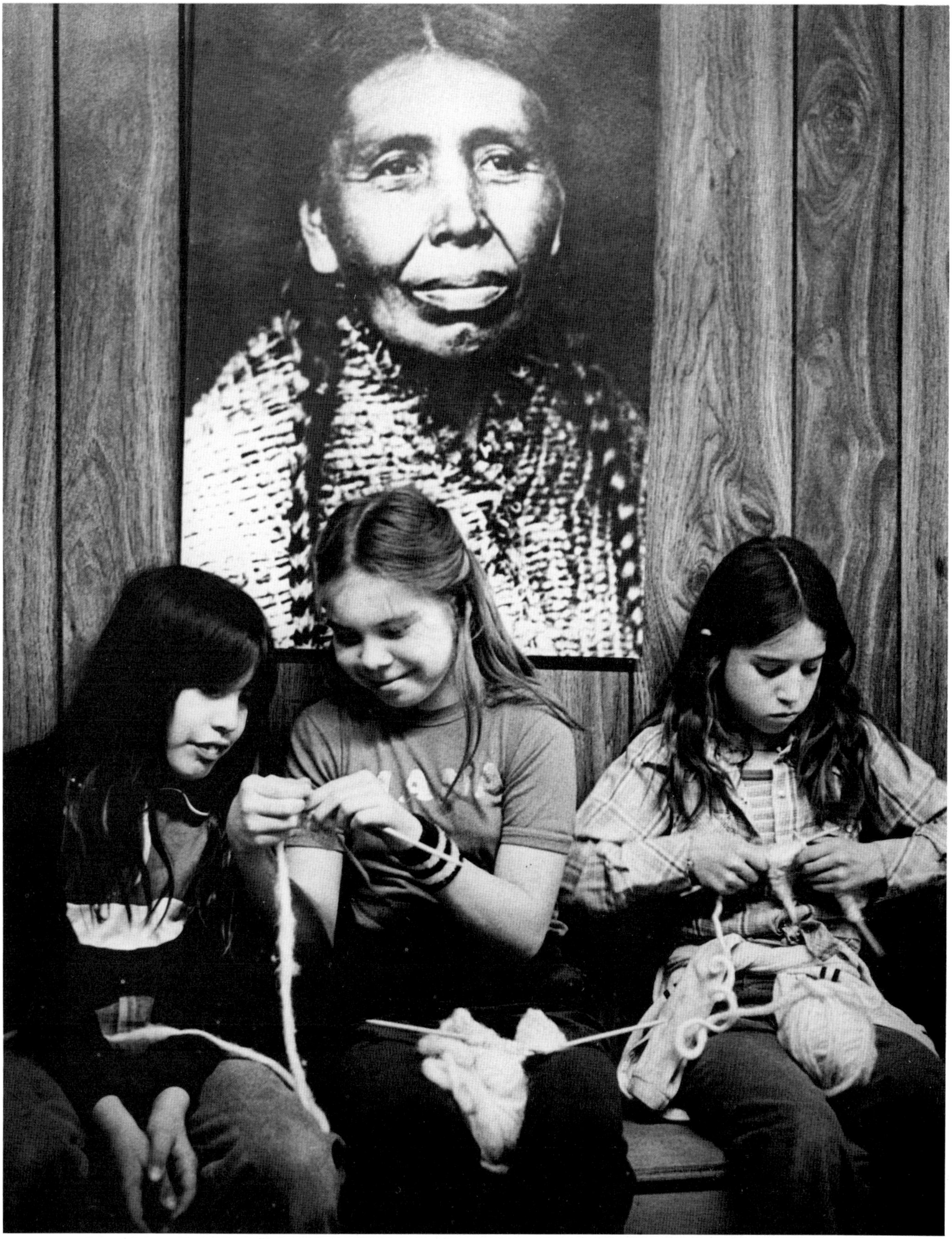

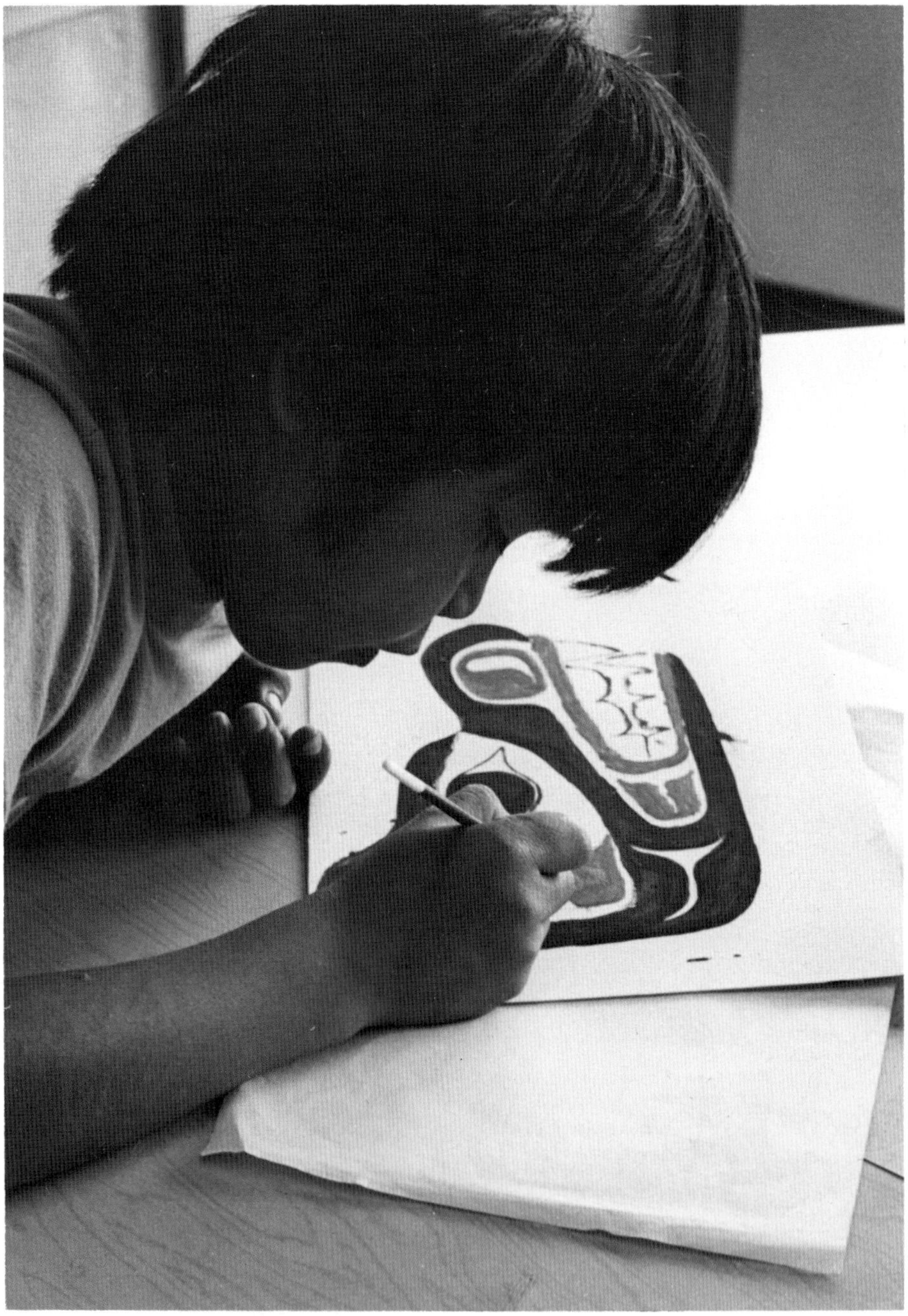

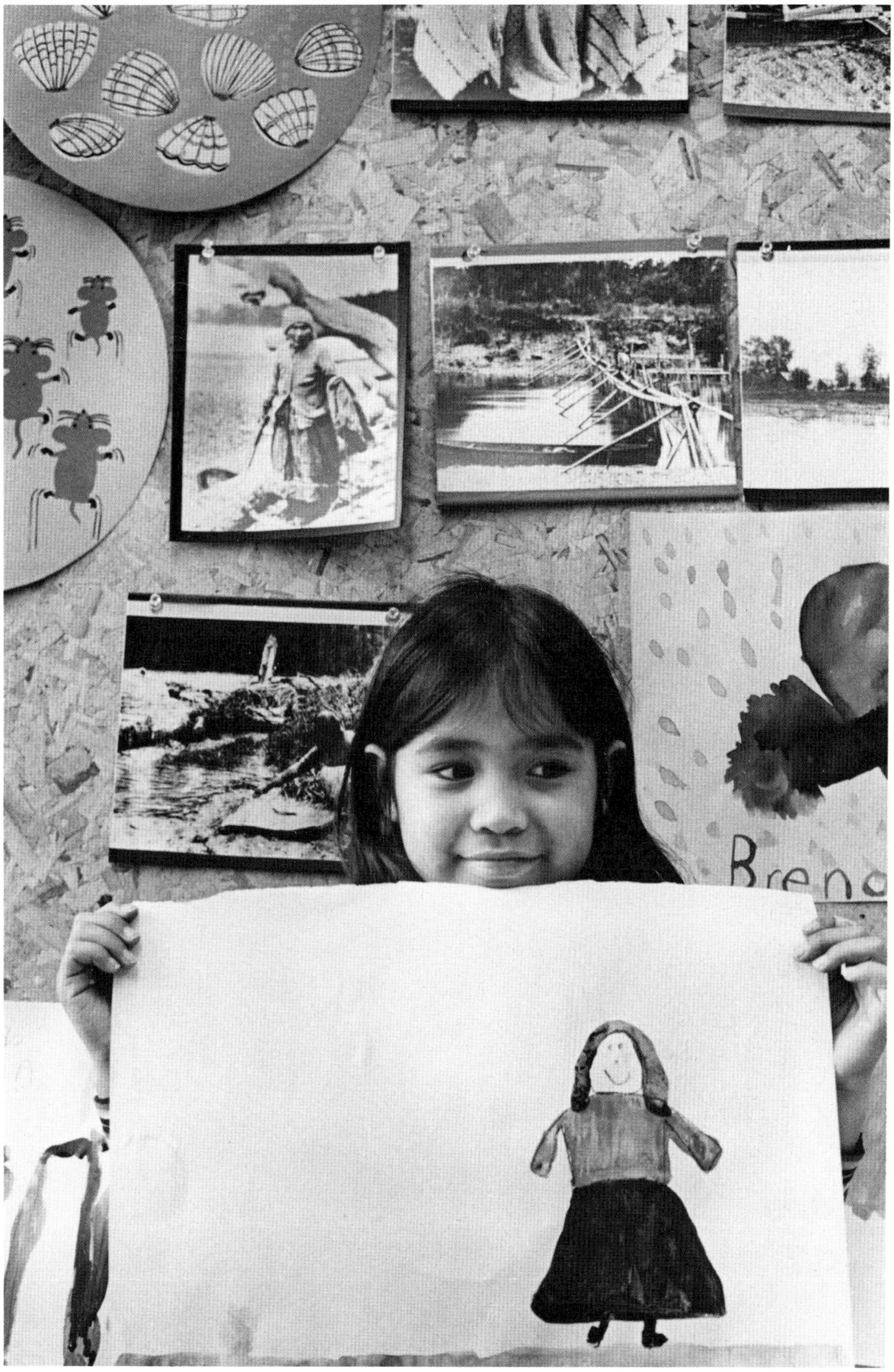

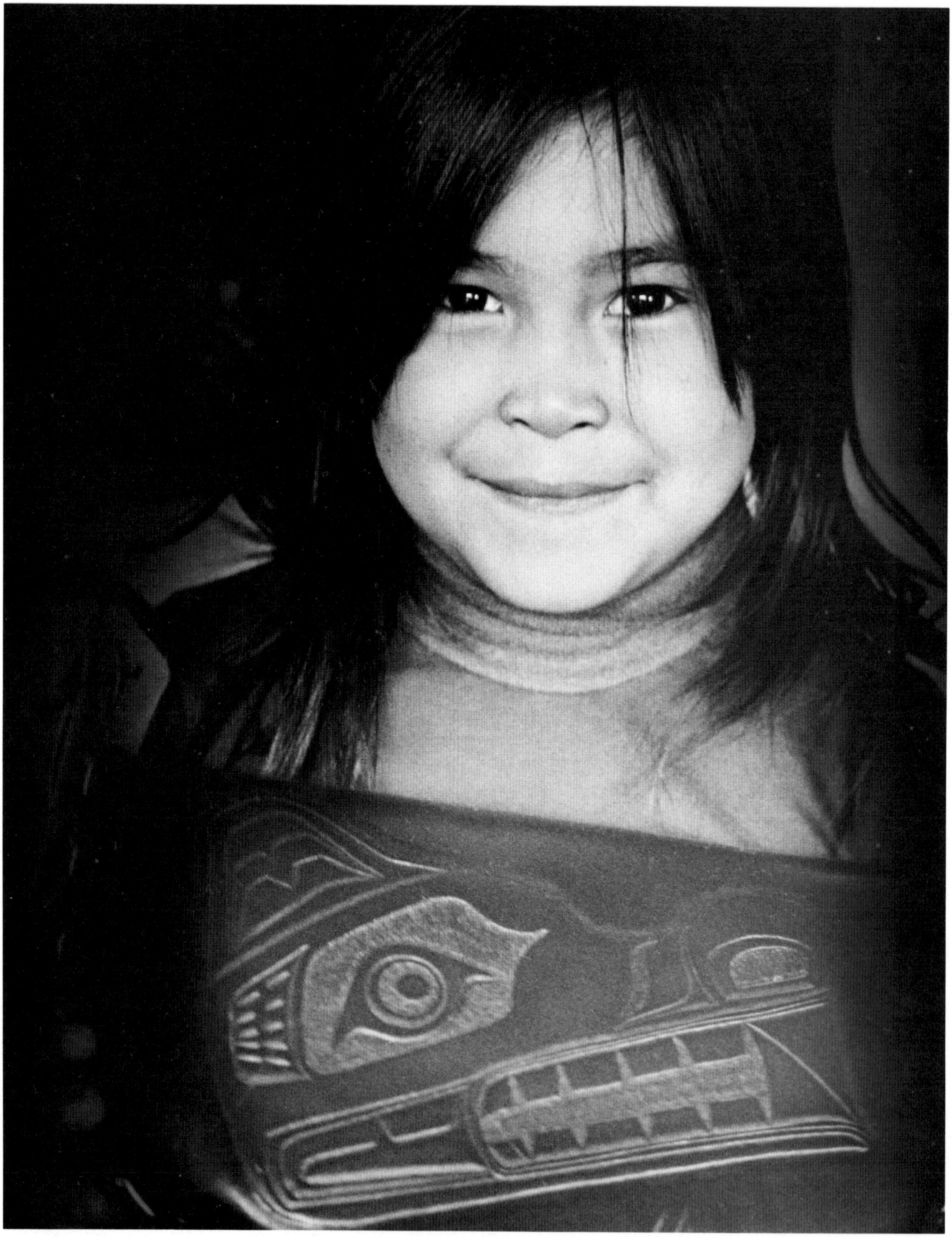

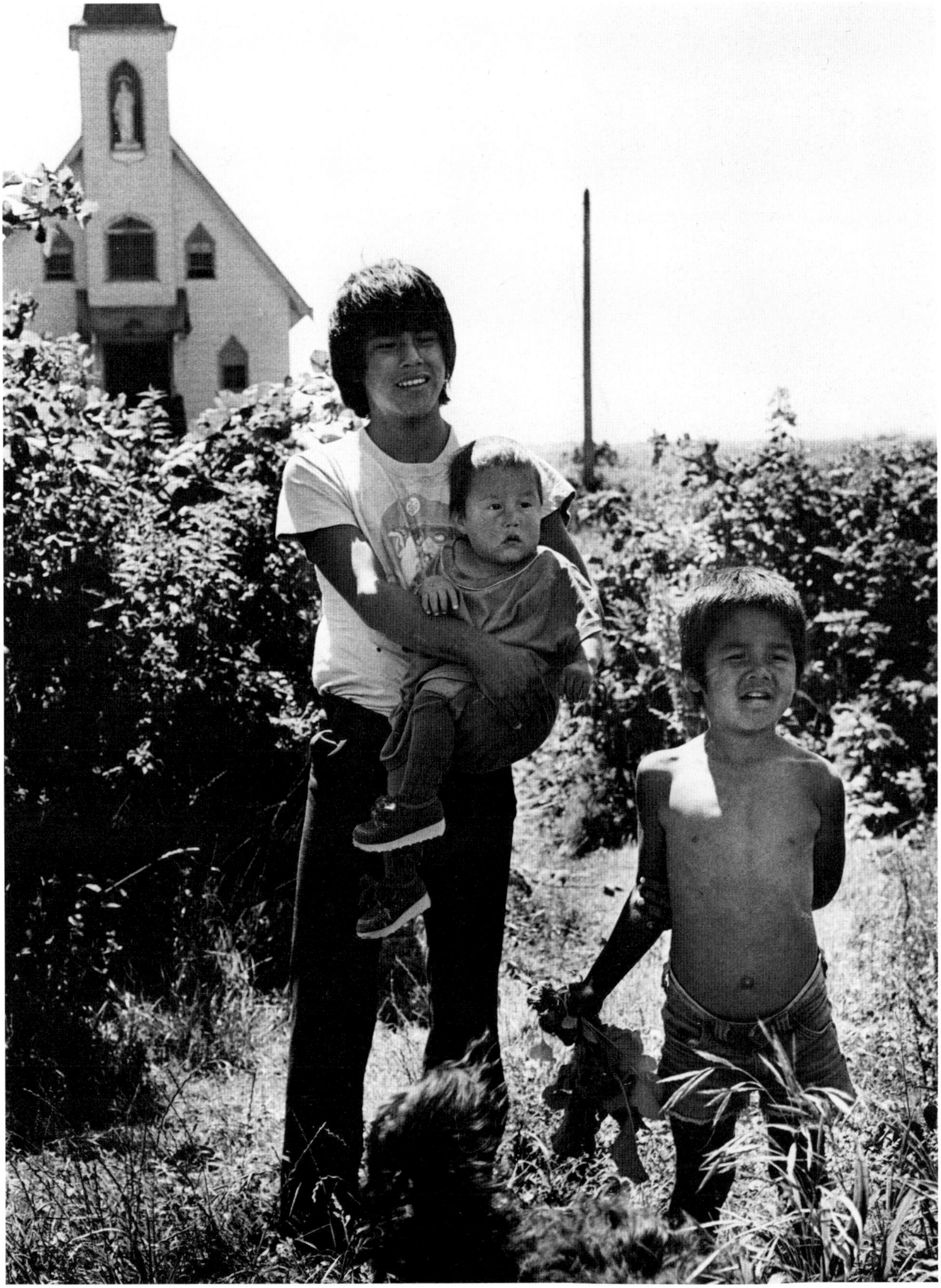

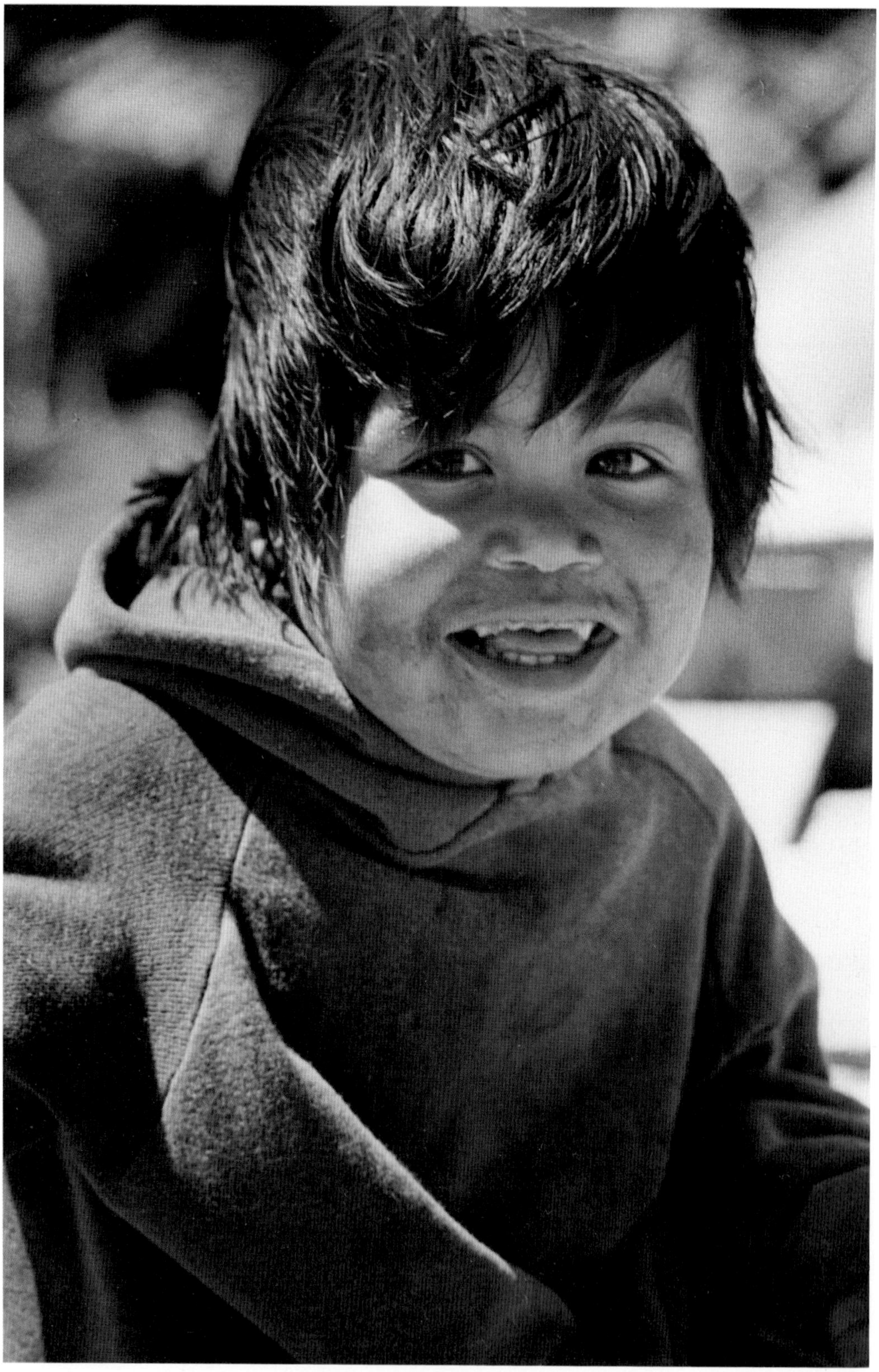

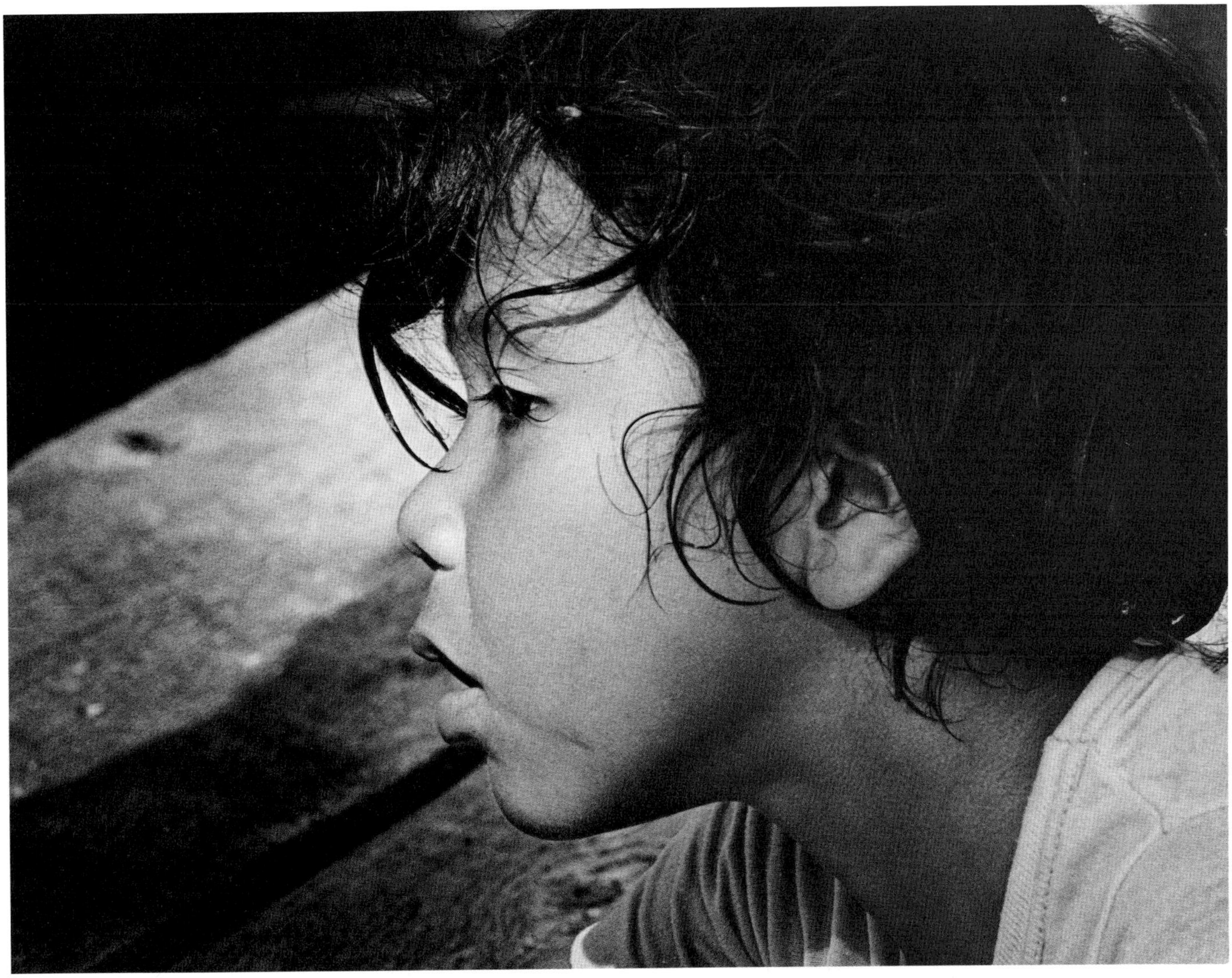

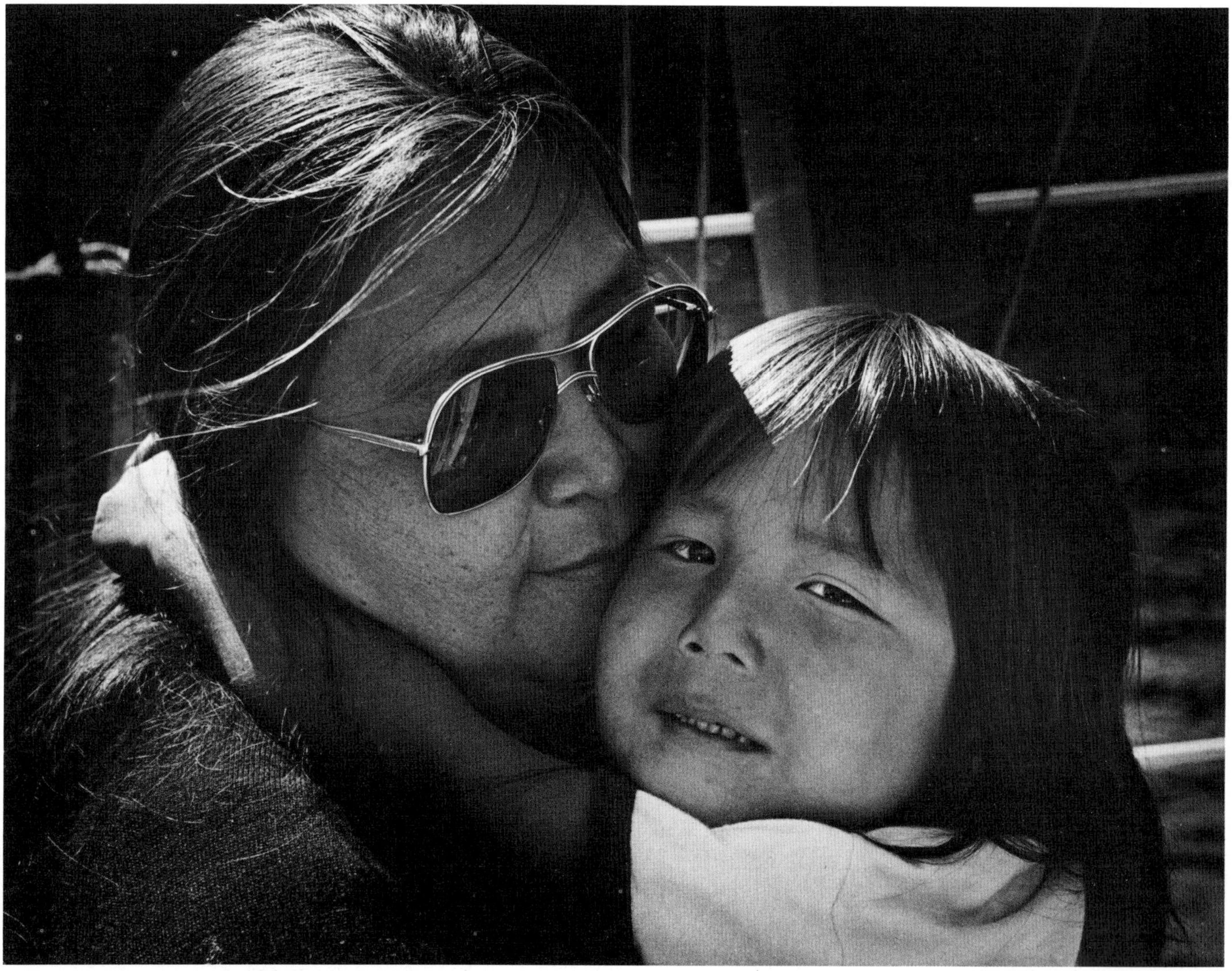

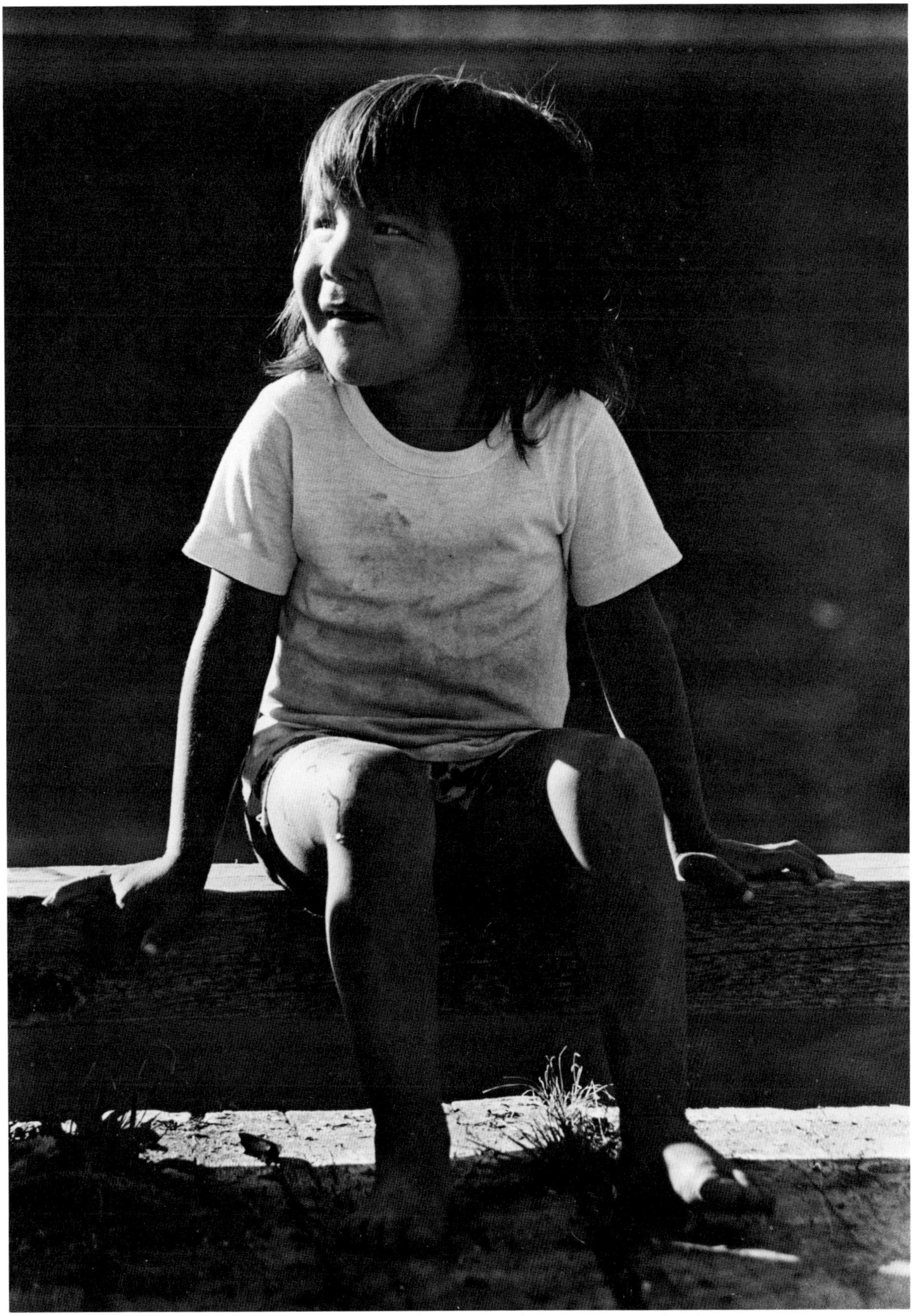

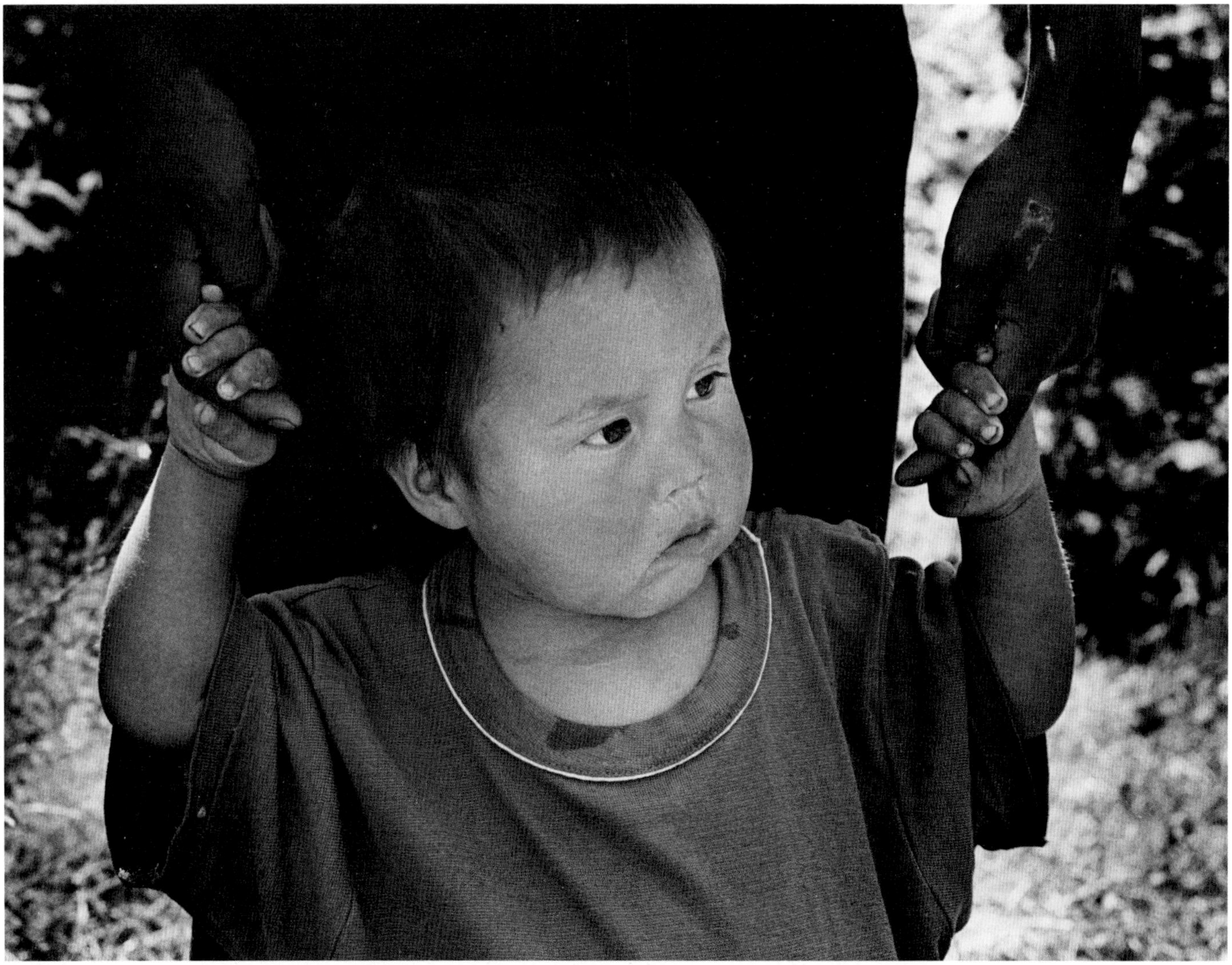

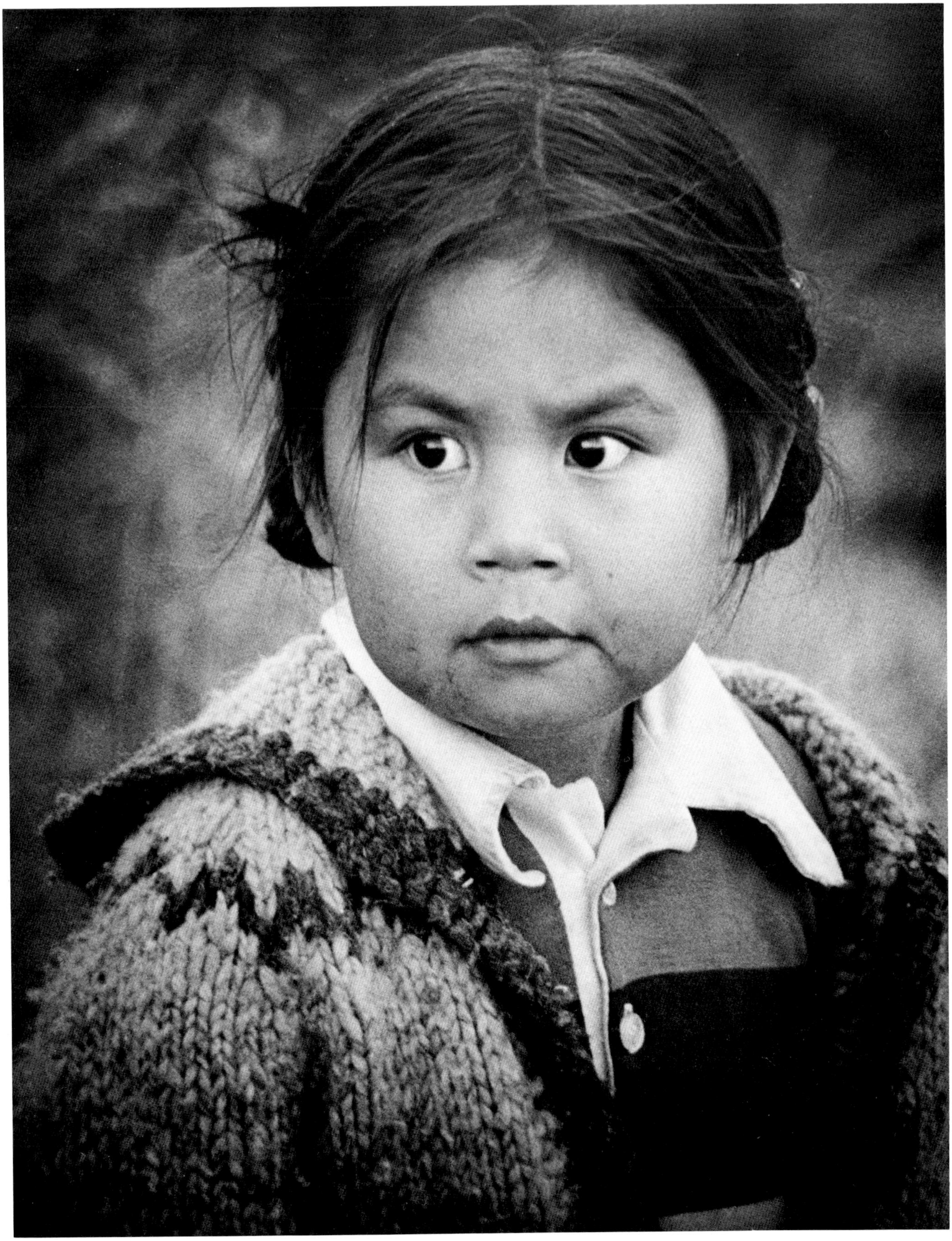

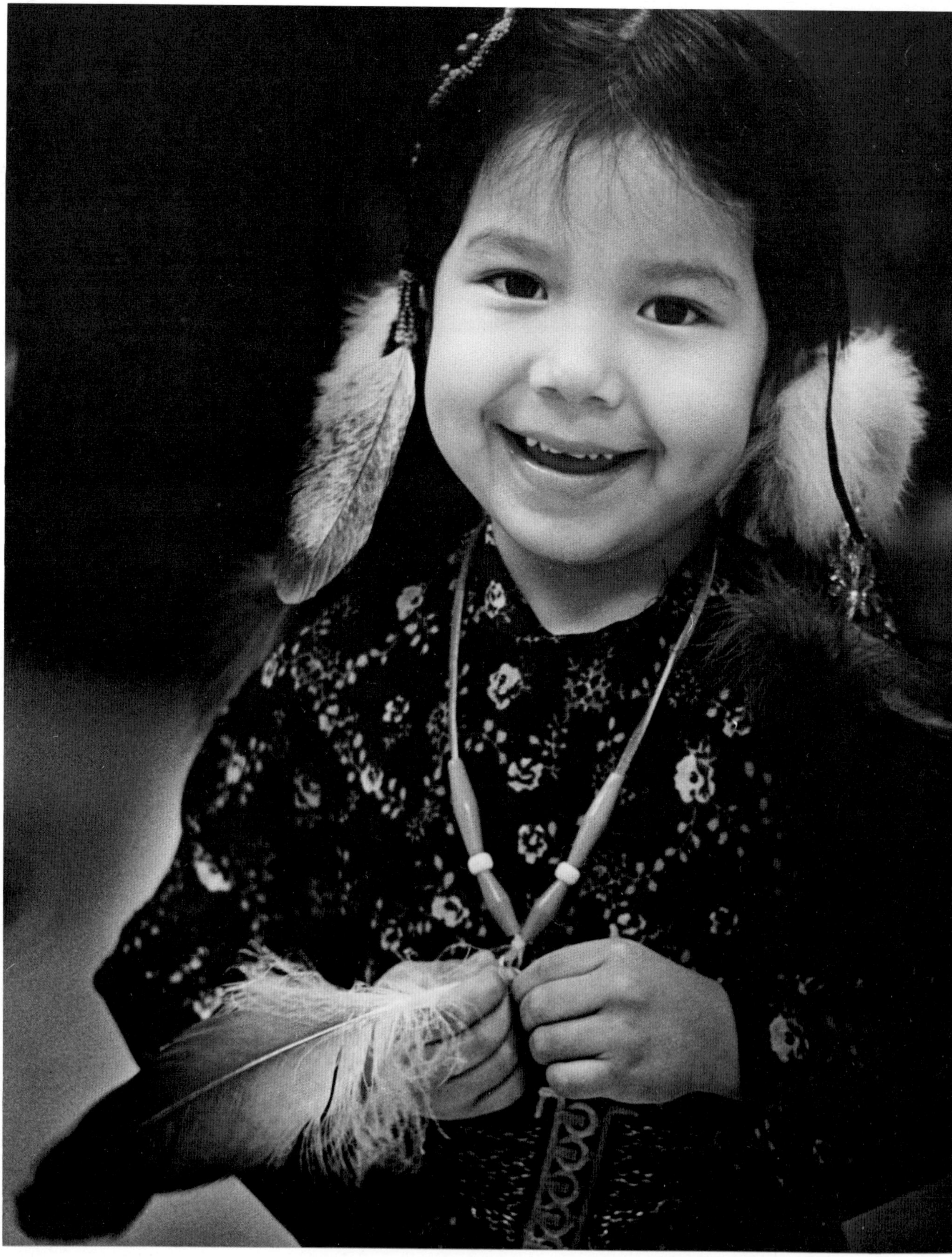

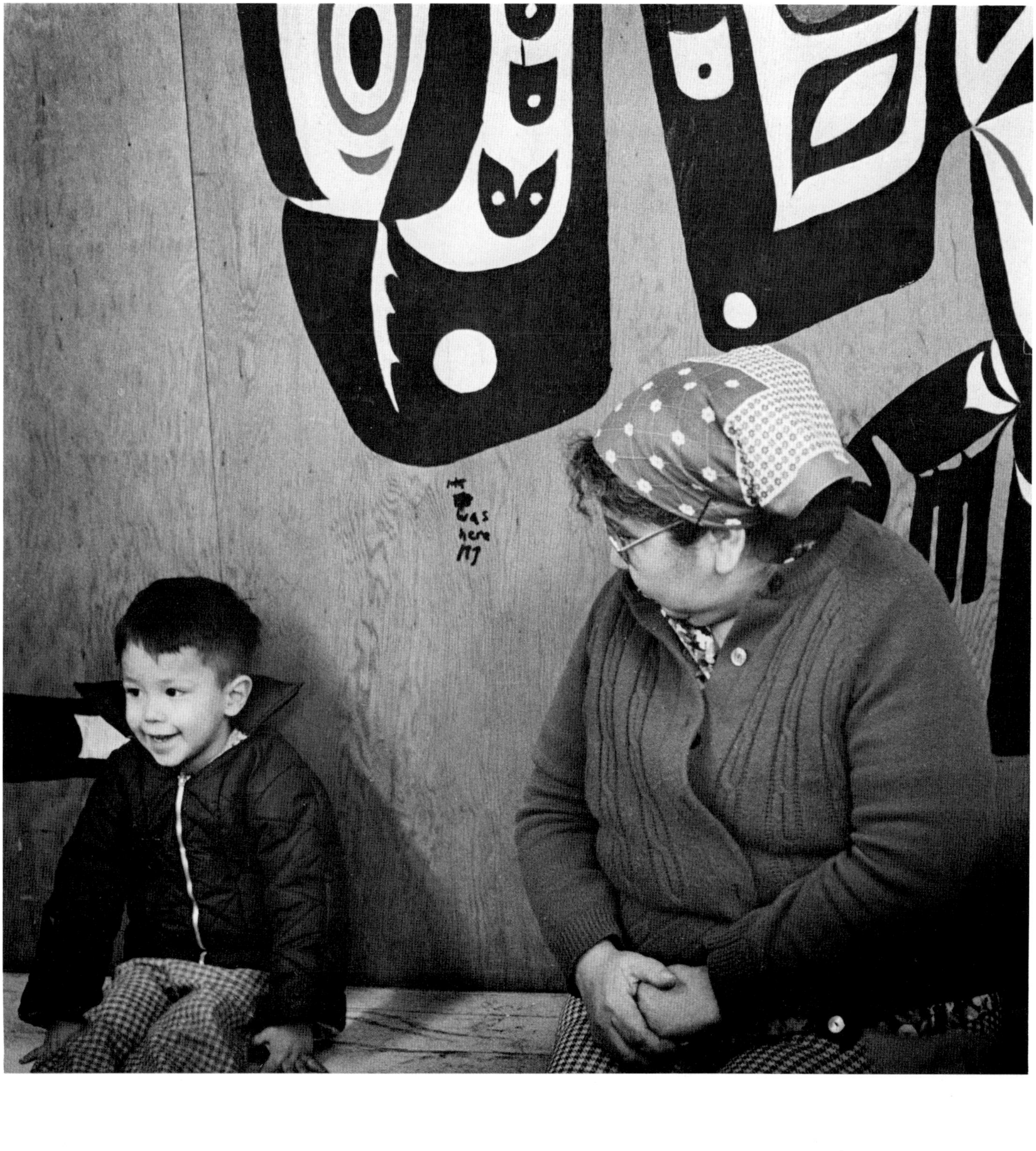
was
here

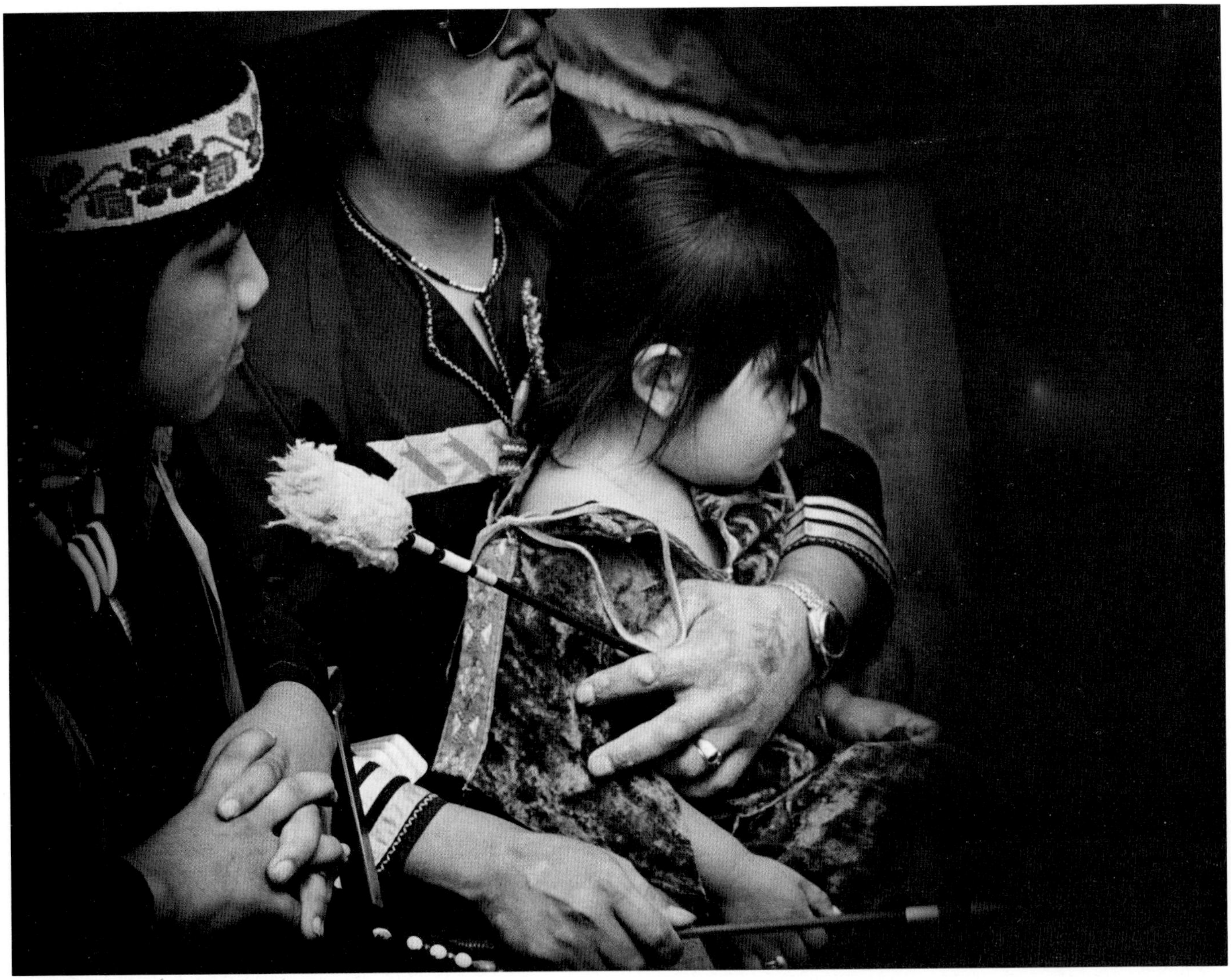

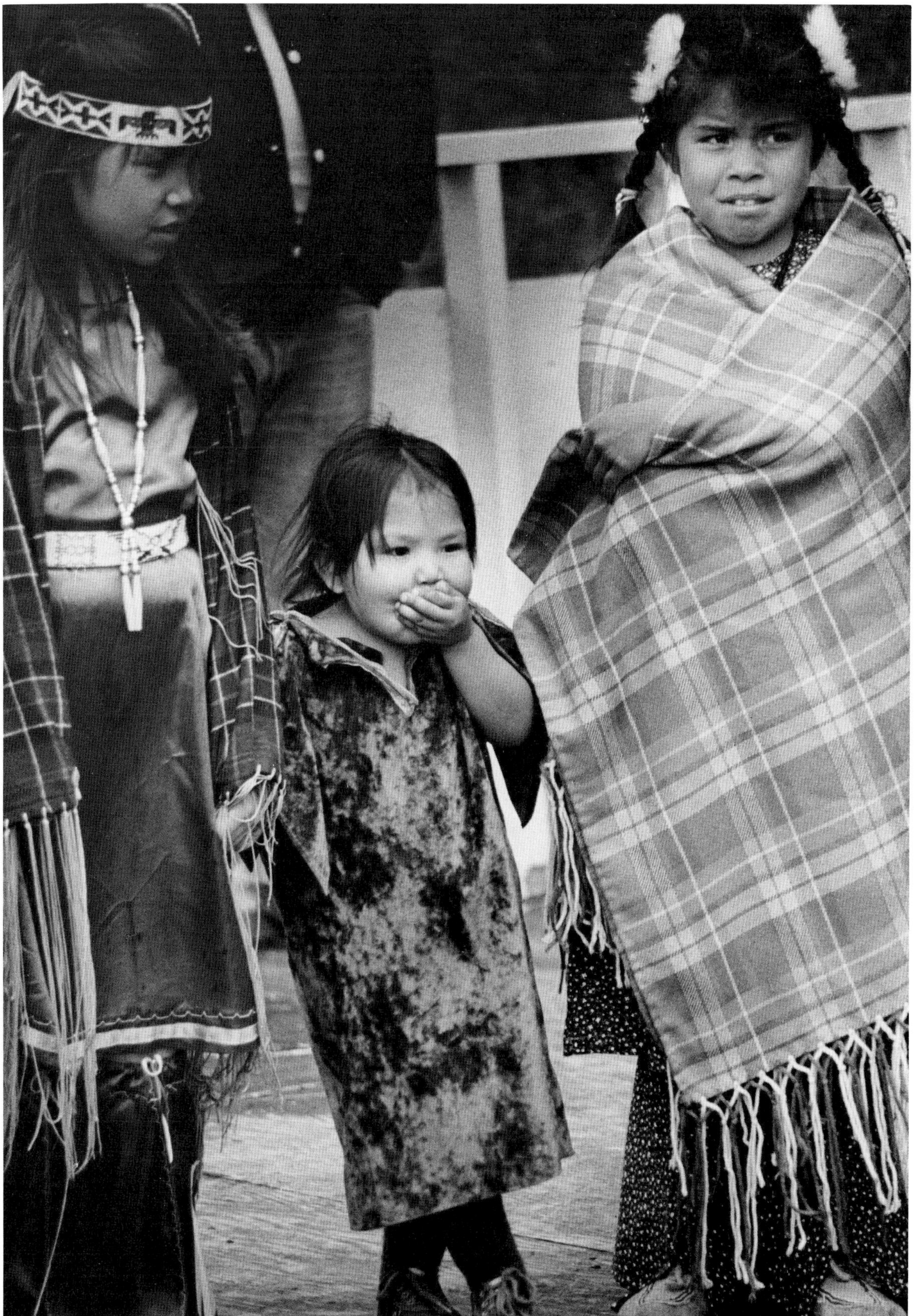

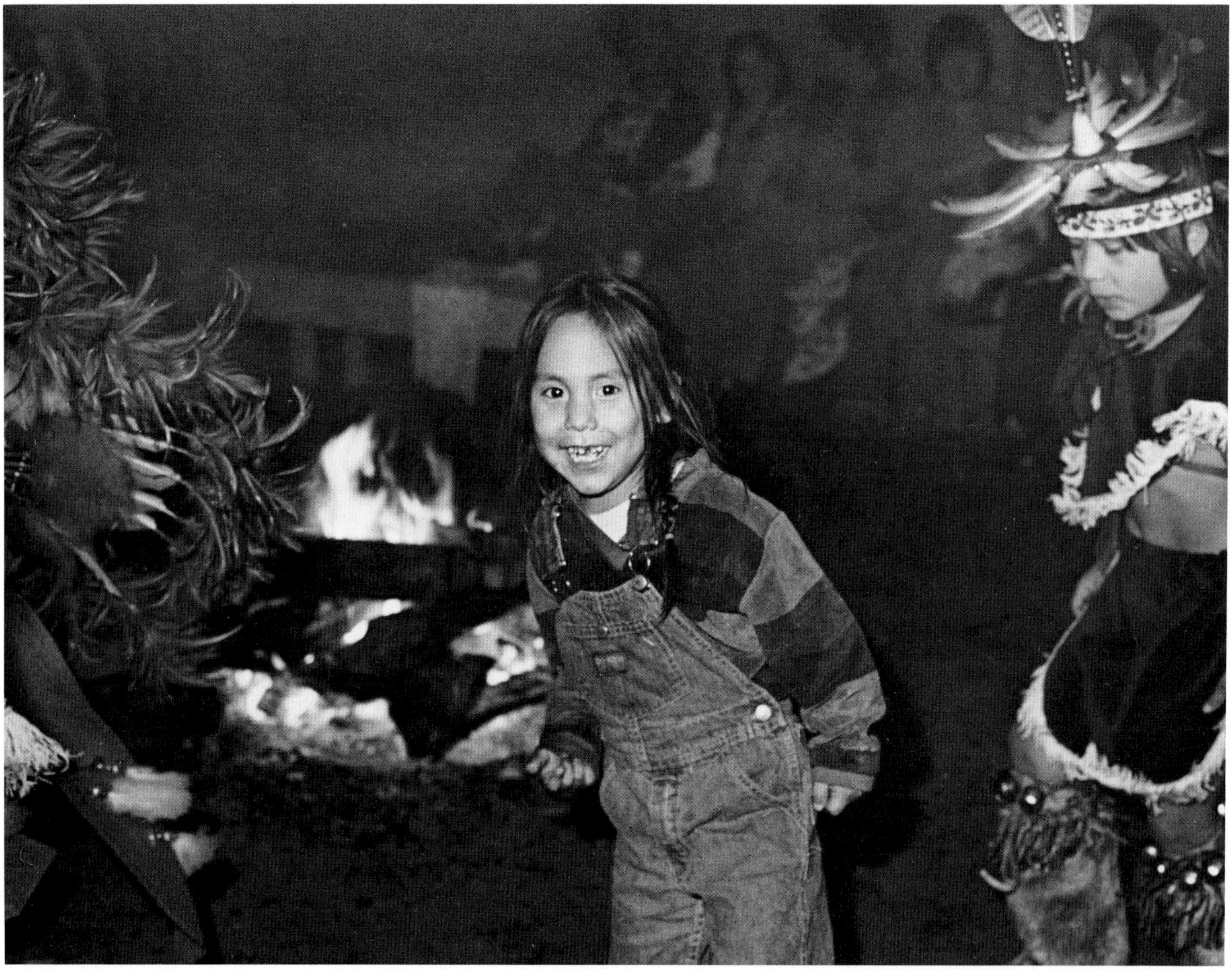

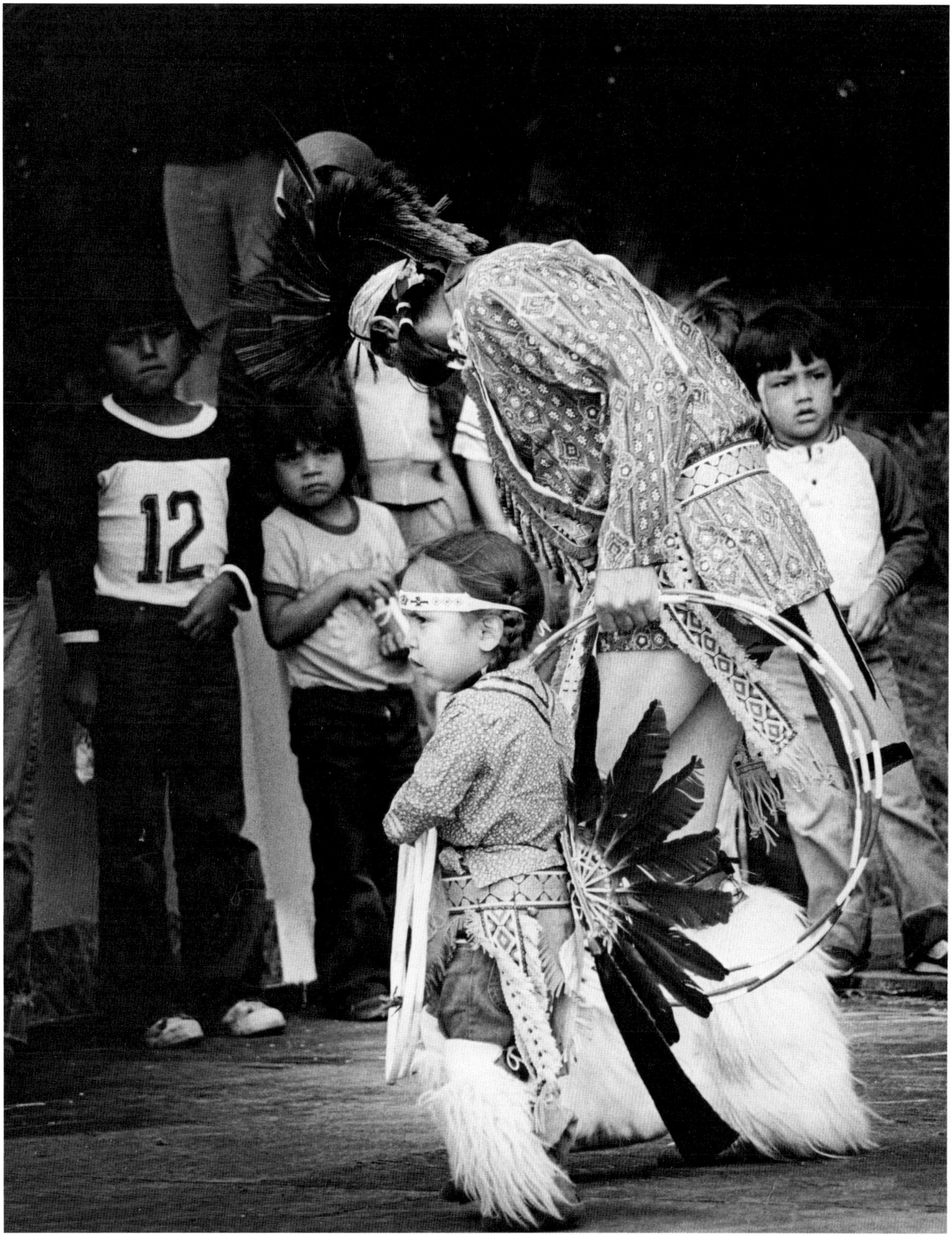
12

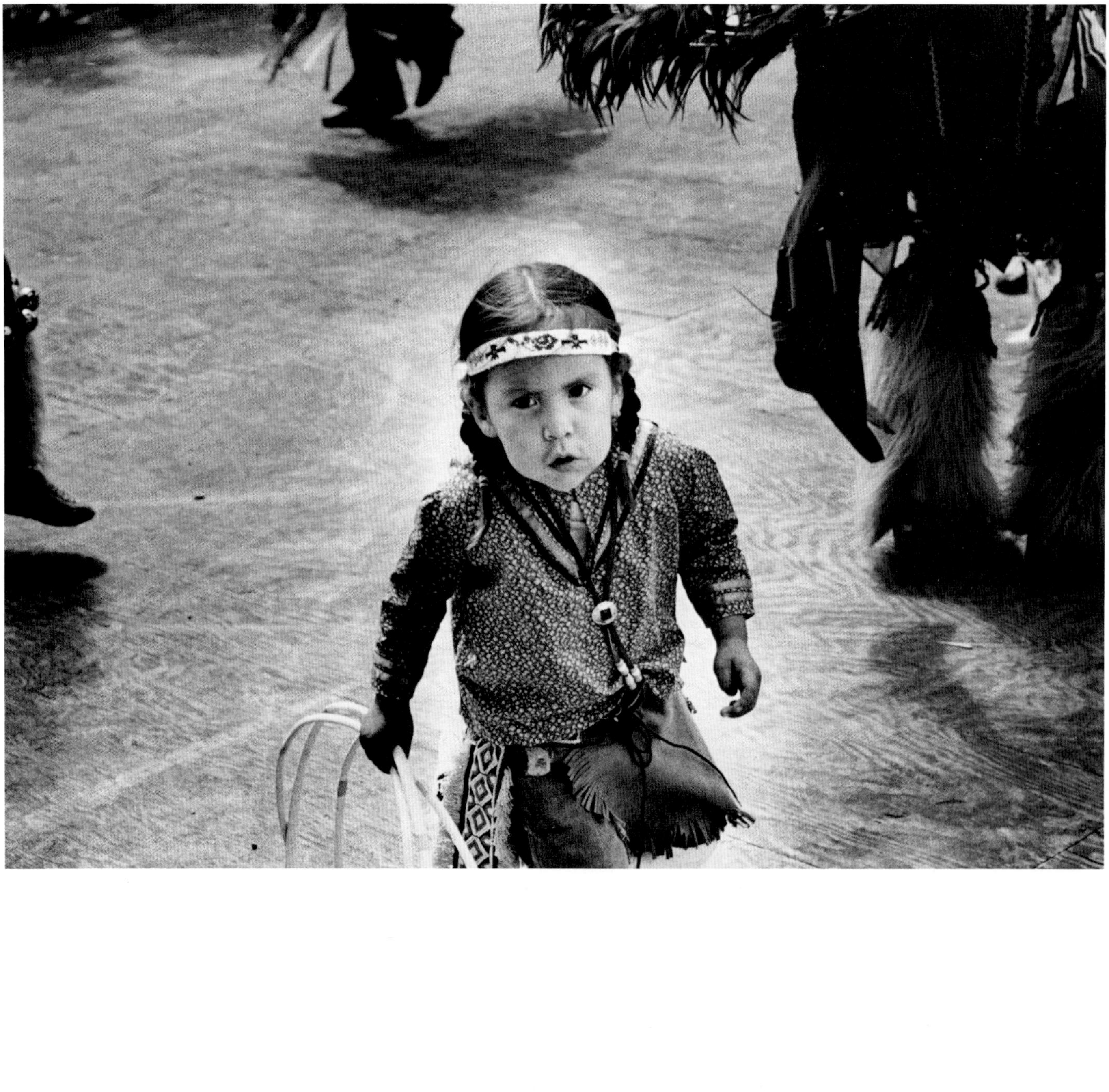

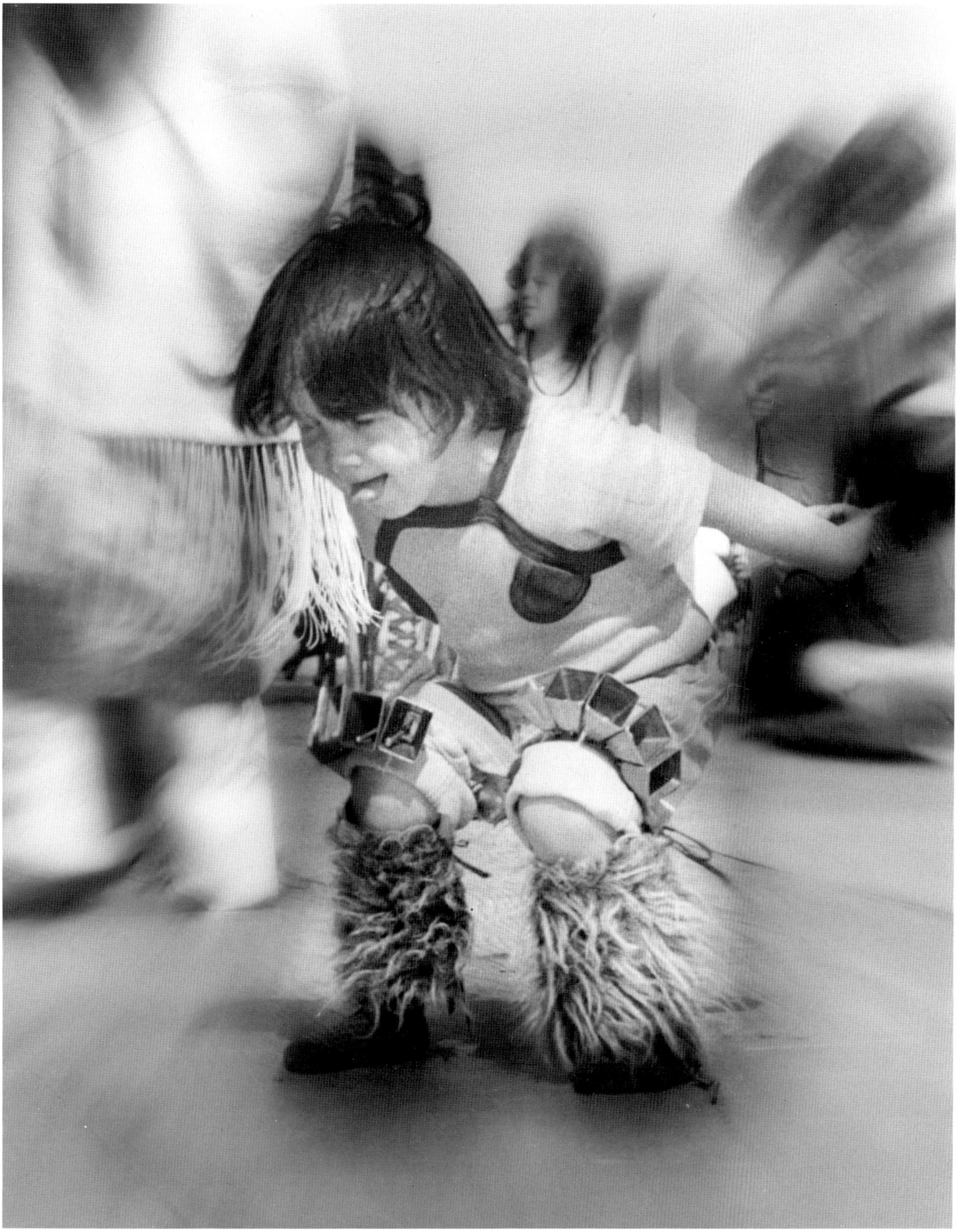

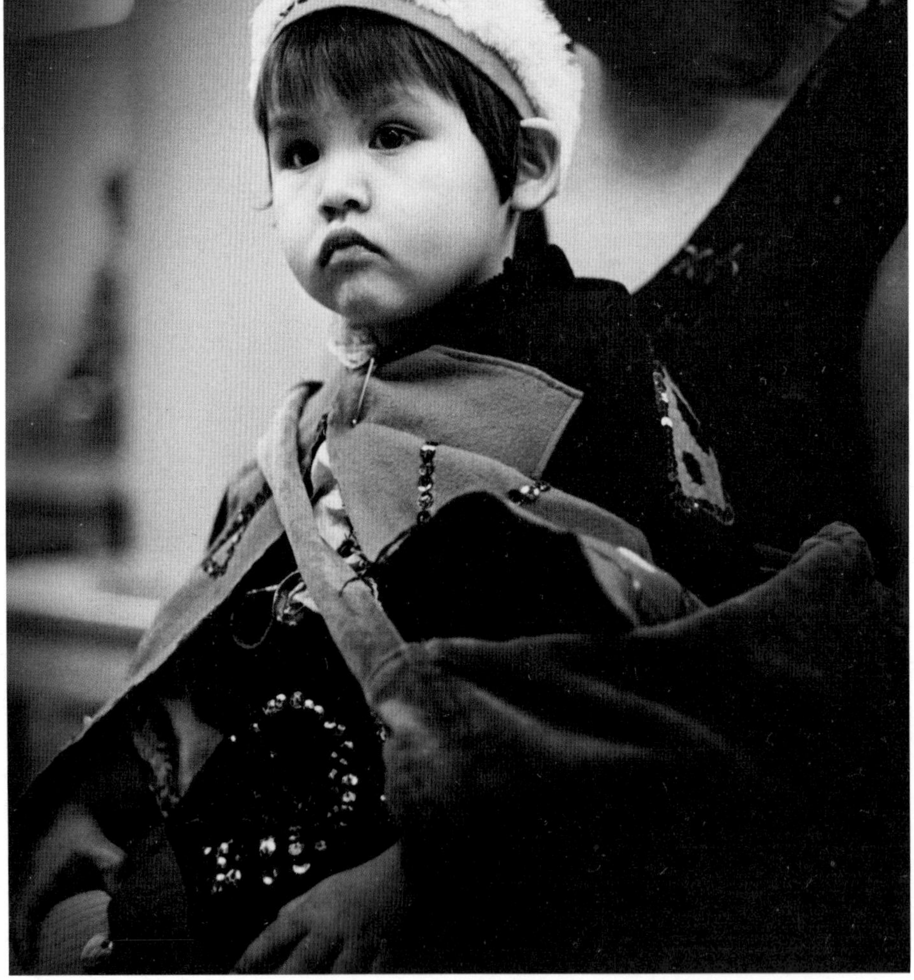

PETER WEBSTER
Ahousaht

As far back as I can remember—we were small children—I must have been three years old, and I remember my father came back from the sealing schooner. It was 1911. Yes, it must have been. Mind you, I didn't know a word of English.

In the first place, we were close to nature—how our great-great-great-forefathers used to be. Because there was no civilization in their time. But in our time, that's seventy years ago now, there were a few settlers coming in—traders coming in to Clayoquot Sound where we were raised. It was a village called Yaaqsis and the neighbouring place would be called Kluthpich.

Now in my young days as a small child—I don't think I had any shoes. There were no shoes, no pants. I don't know what I wore before I got to know that I was in the world. I remember watching my mother—she cleaned that flour sack and she had to sew it together, you know, to make me a shirt. That's how we were in our way of living. Although my mother was learning to make capes of cedar bark which I wore as a little boy. And when the cloth came my parents bought me a little cape, a black one. I remember it with just one button or loop.

We had a hard life, the way I was living, but we had food from the sea, from the land, and we followed the food in different seasons. I would start from where I was born—that used to be called Bear River but they've changed it to Bedwell Sound, Bedwell Inlet. People used to be up there in the fall to dry and smoke fish or deer meat. We were pretty well off with our food as children. Lots of food—they were all preserved too. Summer food, summer berries. I still recall my grandmother and the way I used to watch her with salal berries. She used to crush them and stir it all up and lay it out in the sun. She'd put them up in squares, just so thick. So those salal berries got dry, and in the winter, when there were no berries around, you could break a square and soak it and it would become salal berries again. Like the deep-freeze today, but they were sun-dried. That's what we called *chamas*—anything sweet.

Salmon berries came in early spring when the bushes were green—pale green branches of the salmon berry. My mother used to pick them and I used to eat them all right—peel the skin off and dip them in brown sugar.

When you got dogfish roe, you sun-dried it. It was a cheese colour. And there were sea grass roots—they're sweet, just like sugar. And sea urchins—blue, yellow, purple. They're big and small. They all have different names in our language, but I

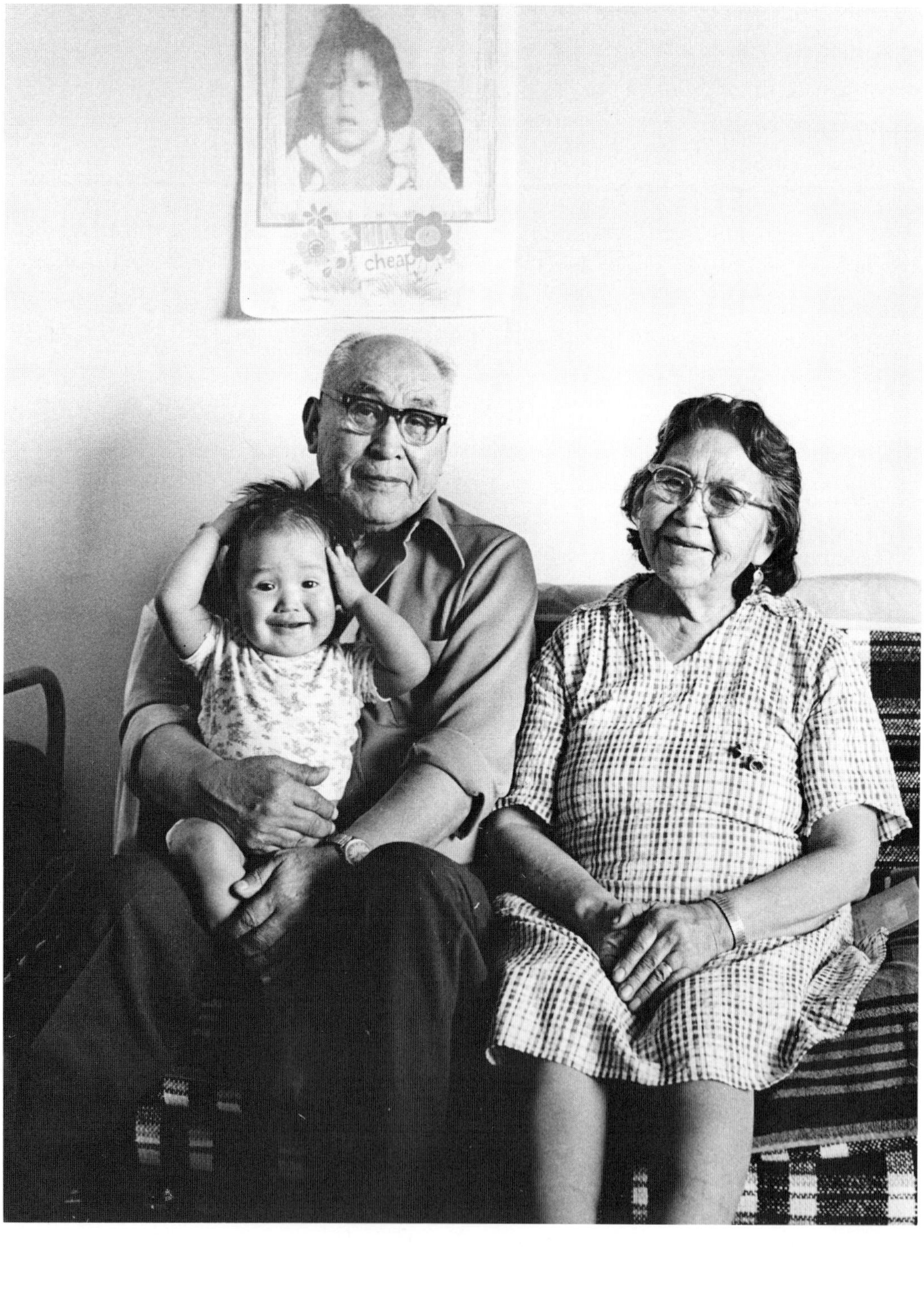
cheap

don't know about white man's language. And there were abalones. We used to spear them. And rock chitons, which are still a favorite today with our younger generation. After all, you can always go out in low water tides. Blue mussels – we call them *kluchim.* They're really good either steamed or roasted on the open fire. Gooseneck barnacles, they're the thing I like best. I'd say we were pretty well off. Nobody would starve.

It was in our family life, with grandparents, the old parents – this is the way I got educated. I would say I'd be a doctor in my own language although I don't know all that my great-grandfather knew. But I would say that I have many new things that my grandfather didn't know. So I'm just about equal to what I missed. They missed what I have now, understand? I was raised with my parents and with their parents who taught me how they lived. They taught me all the songs, prayer songs, potlatch songs, introduction songs – we call it *tsee-kaa.* And how to hunt for food. And the legends came along at the same time. There'd be nights for telling us what to be like – how to become a real he-man or a real he-woman – she-woman, that's a strong-minded woman. These were the teachings we got from our grandparents. Although these teachings were passed on to our parents, now again they passed them on to us. They would just review the teachings of the grandparents. And we were taught how we related to different tribes up along the coast: *Uchuklesaht, Kyuquot, Nuchatlaht, Mowachaht, Hesquiaht, Ahousaht, Clayoquot, Ucluelet, Toquaht, Opetchesaht, Pacheenaht, Nitinaht.*

We used to play with little spears about three or four feet long, spearing kelp, in teams – boys on both sides and the target would be the kelp. That game was called *tsaks-tal.* Another game was running races or jumping or a combination – competing with other children. It was usually children from one end of the village and from the other, in teams for foot races, wrestling. We used to play with cans – when they came around – and before the cans, stones – round stones just a little smaller than a baseball, big enough to throw. This game was called *teeka*, similar to horseshoes. We had a sandhill and a stake in front of it. We tried to hit the stake, but if a stone was close to the stake, the other team would try to push it a little farther away. There would be one judge who had a little measure and whoever was closest got the point.

As we get into today's problems, what I would say is 'Calm alcohol down.' It's what it costs some people who work hard and still have nothing to eat. But I don't think it is only the Indians because white people do that too. Now this is all connected to our lives. Jessie and I got together in 1928 and we were all right. Now alcohol hates us and we didn't know how bad it was. We had good food, like I was saying. But that booze is really powerful so I learned about it. If it wasn't for a man from Duncan by name of Able Joe—he was the man that woke us up. So our children saw what we were doing and we didn't know we were giving them a bad example. Now today they're happy, some of them. It's really too bad that we tried that stuff. I'm still kicking about that alcohol today. Although we're not drinking anymore, it hangs on to our children and our grandchildren.

I am fully educated, with my knowledge of the traditions, culture, history and songs that belong to my Indian way and language. But I haven't got much white man's language because I only spent two years in a boarding school. It was Ahousaht School. I didn't even know how to say 'yes' and I used to get kicked or slapped or sent to bed without supper if the staff heard me use my own language. So if any of those teachers are alive today, I wish they could take a look at Peter Webster. What is he doing in university? He's a man who didn't know a word of English and he's teaching his language back to his tribe.

My wife attended Christie School. We had a mixed marriage, but we're still together for the last fifty-three years.

I've been a language teacher for the past three years and children today are having a hard time. In the writing of the songs, some kids are really good but some don't know what they write. They don't understand what it means. Others seem to be more understanding.

I believe we need more teachers to teach them our language back. First teach them what we were taught by our grandparents in the past. This might be the only way to get them to change. If we don't it's going to get worse. So if I live another ten years, I hope I'll see a difference in the future. Again, if any of these young children of school age would get interested in it—teaching the language—if one of them gets the idea, I'll help them. I'm saying this because I want somebody to finish the Indian dictionary.

FRANCIS CHARLIE

Keltsomaht

Well, I'll tell you some things I remember
about sixty to sixty-five years ago.
I remember a house—open fire, no floor,
just mud where they slept.
I don't think there was pants or anything—
we went without pants, shoes—
I don't remember being sick or anything like that
—cold or sick, just run around in a shirt.
There weren't many children when I was growing up.
They died off, very few lived, I was a lucky one.
I come from a big family—twelve children,
and there were eight children when my father died.
There's only three of us left.
We're all getting old.

Well, nobody was there, just us in that village
where I came from—Keltsomaht, not Ahousaht.
Not too long ago, we amalgamated with the Ahousaht tribe,
but we have always been allied with Ahousaht.
We speak the same language, but Ahousaht speak very slow.
—we speak fast.
There weren't too many when I grew up.
They're all gone now except me and my brother and sister.
There's very few people left.
People died. They drowned in a schooner—
it capsized off here, off the shore here, up off Clayoquot Spund.
It got into a ninety-mile southwester—
that was my people on the boat—the Kelsomat tribe—
and they left their wives and children.
They had to find a way of living, you know,
a lot of them died. My mother's father died on the schooner.
That's how we're a small tribe, very small,
but today we have really grown—
we're with the Ahousaht tribe now, we've always been with them.

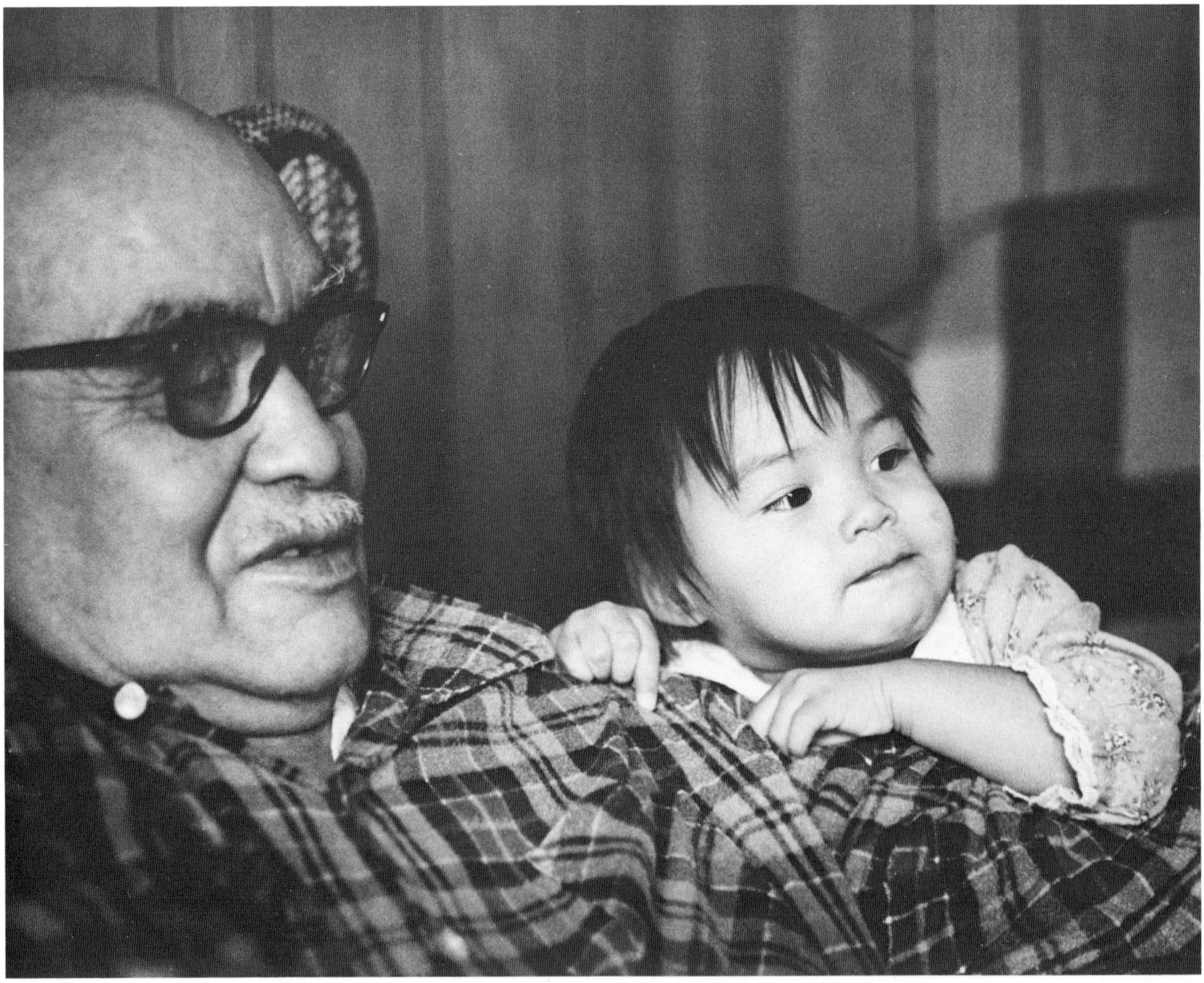

Our main diet was fish – it's all we had.
There was deer and duck once in awhile.
In the summer we had berries, we had flour,
mostly what we call 'pilot bread' – you call it biscuit.
Fish in the morning, fish in the afternoon,
we had a big supper – there was fish again.
There was no such things as bacon and eggs.
Different kinds of fish – dried fish, fresh fish, smoked fish,
different parts of the fish like the bones, the backbone,
the tail, the head – we never wasted any fish.

I remember living with my grandfather
– he was my grand uncle, my mother's uncle –
he was a crippled man, crawling on his hands and knees.
He had a mother and aunt and me,
there were four of us living there in one village.
We stayed with them all winter, we never moved,
and this man hunted.
He was a great hunter although he was crippled.
We had ducks, we had meat – anything we wanted.
I remember a fire started on the roof. There was snow
on the ground, and we threw the snow up, put the fire out,
and he climbed the ladder next day to fix the roof –
he was crippled, mind you, crawling on his hands and knees.
He used to pray every morning, pray at night before sleep.
Those were the main things we learned –
how to go hunting and how to pray before you went out.
What you call religion today – it's not new to us,
it's always been with us, the Indian people.

In the 30's we fished up the inlet.
miles and miles up the river. My uncle was trapping.
I used to watch and follow him around
and get a deer now and then – during the Depression.
You had to be careful with your shells –
you had one aim and that was it. You couldn't waste any.

The house had been standing there for many years—
the smokehouse—and we all lived in there,
I don't know how many families, three or four in that house.
We all dried fish up there, and soon as it got dried
it was put aside. Some did about 500 fish for the winter
till spring when the herring came in,
then they dried the herring.
They moved, they never stayed in one place.
Up the inlet they went and smoked their fish
and then they moved to the main village.
There were houses, then—they had boards and stoves
and everything, but up the inlet there was an open fire.
In the 30's people were hungry—we never went hungry.

In the spring, they went outside again, way out, to see the ocean.
They lived there and went halibut fishing and seal—
not hair seals, fur seals—
they went out, miles and miles out, way out—way, way out.
You couldn't see the land anymore, just the hills, just the mountains.
You had to be really prepared to go out.
Start coming home with the oars and sails.
This was the teaching. They had to prepare themselves,
get ready to go out seal hunting or go fishing,
and, you know—the prayers they had to say.

When I was nine I went to school.
I didn't know a word of English then, I went to Christie School.
Boy, that was a good seven years.
That was a religion taught—you were taught to behave,
you were taught to listen—it was good.
We only had two hours of classes when I went to residential school.
We worked—
we had a farm—we had cows, chickens, we had to look after all that—
we had to cut our own wood—the old saw they had wasn't even sharp.
Sometimes four people on that saw, two on each end, hardly cutting.
I went back to the village—you had to get out as soon as you're sixteen.
I didn't get much education, very little education.
I went home, I knew what to do, I wasn't lost.

I went fishing then and got a boat,
got on my own, got married—I knew what to expect.
I had responsibilities after I started raising children.
Ten children—four boys and six girls,
but now I have eight—lost two, two boys.

Here I am
I've been a father and mother to my eight children.
Although they're on their own, they still come, can't get away.
Sometimes I wish to go, then I think—
we're a very close people, Indian people,
very close, very, very close.
If I move, they all move, you know—
that's the way of the Indian people.
It's different with white people.
Like me now, I move here and everybody's here, all my kids are here
—just one boy is not home, the rest are here.
When we get together, there's a big crowd—there's forty-one of us.
I have thirty grandchildren, and two great-grandchildren.
We're a small tribe, our one family.
One man at home, he's got about one hundred grandchildren.
He had twelve or thirteen children.
One of them had thirteen children.
Today we're one of the biggest tribes on the coast. We're called Keltsomaht.
We always had a god, before even the white man came.
When the ministers and priests came in, they took all that away.
Couldn't pray in our own language because it was called 'superstitious'
or something—we're 'savage' and we prayed to something, like the sun—
but we didn't pray to that.
We prayed in the morning and we prayed at night. We thanked god at night.
This is what we believe and still we believe today.
I believe in prayer, I've gone back to my own way.
I don't think my children will go back to the old way—
like me living in town, how can they do it?
Where can you take them? We had to walk in the woods. But here in the city,
you can't go in the woods—you're trespassing.
I think this is the end.
I had a pretty good life, I'm telling you.
We lived well.

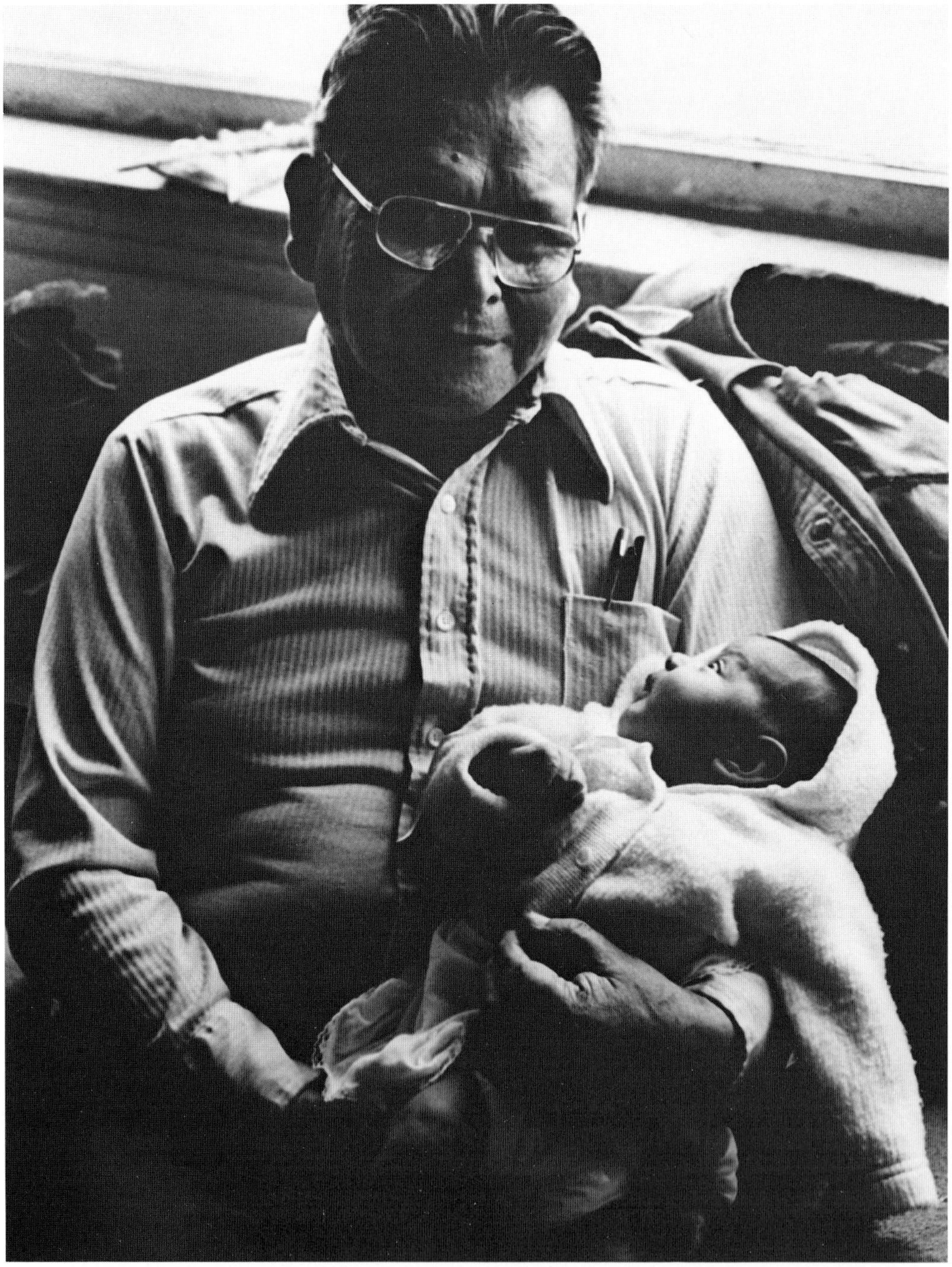

GEORGE LOUIS

Ahousaht

A little girl got her teachings from her grandmother from the time she was old enough to understand. And the same with a boy. We were all brought up to listen to my grandfather. The same with my cousins—I didn't have any sisters, just cousins at that time. First thing in the morning when Granny woke up, she used to sing a song, although we didn't understand the tongue. We listened to that song. 'It helps each person,' said my Granny. And when she sang it, there was a feeling, a feeling inside, because there was something there—a creator.

The girls learned to make baskets, and every morning had to do their chores. If they slept in, Granny used to say, 'Oh, your basket is crying! Wake up, dear, come on, start working on your basket.' I had to have a bath before breakfast. Every child did. You had to go down to the beach and have a swim. Lots of mornings I didn't like that, but it was part of our training. All my cousins and relations went through that.

The girls were taught how to prepare a meal and how to barbeque. There's certain ways to clean a fish. When we clean a fish we don't slit down the belly. We slit it from the back and then cut down both sides of the head. If it's for barbequing we leave the tail on and we had to be real careful not to spill the insides. If there was a little spill, Granny used to use a moss to sop everything up, and to take that slime off first. You don't wash it. West coast natives, when they barbeque their fish, the tail end is up—it goes onto the stick like that. Sockeye—real rich. Everything was saved, except the guts. Eggs were saved too, or they could be barbequed right away. Drying fish, we had to lay it on a pole like that, and be real careful, especially about flies. We had little smudge fires to keep the flies away.

At ten, a girl learned about what she was going to be like when she was grown up. At about thirteen girls are maybe more mature than boys and they have their periods and all that. They were real careful. When a girl had her first period, she was put away in the house for about four days. After that there was a certain place where she would bathe. After her period, she wore two braids and sometimes put rouge on. Today it's very expensive. This rouge was used for dancing. Six months later, the father would give a feast just to show that the girl is now mature. She is a little lady.

The boys were taught about sex too. Which is very important to us. We don't talk about sex in public, my grandfather used to tell me. He used to take me aside, so nobody would listen. When I was growing up I was taught to respect people. That was part of the training—to respect people no matter who they are.

Another thing about training a young man—we had to pray. And we didn't pray in the open public. My grandmother used to tell me the best time to have connection with the creator was when you're walking. Nobody knows you're walking there, you're all by yourself. That was part of the teaching—go up in the bushes. The praying used to last four days. Sometimes eight days. After that you had to stay home for awhile, and not go into other homes, because if you did, all your blessings went to the other person's house and you lost that.

My grandmother used to get up early in the morning and go out and look for thick grass—and she'd rub the dew on her face. And you know, she never had any wrinkles in her face. And there was a rock used too, the river people used it too, as far up as Lillooet. I met a woman who told me that her grandfather used to dive into the deepest part of the river there to get this rock. It was rubbed over the face. Granny used this rock to that dust out of there. She used to make me drink it, and there were herbs that we had to take from the new moon till the fourteenth day.

Our calendar starts on the first day of the new moon. There are a couple of months that take about sixteen days from the new moon to the full moon. After the full moon it takes fifteen days to the new moon—comes to thirty-one days altogether. We have four seasons and our equinox falls on the twenty-first of March and September.

In the winter months, the people had to be careful. In December there was a lot of praying. Some people would pray for ten days. Some would take a month off, and wouldn't do anything. But before they did that, everything had to be ready—lots of wood and lots of food. It was just like going to church.

There was more training. There were times when you weren't supposed to touch your wife—no intercourse, no relations. If you met a girl and broke that tie, then you lost everything. And if you went hunting or fishing, you'd be unlucky. They claim that some women bring good luck, but I never tried that. Our sex life was very important. The only time for sex was from the new moon to the full. You had to go certain times to your better half. They claimed that if you had too much sex then your life would be short. That's what Granny used to tell me. You don't fool around, or you'll lose your blessings.

Making a canoe, a man had to do certain things, and he'd pray so he wouldn't have an accident. Because that tree's a living thing. When a tree's cut it dies. He had to pick a certain tree, so that when the cedar fell it wouldn't shatter. He had to line it up. Take this part here, where the sun shines, and this part where the moss grows – that would be the bottom of the canoe. It gets seasoned, gets dry. It's much harder. The other part there, save that for lumber, for boards. Nothing wasted. And when a man made his canoe he couldn't burn his own chippings. He had to let someone else burn it. My grandfather used to say, 'Don't burn your own chippings. Let somebody else. You got to be generous.'

It took a long time to make a canoe. Today, you got this power saw. That's what I did in Toronto. I'd start at five in the morning and work till nine. Then I'd put away the power saw and sweep up the chippings and the tourists would come in at ten. From ten o'clock on I'd be out there with my hand chisel, relaxing.

When kids today hit a city or a town, most of them think they're in a free world. But, no – I worked for the Native Friendship Centre in Victoria and we had every problem. Whose fault is it? It's pretty hard to say. It's not only in Victoria. It's like that clear across the continent.

Today grade twelve is nothing. You have to have a university or college degree. Take the fish – it's going to be finished, and the same with logging. In B.C. twenty-five years ago they were clearing one hundred acres a day. Just imagine. Vancouver Island is only 12,500 acres. That's not very much. It's going to be harder for children now. That's why a lot of native girls are going into nursing or secretarial. Back east, native people are going for doctors, lawyers, highrise builders. These people are qualified. I tell my children, 'You got to go to school. You got to. You can't ask for a handout. No. Especially a native guy.'

In dances, like the wolf dance – well, this used to happen at night.
We'd hear this wolf make ooo-oo-oo – all kinds of noises,
and they'd put the lights out in the big house.
And there'd be knocking and pushing the door in –
it would be real scary.
And the women would be singing their song,
and the men would be singing their song,
and these wolves, they always came in this way – they don't come on the left side,
they come on the right,
Make a circle this way
– and they pick up a chief's son or a chief's daughter.

After everything was quietened down, the put the lights out –
douse the open fire with water.
It would get real steamy in there.
Two men marked their faces with ashes – we call it Wolf. And they'd be looking for him. 'Is everybody in here?'
'Oh, there's one missing – it's this one or that one!'
'They were taken away –
Was it their forefathers – they came with the wolf.'

You know, next morning the wolves used to come out –
they were down on the beach, every morning, twice a day.
Same in the afternoon.
Some of the people were put among the wolves.
That's how they formed the dances and how they got a name –
a child that was in with the wolf.
The ceremony lasted eight days, lasted till way after midnight.
It's not like this dance we have here. The village was sectioned off –
three sections – there was the head chief, second chief, and the third –
people would get in there – it was scary –
and all the masks used to come in during the day
– real fierce looking.
Well, they claim it was like a gorilla – it used to be around long ago.
Indians in Alert Bay, they call it *Tsonoqua*, and *Bookmis, Puqmis*
and they used to carry a staff six feet long with sharp ends –
if there was anything on the floor, they'd rip it up.
Someone would put a sack of flour there, and they'd creep up
– fierce looking creatures – and take a handful
– throw it all over the place. They even used salmon eggs, let them rot first.
Oh, I never did like that.
Well, everyone went from house to house, it was like Christmas season –
everybody would be singing, chanting, and having a good time,
and that's the way it went.

Contributors' Notes

HELEN ALPHONSE was born in Koksilah, B.C., and lives in Victoria. In addition to being a mother and housekeeper, she has worked at a number of other jobs, including caring for the elderly in a number of west coast communities, and custodian in a school in Duncan, B.C. She has also spun wool and knitted traditional Cowichan sweaters all her life. She has had seven children, thirty-seven grandchildren, and eleven great-grandchildren. Her son, Dennis Alphonse, is Chief of Cowichan.

ALEX AMOS was born in 1898 in Hesquiaht, on the west coast of Vancouver Island, and was a fisherman for most of his life. After his retirement, he worked in Hesquiaht as a language teacher during summers, and in winter worked on linguistics projects with Dr. Barbara Elliot. He had approximately sixty-nine grandchildren, one hundred fifteen great-grandchildren, and eight great-great grandchildren. He died in 1987.

FRANCIS CHARLIE was born in 1910 in Ahouset, B.C. He was a commercial fisherman for thirty-four years on a seine boat on the west coast of Vancouver Island. After retirement, he went to school and taught the Nootka language for two years at S.J. Willis Junior High School in Victoria. He has had ten children, thirty-one grandchildren, and two great-grandchildren.

RUTH COOK was born in 1931 in Charles Creek, B.C. She worked in a cannery at the age of eleven, and has been variously employed as a housekeeper in a hospital and a residential school, as a hotel chambermaid, a teacher's aide, home and school co-ordinator, and language teacher at the Nimpkish Band School. She has had six children and thirteen grandchildren.

DAVE ELLIOTT was born in 1910 at Wjotep ("Place of Maples"), Tsartlip, B.C. He lived on southern Vancouver Island, the San Juan Islands, and in Tsartlip, for some sixty years. He was a commercial fisherman for most of his life, and was also custodian at the Tsartlip school for sixteen years. He also worked as a Native Studies resource person. He had eleven children and thirty grandchildren. He died in 1985.

DOROTHY HAEGERT was born in Toronto in 1938 and moved to Victoria in 1945, where she eventually opened a photography studio. She studied art at the Vancouver School of Art, Banff School of Fine Arts, University of British Columbia, and under Arlette Carreau-Kingwell in Montreal (1965-66). She has had extensive training in photography, and her paintings and photographs have been shown in galleries and museums in Montreal, Victoria, and Seattle. Her show, *Children of the First People*, was exhibited at the British Columbia Provincial Museum, 1979-80. In the last few years she has embarked on an ambitious project, photographing the children of China; exhibitions of her Chinese photographs were mounted in Vancouver in 1988 and 1989. In 1989, she married a professor from Haikou, China, and currently divides her time between China and Victoria.

STAN JAMES was born in Nanaimo, B.C., in 1911. He attended boarding school in Chilliwack and also lived for a time in Victoria. He has worked as a labourer and carver. He has seven children and twelve grandchildren.

GEORGE LOUIS was born in 1912 at Sidney Inlet on Vancouver Island. He has worked for Parks & Recreation in Port Alberni and at the Ontario Science Centre in Toronto. He is also involved in the United Native Nations, and sat on the School Board of Greater Victoria. In 1987, he received an honourary law degree from the University of Victoria. He has had twelve children, seventeen grandchildren, and three great-grandchildren.

DOROTHY SANVIDGE was born in 1925 in Nootka, B.C., and lived there and in Friendly Cove, Gold River, Alert Bay, and Campbell River. She was a cannery worker, kept a rooming house, and run a foster home. She had ten children, eighteen grandchildren, and five great-grandchildren. She died in 1985.

JOHN THOMAS was born in 1913 at Clo-oose on Vancouver Island. He has been a fisherman and logger, and has studied and taught linguistics at the University of Victoria. He has also taught language at Neah Bay in Washington state. He has had thirteen children and twenty grandchildren.

PETER WEBSTER was born in 1908 in Bedwell River, Vancouver Island, and has lived in Keltsamat and Ahousat. He has been an independent fisherman on the coast, a carpenter, and an author, and has acted in three films. The holder of a honourary degree in Linguistics from the University of Victoria, he has also taught his Native language in his own school in Ahousat. He has had six children, thirty-six grandchildren, and thirty-three great-grandchildren.

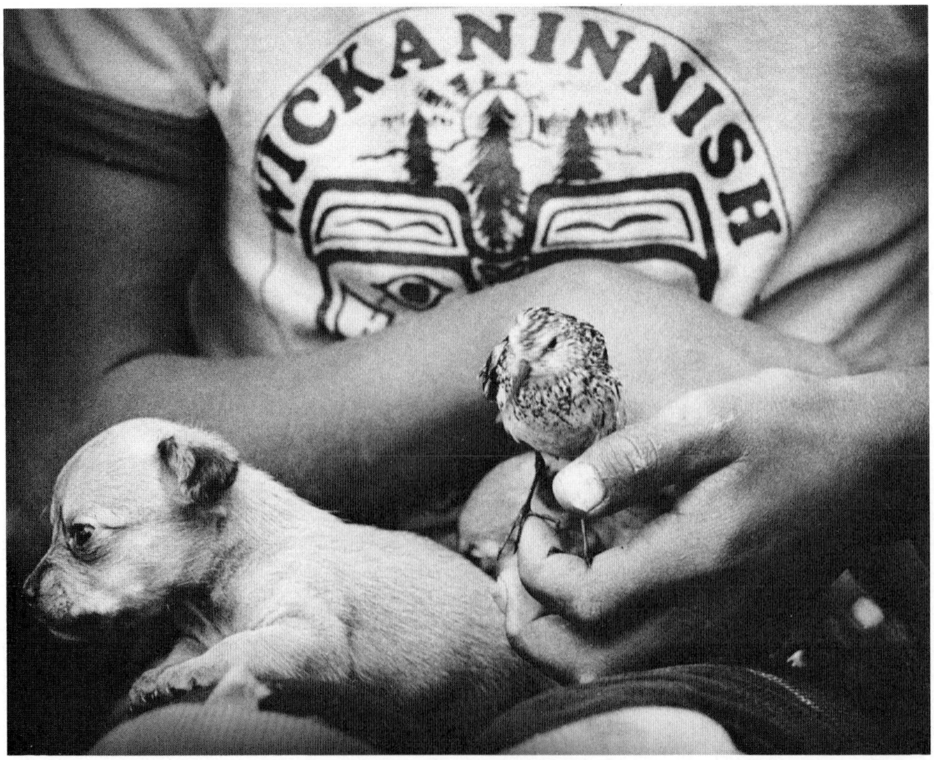

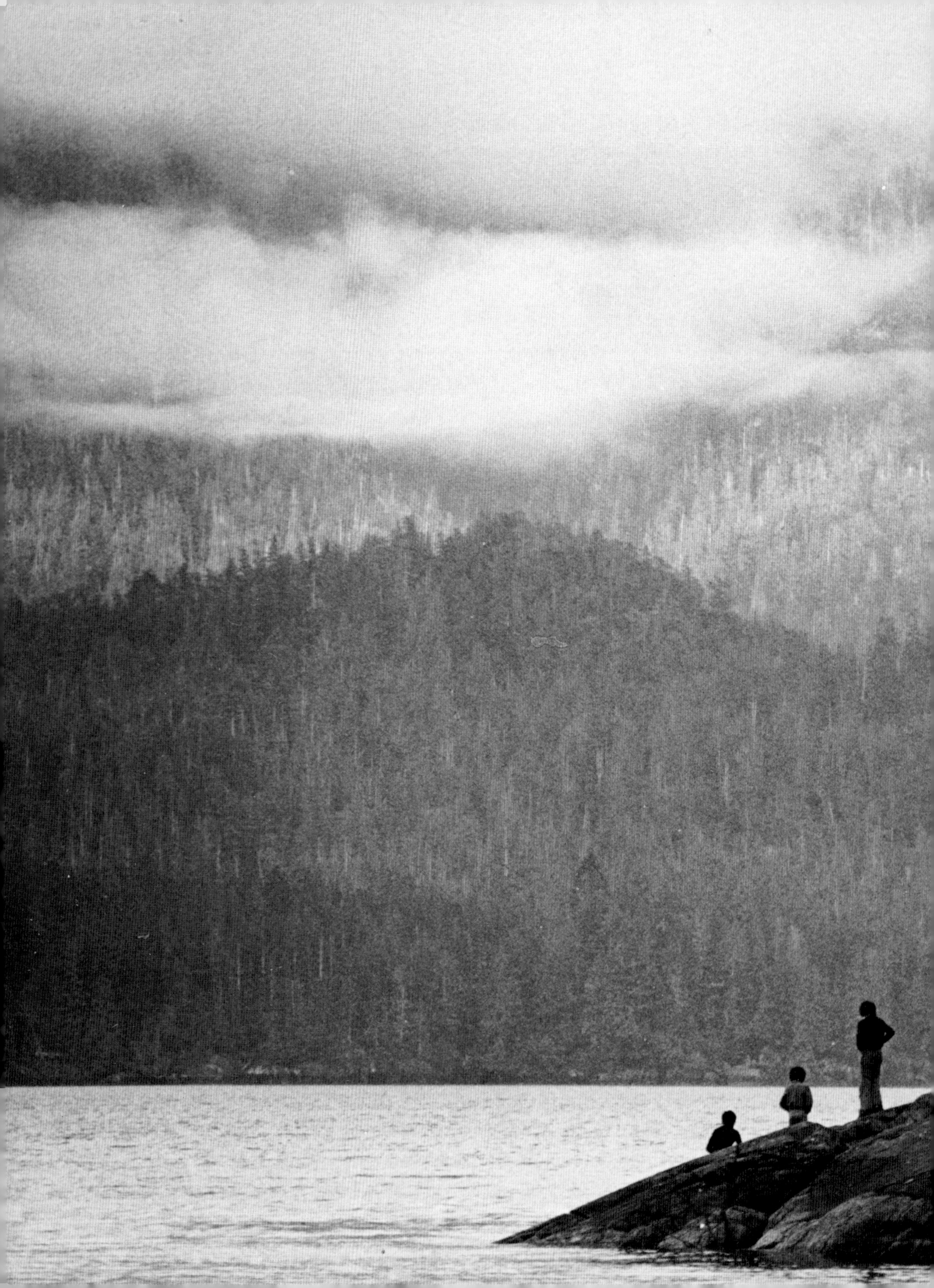

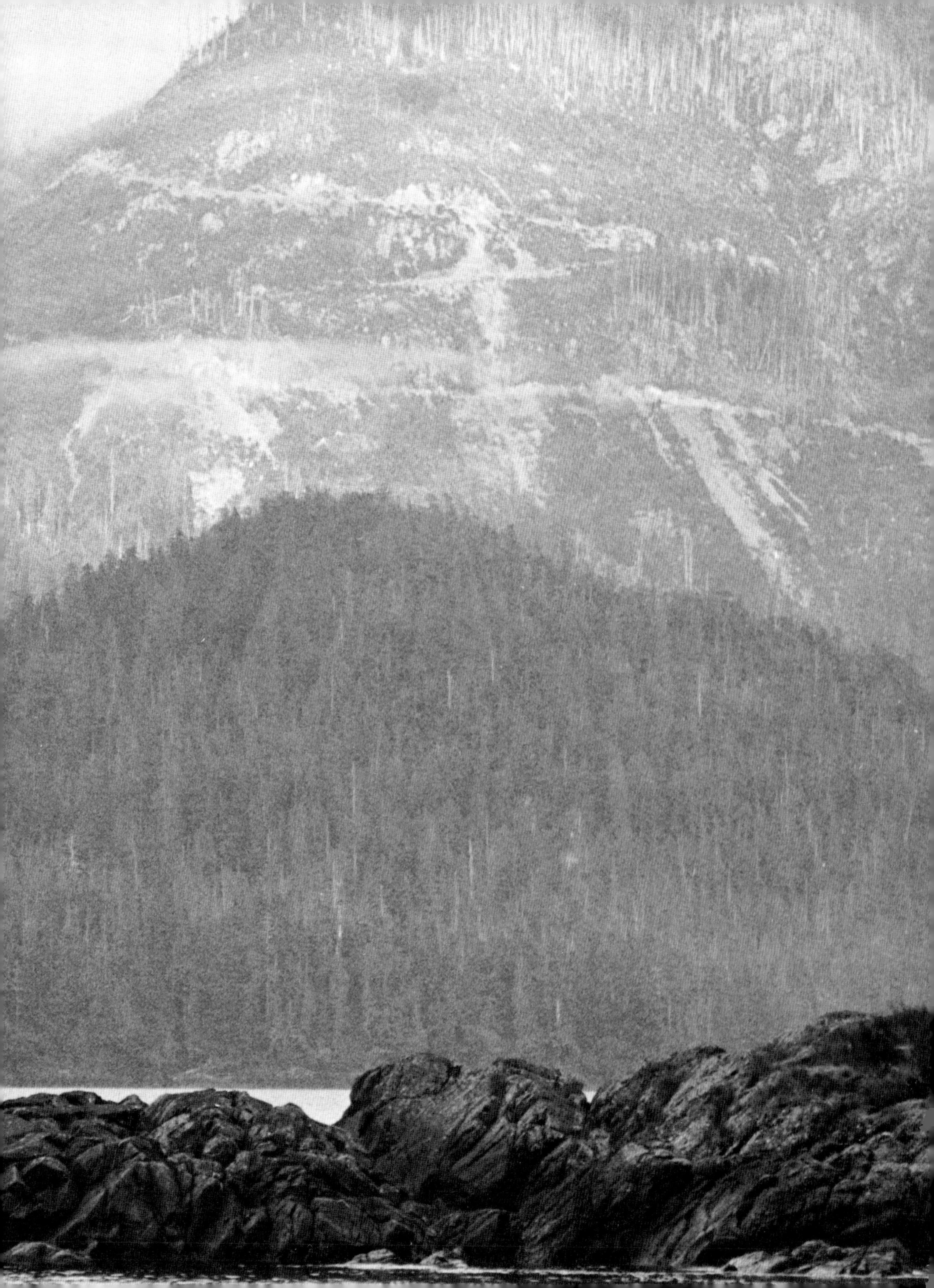